MUD SWEETER THAN HONEY

MUD
SWEETER
THAN
HONEY

Voices of Communist Albania

Margo Rejmer

Translated from the Polish by
Zosia Krasodomska-Jones and Antonia Lloyd-Jones

With an Introduction by Tony Barber

RESTLESS BOOKS
BROOKLYN, NEW YORK

First Restless Books hardcover edition November 2021

Hardcover ISBN: 9781632062833
Library of Congress Control Number: 2021937471

This book is supported in part by an award from the National Endowment for the Arts.

This publication has been supported by the ©POLAND Translation Program.

This work is published with support from the Sons of St. Mary's Albanian Orthodox Church, Worcester, MA, and the Massachusetts Albanian American Society (MAASBESA).

Cover and text design by Sarah Schneider
Map © Bill Donohoe
Cover photograph by © Nikos Economopoulos/Magnum Photos
Photographs on pp. xviii and 226 by © Nikos Economopoulos/Magnum Photos
Photographs on pp. 48, 108, and 176 by © Ferdinando Scianna/Magnum Photos

Printed in the United States of America
1 3 5 7 9 10 8 6 4 2

Restless Books, Inc.
232 3rd Street, Suite A101
Brooklyn, NY 11215

www.restlessbooks.org
publisher@restlessbooks.org

CONTENTS

PART THREE: Circles

PART FOUR: Stone on the Border

PART FIVE: The Fortress Crumbles

Where is mud sweeter than honey? In your own country.

ANDON ZAKO ÇAJUPI, "Where We Were Born," 1902

I love you, muddy Albanian soil,
Magic,
Sweet as honey,
Bitter as wormwood,
I love you
Ferociously,
Desperately,
Like a wolf loves the forest,
Like a wave loves a wave,
Like mud loves mud!

MITRUSH KUTELI, "The Muddy Albanian Soil," 1944,
translated by Robert Elsie

Albania (before the breakup of Yugoslavia)

KEY EVENTS IN THE
HISTORY OF ALBANIA

1912   Albania declares independence from the Ottoman Empire.

1914   Albania becomes a principality under Prince Wilhelm I of Albania, although Wilhelm flees in September 1914 and is head of state only nominally until 1925, when Albania becomes a republic. The First World War plunges Albania into political chaos, but in the aftermath it avoids being partitioned by neighboring countries, forms its own government, and expels foreign occupiers.

1922   Ahmet Zogu becomes prime minister.

1925–8   The First Albanian Republic. Ahmet Zogu becomes president.

1928–39   The Albanian Kingdom. Zogu becomes King Zog I.

April 1939   Italian invasion of Albania. King Zog flees to Greece.

November 1941   Creation of the Albanian Communist Party led by Enver Hoxha.

September 1943   German invasion and occupation of Albania.

1944   The communist National Liberation Army liberates Albania, fighting both the Germans and Balli Kombëtar, a nationalist anti-communist paramilitary and political organization that had fought against the Italians and then sided with the Germans. A government led by Enver Hoxha is formed.

1946   Albania and Yugoslavia sign a treaty of friendship and cooperation.

1948   Albania breaks its ties with Yugoslavia.

1951   Albania and the USSR sign an agreement on mutual economic assistance.

1954   Mehmet Shehu becomes prime minister. Hoxha remains first secretary of the Communist Party.

1961   The Soviet–Albanian split. Albania shifts closer to China.

1967   Hoxha declares Albania an atheist state. A campaign of religious oppression begins.

1972–8   The Sino–Albanian split.

1980   Hoxha chooses Ramiz Alia as his successor over Mehmet Shehu.

1985   Enver Hoxha dies. Ramiz Alia takes over as first secretary of the Party.

1990   The communist regime collapses.

March–April 1991   Elections are won by the Communist Party. Ramiz Alia is re-elected as president.

March–April 1992   The Democratic Party wins a majority in new elections. Sali Berisha becomes president; Alexander Meksi heads the first non-communist government.

1997   A financial crisis triggered by a collapse in fraudulent pyramid investment schemes leads to major riots, mass looting of weapons, and the resignation of the government. More than 2,000 people are killed in the violence that spreads nationwide.

1997–2017   Political unrest and instability continue. Power continues to shift between the Socialist Party and the Democratic Party.

1998–9   Refugees from the conflict in Kosovo flee to Albania.

2006   Albania and the European Union sign a Stabilization and Association Agreement.

2009   Albania joins NATO and applies for membership of the European Union.

2014   Albania becomes a candidate country for membership of the European Union.

2021   The general election held in April results in a clear win for the Socialist Party led by Edi Rama.

INTRODUCTION

BY TONY BARBER

AT THE STATE FUNERAL for Enver Hoxha in April 1985, the dictator's body was buried next to the Mother Albania monument in Tirana's Cemetery of the Martyrs of the Nation. A red marble slab with the inscription ENVER HOXHA 1908–1985 was placed over the coffin. Ramiz Alia, Hoxha's successor as Communist Party leader, solemnly told the mourners: "There should be no date of death on this marble stone. . . . There is just one date for Enver Hoxha, his date of birth, and that is how it will always be, there is no death for him. Enver Hoxha is immortal."[1]

Intended as a prophecy—and doubtless as a warning to the Albanian people—that Hoxha's repressive apparatus of power would outlast the tyrant himself, Alia's words proved mercifully off the mark. Less than six years after the funeral rites, a crowd tore down the bronze statue of Hoxha that towered over Skanderbeg Square, Tirana's main plaza. In May 1992, Hoxha's remains were transferred from their grand resting place to Tirana's plain municipal cemetery. A little later than other countries in east-central Europe, but not a moment too soon for most Albanians, the nation was embarking on a rocky journey to political pluralism, civic freedoms, a market-based economy, and integration with the outside world that continues to this day.

Despite the undeniable progress made over the past three decades, the legacy of Hoxha lingers on. It could hardly be otherwise, given that the tyrant had ruled, by the time of his death, for forty-one of the seventy-three years that had elapsed since Albania claimed its independence from the Ottoman Empire in 1912. Yet the desire among political elites and ordinary citizens alike to look to Albania's future rather than its past is understandably strong. On a visit to Tirana in 2015, I had dinner with Edi Rama, who had been elected Albania's prime minister two years earlier. Recalling the brutality, desolation, and, at times, somewhat surreal quality of Hoxha's dictatorship, Rama told me: "I've stopped telling my son about those times, because he looks at me as if I'm crazy."

Mud Sweeter than Honey serves as an essential reminder that to move on from a painful national past should never mean to forget it or brush it aside. This is as true for western countries with complicated legacies of imperialism, racial injustice, and lapses from democracy as it is for former communist societies once held in the grip of fear and silence. It is important for the voices of victims of Albanian communism to be heard, writes Margo Rejmer. For many Albanians, "the suffering of the past is so vivid that it feels as if it only ended yesterday. They're hurt by the failure to settle accounts or to provide compensation, and by the feeling that in today's Albania no one cares about the criminality of the old system."

Measured against other communist regimes that emerged in east-central Europe around the end of the Second World War, Hoxha's dictatorship stands out as one of the most unrelentingly cruel. With the passage of time, it also became the one that was most cut off, by its own choice, from the rest of the world. In these respects it bore a closer resemblance to Kim Il-sung's North Korea than to Hungary under János Kádár or to Poland—Rejmer's native country—under Władysław Gomułka and Edward Gierek. Even Bulgaria under Todor Zhivkov was more open. The pervasive, intimidating presence of the Sigurimi security police in Albanian life was comparable to that of the Stasi in Erich Honecker's East Germany and the Securitate in Nicolae Ceaușescu's Romania. But

the truly distinctive feature of Hoxha's tyranny was that—in contrast to
its counterparts in east-central Europe and, for that matter, the Soviet
Union—the Albanian regime displayed ruthlessness, paranoia, and regular murderous instincts in a manner that scarcely changed at all from 1944
to 1985. Gentian Shkurti, an artist, tells Rejmer that "in the communist
era you felt as if you were being raped on a daily basis."

Stalinism exacted a heavy toll across the communist world in the late
1940s and early 1950s in the form of executions, torture, imprisonment,
purges, and general suffering.[2] But after Joseph Stalin's death in 1953, and
even more so after the violent suppression of the 1956 Budapest uprising,
the one-party regimes of east-central Europe settled into a less ferocious
style of rule. For sure, the Prague Spring liberalization ended with a Warsaw Pact invasion in 1968, Poland's Solidarity movement was suppressed
under martial law in 1981, and repression under Ceaușescu intensified in
Romania throughout the 1980s. Yet the era of high Stalinism had ended
decades earlier.

Not so in Albania. Hoxha, the son of an imam from the southern
town of Gjirokastër, idolized Stalin, the seminary student from Gori
in Georgia. Or perhaps it is more accurate to say that Hoxha admired
not so much Stalin himself as the methods of consolidating a dictatorship—including the leader's personality cult and the liquidation of all
rivals real and imagined—that Stalin perfected. In 1945, Hoxha ordered
the execution of Bahri Omari, his brother-in-law and a former Albanian foreign minister, in an unmistakeable signal that he would spare
no one, not even his sister's husband, as he imposed communism on his
country. Three decades later, the same fate befell Beqir Balluku, Hoxha's long-serving defense minister. In 1981, Mehmet Shehu, Hoxha's
prime minister and closest associate of all, fell foul of the dictator and
committed suicide. Bashkim Shehu, Mehmet's son, recounts to Rejmer
how this episode resulted in prison terms and internal exile for other
members of the Shehu family.

Is it possible to construct any sort of defense for the abominations of
Hoxha's rule? Bernd Fischer, one of the world's leading scholars of Albanian communism, writes: "Views of Hoxha's impact vary rather widely but

most historians suggest that he had some important achievements to his credit."[3] These are said to include improvements in the status of women in Albania's deeply conservative post–Second World War society, a better education system, reduced rivalries between the country's northern and southern regions, and even a modicum of economic well-being— achieved, to be sure, from a very low starting point.

Besides these accomplishments, Hoxha in some ways completed the construction of the Albanian nation-state that had begun in the interwar era under King Zog but was thrown drastically off course by the Italian invasion and de facto annexation of Albania in 1939 and the country's occupation by the Nazis in 1943–44. In contrast to the experience of all countries in east-central Europe except Yugoslavia, the Albanian communist takeover was not Soviet-led but homegrown, though the British helped Hoxha's partisans with supplies of weapons. Then, during his four decades in power, Hoxha preserved Albania's independence against what torrents of state propaganda depicted at various times as the malevolent designs of Yugoslavia, the Soviet Union, and China, not to mention Western imperialism. For a European state, it was an unusual form of independence, perched on the edges of the international system. As East-West détente gathered pace in the era of Richard Nixon and Leonid Brezhnev, the Helsinki Final Act of 1975 was signed by thirty-five countries including the United States, Canada, the Soviet Union, and all European states except Albania. As Rejmer reminds us, Albania was a self-styled paradise held together by barbed wire and dotted with labor camps, a "small country of bunkers, blockades, and barricades."

In *Mud Sweeter than Honey*, a few of Rejmer's interviewees either deny the horror of conditions under Hoxha or, more often, express the despairing view that inequality, poverty, corruption, and political turbulence in the post-communist era make it difficult to discern the benefits of democracy. But a different insight comes from the writer Fatos Lubonja, who observes: "When freedom came, the Albanians were like children who didn't know what responsibility was."

Building a politically stable, economically flourishing society founded on the rule of law has proved to be a formidable task in many post-communist countries, but in few more so than in Albania, where knowledge of the outside world was so restricted that a person might tremble in fear that a can of Coca-Cola was a small, foreign-made bomb. Yet the powerful, often chilling stories in *Mud Sweeter than Honey* attest to the truth that even a regime as atrocious as Hoxha's cannot triumph in the long run over the irrepressible human yearning for freedom and dignity. In one of the most moving passages of Rejmer's book, Ridvan Dibra, a writer and college lecturer, tells the author: "The system wasn't capable of destroying everyday beauty. And that was our salvation. Beauty always found a way around the system."

1   Fevziu, Blendi: *Enver Hoxha: The Iron Fist of Albania*, translated by Majlinda Nishku (London: I.B. Tauris, 2017), p. 258.

2   Connelly, John: *From Peoples into Nations: A History of Eastern Europe* (Princeton/Oxford: Princeton University Press, 2020), pp. 538–48.

3   Fischer, Bernd J.: "Enver Hoxha and the Stalinist Dictatorship in Albania," in *Balkan Strongmen: Dictators and Authoritarian Rulers of Southeast Europe*, edited by Bernd J. Fischer (London: C. Hurst & Co., 2007), p. 266.

The statue of Enver Hoxha erected in Gjirokastër in 1988 and destroyed by workers in February 1991.

PART ONE

CHILDREN OF THE DICTATOR

ONCE UPON A TIME, PARADISE was created in the most perfect socialist country in the world.

Where everything belonged to everyone, and nothing belonged to anyone.

Where everyone knew how to read and write, but they could only write what the authorities endorsed, and they could only read what the authorities approved.

Where electricity, buses, and propaganda reached every village, but ordinary citizens weren't entitled to a car or an opinion of their own.

Where everyone could rely on free health care, but people sometimes vanished without a trace.

Where mass education was a priority, but every few years purges were carried out among the elite.

Where everyone was entitled to celebrate progress and cheer at public parades, but telling a joke meant challenging fate and the authorities. For that reason, the citizens were advised to feel enthusiastic and happy, because complaints and stupid jokes—in other words, agitation and propaganda—carried the threat of anything from six months to ten years in prison.

But there were no political prisons in paradise, only "reeducation camps" designed to alter the consciousness of enemies of the people, with the aid of prescribed literature, torture, and penal hard labor.

In paradise, everyone was equal, but people were divided into better and worse types—those with a good family background, who led an upright life, and those with a bad one, who were oppressed from birth. The good had to keep company with the good, and the bad with the bad—sharing their suffering. The good could become bad at any moment. The bad generally remained the worst until death.

The authorities held the life of every citizen in their grip and decided who would go to university and who would work on a cooperative farm, who would become an architect and who a bricklayer; who would be a human and who would be a wreck.

Who would prosper, who would languish, and who would have their life stolen from them.

The authorities controlled ambitions and cut them down to size, so people eventually taught themselves not to have ambitions.

In 1967, God was formally declared dead—or rather, never to have existed—and consequently, all religions were officially futile. From then on, the only religion was to be socialism and a common faith in the power of the new man.

From 1978 onward, this paradise on Earth stopped looking to other countries for support; it stopped owing them anything or wanting their help. It had no inflation, no unemployment, no loans, and no debts. It was self-sufficient.

Its borders were marked out on all sides by barbed wire. Anyone who tried to cross them was to be shot without warning. Those who lived according to the rules of paradise believed they were the happiest people in the world. In fact, as they fell asleep at night, some of them did wonder what freedom was, but others were sure they wanted for nothing. The authorities gave them food, shelter, education, and work, so the citizens had nothing to worry about. They merely had to mind what they said, did, and thought.

From 1976, their paradise on Earth was called the People's Socialist Republic of Albania.

Its only rightful god was Supreme Comrade Enver Hoxha.

What Was Meant to Be
Has Already Happened

THE MOUNTAINS GAZE DOWN AT YOU, but their eyes are empty. You look up at them and see a shining, austere beauty. At the bottom of the Zagoria valley, at the foot of the slopes, we're smaller than shards of stone. The great open space reduces our bodies to shadows.

All around, time is destroying the houses and distorting memory. There's too little of anything to live on. The people are growing older, broken by what has passed, and longing for what has never happened.

Those who are strong enough and don't consider the humiliation flee Zagoria for a better world. They abandon their crumbling houses and walled enclosures. They take their children, the growing hope for the future, and they leave.

The public bus doesn't come here anymore, so there are only private off-road vehicles and a battered van juddering along the gravel road. The old people raise a hand in farewell to those who are leaving the rotting walls, collapsing fences, and caved-in roofs behind them.

You can count the children here on the fingers of one hand; nearly all the schools in the area are deserted, but you can still cross their sunken thresholds to take a look at what used to be. There are blue display cases crammed with three-dimensional models of the human body, lifeless ammeters and voltmeters cloaked in a layer of dust, and a plastic brain lying in the corner. The peeling walls still carry the burden of the propaganda noticeboards.

To be a friend of books is a great honor.

In a faded stack of abandoned works by Karl Marx, Friedrich Engels, and Enver Hoxha, a red album bound in imitation leather cries out for attention. It was meant to tell future generations about the glory of Albanian socialism.

In the Orwellian year of 1984, the authorities made the following declaration:

> In forty years of titanic efforts, the Albanian people have achieved tremendous successes under the leadership of the Party and Comrade Enver Hoxha.
>
> They have consigned the Middle Ages to museums once and for all, and have shown themselves to the world as the people of a completely independent country, who by their own strengths are creating a flourishing socialist society. Our citizens have become the masters of their own destiny, and today they are building and protecting a new life—without persecutors and their victims, without oppressive treaties, without poverty. With every passing year we take another step forward.

The abandoned village school is filled with a vast, unbroken silence. As though there were nobody left for miles around.

> All this we have achieved by waging a fierce class war, conquering backwardness and frustrating the internal and external plots of our enemies. Albania is the land of a reborn nation, a people with a completely new countenance. Among the ancient fortresses, which symbolise tenacious resistance in times of historical aggression, the iron fortress towers of this new life have arisen: factories, industrial plants, drilling shafts and hydroelectric dams. This powerful, modern industry is one of the principal victories of the working class and the Albanian people.

Finally, a sound: from afar comes the harsh jangle of tin bells, and sheep bleating in pained chorus.

> Socialist Albania enjoys great authority and a strong international position, as well as having many friends and benevolent allies around the world. Surrounded and harassed by perfidious enemies, it resolutely resists imperialist hostile intentions and blockades. [. . .] In forty years we have achieved more than in entire centuries. The Albanian people have created this wonderful reality and now they are moving forwards without a shadow of doubt, with the optimism of a society certain of its future.

After this introduction there follows a series of admirable photographs showing grand buildings, exemplary parks, hardworking men, and virtuous women. Each is in their place, each is happy with the task assigned to them. They have the faces of static, cheerful dummies.

As I wipe the book's cover, a thick layer of dust sticks to my fingers.

Less than a year after the album was published, on April 11, 1985, the beloved leader's heart stopped beating, and the country froze in despair and disbelief. Six years later—a short time that went on for so long—protestors in Tirana smashed the statue of the immortal one to pieces.

In July 1991, an amnesty was issued to all political prisoners, and the regime's crimes became statistics.

For forty-seven years, the communist authorities held 34,135 political prisoners behind bars.

Over that time, a total of 6,027 people were murdered by order of the Party, in a country with a population of 3 million in 1985.

Nine hundred and eighty-four people died in prison, and 308 lost their minds as a result of torture.

Fifty-nine thousand were detained, of whom more than seven thousand died in labor camps or in internal exile.

The Sigurimi, the Albanian secret police, bugged thousands of homes and enlisted more than two hundred thousand informers. To this day, the Albanians believe that one in four citizens informed on others to the authorities, and when I ask how that was possible, they reply: "The regime could do anything, they terrorized us with fear. It was impossible to escape it."

But according to an OSCE survey carried out in 2016, as many as 45 percent of Albanians see Enver Hoxha as an outstanding politician and good administrator, and only 42 percent regard him as a dictator and murderer. Over half of those surveyed agreed with the statement that communism was a valid ideology in theory, but was badly implemented in practice.

———

I'm on my way to Zagoria with Olti, who comes from these parts, and is now a university lecturer in Tirana.

"No, that's impossible!" one of the passengers in the battered van rudely interrupts when, as part of a typical Albanian introduction, Olti says what he does for a living.

"Why do you say that?"

"If you really were a professor in Tirana, you'd be so rich on back-handers you'd be driving a four-by-four, not slumming it in here with us."

The other passengers nod in agreement. Of course he would! The truth is out! You can't fool us!

"If my child who's at university in Gjirokastër can't pass a single exam without paying a bribe, it must be ten times worse in Tirana," added the man in a tone to end all argument.

Olti is pained, and so am I.

The next day, when we go inside the abandoned school in the village of Ndëran, I think the sight of the dusty voltmeters, plastic models, and faded maps moves him. Most of the equipment in his university laboratory also dates back to the communist era, and, over the years, the students have stolen the valuable collection of rocks and precious stones.

"When freedom broke out, we all lost our minds," Olti says, smiling. "I was a stupid kid, and, flooded with emotion, I ran to my school, picked up a large stone, took a swing, and threw it as hard as I could at the window.

"The whole of Albania was shouting: 'Let's start from scratch!' Every-one came outside, and, in a burst of irrational euphoria, began destroying everything they associated with communism: schools, hospitals, and factories.

"'Why did you smash the window?' asked my teacher. I didn't know what to say. 'I don't want a communist window,' I muttered, my head drooping. And then I looked up and said, in a flash of inspiration: 'Sali Berisha will fit new ones for us!' The leader of the Democratic Party would install better, democratic windows for us! We had no idea what it meant to be free, but we believed that any moment now everything would be the same as it was in the West."

"Whoever could get away from here, did just that—to save themselves," adds Petraq, Olti's uncle who stayed on the family land. "There used to be cultural centers and festivities, work and dignity. Now there's nothing."

Petraq puts white cheese and a bottle of homemade plum raki on the tablecloth. A baby goat that moments ago was getting under our feet will soon, despite our protests, have its throat cut.

"The house of an Albanian belongs to God and to the guest," says the Kanun, a medieval set of laws that were applied for centuries across Albania.

What was meant to be has already happened.

Time smooths out the edges of our recollections; the past is distorted by the weight of the present. The residents of Zagoria are left with just a hazy, deceptive memory.

The Ballad of Uncle Enver
and the Blood That Was Shed

HE WHO SHEDS ANOTHER MAN'S BLOOD poisons his own, but Uncle Enver seems to have escaped that ancient law, because while he took lives swiftly and tactically, without scruples or consequences, he breathed his own last breath at home in bed, having been weak and lifeless for months, but stronger than ever, for nobody had survived who could do him harm, and his anointed successor was humble and happy to assume power.

Enver departed this life propped up on his pillows, hands clean and conscience gleaming, with all those who loved him gathered at his bedside, while all those who feared him timidly stood watch, and all those who hated him were far away, barely alive from hunger and daily torment; or else they were dead, forever silent and fading from memory, with a bullet in the chest or the back of the head, or with the mark of the hangman's noose faded long ago.

The wind dropped, the walls listened and the earth waited, trying to catch the sound of breathing in the silence, just as in their homes people strained to hear the noise of unfamiliar footsteps, the creak of the garden gate, and a knock at the door. Some had to suffer so that others would tremble as they fell asleep for fear of the terrible fate that might befall them, too, in that small country of bunkers, blockades, and barricades.

Yes, dictators die comfortably, degenerate and unyielding to the end, men who have grown more relentless over time, who never spared a bullet for the next purge, who mistook paranoia for intuition, who knew only one form of justice: the earthly kind, meted out in the name of the Party. And that's why ruthless Enver never slid to the ground, shot against a wall in some unremarkable town; nobody came onto the street to demand his head, no man in uniform tied a noose for him, and when the news of his death spread across the country, the people's faces froze in trepidation as they struggled to see the future through a wall of tears. When the heart of the nation dies, the whole country quickly grinds to a halt.

Dead and gone—dearest Uncle Enver, who cradled his children so lovingly, who took every youngster in his arms, who danced with a delighted little girl, who clapped, sang, and smiled so brightly that a great light shone from his eyes, who greeted the people by raising a benevolent hand that tightened to a ruthless fist in the name of the Party.

Dead and gone—dearest Uncle Enver, who held the good children close to his heart and chastised the bad ones by sending them far away, our hero, a paranoid and murderer, a loving leader, who encouraged people to write letters, to praise, to protest and complain if harm was ever done to anyone. He would answer every question, ignoring the trick ones such as: "How many times must you wash your hands to get rid of the blood?"

Dead and gone—dearest Uncle Enver, the great leader and brilliant statesman, but his work shall be immortal, his thoughts shall remain in our heads, glory be to his undying deeds, glory to his everlasting words!

Dead and gone—dearest Uncle Enver, but lo, white light shines from his tomb, and people say they have seen a pale, spectral figure floating in the darkness, not a vampire, nor a ghost, but a *kukudh*, a hungry, thirsty demon, who whispers to the old about the beauty of days gone by, and lectures the young about peace and valor. Forty days have passed, forty years will pass, yet he shall still wander, a reminder of the blood that was shed, a taunting reproach that where there was terror, there was also peace, and where there was a fist, there was also a plan.

The Trial

"SOMEONE MUST HAVE SLANDERED JOSEF K., for one day he was arrested even though he had not done anything wrong."

Sixteen-year-old Bashkim Shehu stops reading; he's feeling an emotion he can't identify. The year is 1972. In ten years' time, the sentence he has just read will become his destiny.

In communist Albania, Kafka's *The Trial* is on the list of proscribed texts, but Bashkim got the book from his elder brother Vladimir, or Ladi for short, who has on his bookshelves the scribblings of Western vermin such as Sartre, Joyce, and Camus. Bashkim and Ladi are the sons of Mehmet Shehu, the second-most important man in the country after Enver Hoxha, and they live in Blloku, Tirana's neighborhood for Party officials, closed to ordinary citizens and guarded by policemen who surround it like beads on a string. Blloku doesn't need walls; no one from outside would dare approach it without permission, anyway.

It's a village of prosperity within a land of poverty, an enclave of luxury of a kind found nowhere else in the country. The most important residents of Blloku have maids and chauffeurs, washing machines and dishwashers, clothes imported from abroad and food that most Albanians have never heard of. Blloku has Coca-Cola and pineapples, jeans and jazz.

After work, the officials check in at the party clubhouse, where they have debates, play billiards, and watch forbidden films at a special cinema. But the fun and games aren't entirely carefree: If someone fails to show up at the club for some time, people start whispering that they must have something on their conscience, which means their end is nigh. And then the gossip turns into fact.

The real heart of Blloku is Hoxha's villa, impressive by Albanian standards, though extremely modest by the standards of dictators. On the opposite side of the street is house number two: the residence of Mehmet Shehu, long-standing prime minister of Albania, and, from 1974, minister of defense as well.

Because for forty years, Albania's God had two heads: Enver Hoxha, the kindly father who kissed children and promised a beautiful future, and Mehmet Shehu, who wielded the sword of the dictatorship of the proletariat to cut off the heads of traitors and enemies. But in 1981, invincible Comrade Shehu, for years the leader's anointed successor, was exposed as a Yugoslav spy, a British, French, Soviet, and even fascist agent, and under the watchful eye of Sigurimi officers, he committed suicide. Then Mount Olympus was left with just one, almighty God.

———

No comedy—when I think about Hoxha, and try to piece together an image of him from dozens of accounts, I feel that this was a person with nothing comical about him. He didn't appear coarse and clumsy like the Romanian communist president Ceaușescu, he didn't play the exuberant joker like Yugoslavia's Marshal Tito, and he had none of the carefree artlessness of the Polish leader Gierek. He preferred to be seen as a reserved intellectual, analyzing the most advantageous scenarios for Albania amid shelves full of books. Here is the leader, sitting at his modest desk, reading letters from his dear people, the Last Judgement personified, the embodiment of legitimacy and law.

"A scholar," the Albanians would say. "A polyglot," they boasted—he'd studied botany in France, after all, although his official biography omitted the fact that he'd been struck off the list of students. And that he worked as a secretary at the Albanian consulate in Brussels, which was quite a surprising occupation for someone who spent his whole time at university in the company of French communists. When things started to go missing from the consulate's coffers, the young Enver lost his job and returned to King Zog's Albania, which was increasingly dependent on Italy. Barely eight years later, the failed botany graduate would become leader of the Communist Party, a war hero, and scourge of the elite. Those who had granted him a scholarship to study abroad would end up on the list of traitors to the nation; they would survive if they managed to escape in time.

The steely gaze of authority was accompanied by a deceptively warm smile. In the eyes of most Albanians, Hoxha was as kind as a father and as infallible as God; amid the uneducated Party hacks, he stood out and shone, perfect and flawless. But the layer of soft moss concealed a rock. As soon as the Supreme Comrade decided that someone was becoming too strong, that their ambitions were growing and their loyalty declining, after a courtesy trial the enemy was shot or exiled to the far end of the country to waste away, be reduced to rags, and disappear.

According to Bashkim Shehu in his book *The Autumn of Fear*, when you became an element of the system, you had to leave friendship behind. To his mind, the man at the top, Enver Hoxha, had no illusions: There was no talk of friendship or camaraderie. He kept his people on a short lead, and they tried to give him proof of their loyalty and devotion, hoping he might mention them in one of his books.

———

On the one hand, there are the dictator's numerous works, in which he rewrites the memory and history of Albania according to communist expectations; and on the other, there are the books that are banned, to which none but a select few have access.

"According to the system, literature had to be transparent, and it had to have a clear message following the Party line."

Sitting before me is Bashkim Shehu, the author of around fifteen books in which he tells his own life story and that of Albanian communism.

More than anyone else, a writer is the hostage of their own past; in their search for literary material, they must constantly dive into the maelstrom of their life and dig out the pearls, the rubbish, and the rocks buried inside themselves.

In some ways, Bashkim Shehu's family history belongs to the whole of Albania. At home, at the dinner table—his father, Number Two in the country. On the other side of the street—Him, Number One. A childhood in an enclave that in the eyes of the Albanian people became a sinister wonderland, a kingdom of gold, collusion, and privilege. Bashkim had access to the forbidden: luxury, travel, and freedom.

In theory, there was no reason to expect a catastrophe. In practice, the atmosphere in Blloku was even more intense than anywhere else in the country. Everyone was connected to everyone else—by marriage, blood, business, or shared glasses of raki. Everyone kept an eye on everyone else. Everyone was prepared to inform. The only loyalty they knew was loyalty to Enver Hoxha. If someone came crashing down, the others looked on attentively. Afterward, they said: "He deserved to crash."

———

Literature was meant to serve the Party, and yet Bashkim's first stories were parables inspired by the works of Kafka. In one of them, medieval warriors appear in Albania to arrest the narrator and his loved ones, and the whole country steps back in time.

"It was like living in *The Trial*," says Shehu. "You were hauled out of your house for interrogation and asked, 'What do you have to say?' You hadn't done anything wrong, but the authorities had their own opinion about you, and were particularly resolute about inflicting punishment on suspects and innocent people. You need only have said something at a committee meeting that someone else found disturbing. You might not have realized it yet yourself, but they already knew you were having doubts."

In the typical Stalinist manner, Hoxha was ruthless and paranoid.

He had started the purges during the war; to strengthen his own position, he had even eliminated staunch communists fighting for the country's independence—anyone more charismatic and better educated than he was, if there was the merest shadow of doubt about their loyalty.

In 1944, he instructed General Dali Ndreu to kill collaborators on the spot, and to arrest and shoot influential individuals as an example to others. The general obeyed the orders; twelve years later, he and his wife Liri Gega would face the firing squad, too—both were accused of spying.

Hoxha also targeted members of Balli Kombëtar, the nationalist movement that was the communists' greatest competition, as well as representatives of Legaliteti, who supported the king, and anyone who had studied abroad or had ties with the West. Some were dragged out of their houses and shot, some were condemned at show trials, and others were interned. The seventeen traitors who were executed included Hoxha's own brother-in-law, Bahri Omari, a minister in the fascist government who collaborated with the Ballists but had also provided shelter for Enver and his fiancée, Nexhmije, during the war.

The purges would keep recurring like floods, drowning Party members on a regular basis, every few years.

In 1948, when Albania cut ties with Yugoslavia, the arrests and executions affected all the "Yugoslavs" in the Party. The first to stand before the firing squad was Minister of the Interior Koçi Xoxe, who had been groomed by Tito as Hoxha's successor. For over a decade, Yugoslavia—which was aiming to annex Albania—would, in Hoxha's eyes, remain the country's greatest enemy. But after the death of Stalin, even the Soviet Union started to betray revisionist urges. In the early 1960s, when Khrushchev had come to terms with Yugoslavia and Greece, and later advised Albania to bet on oranges and lemons rather than chrome and steel, Hoxha branded him an imperialist and broke off their eternal friendship. In Tirana, a wave of repression gradually engulfed the elite who had been educated by the traitors—in the USSR, Poland, Czechoslovakia, and Hungary. Never again would the intellectuals enjoy carefree evenings dancing together to Soviet songs; from now on, they would spend lonely nights in internal exile or hold brief conversations in the prison yard.

———

Toward the end of the 1960s, Hoxha loosened his iron grip. Radio Tirana started playing the Beatles and the Rolling Stones, and the authorities began talking about liberalization and consideration for the needs of young people, because they were the country's future. Bashkim Shehu would meet up with friends who wore jeans and had long hair and furtively listen to illegal records with them, or else he would sit by the wireless in the middle of the night, tapping in time to the beat: Radio Rai, Radio Monte Carlo, the BBC, Radio Free Europe, rock 'n' roll, jazz, Romanian hits. . . . When their infuriated father destroyed his brother Vladimir's Italian records, Shehu switched to American music—Elvis Presley, Ray Charles, Carlos Santana—and became better at hiding the acquisitions smuggled in from trips abroad.

"I always thought my father was conservative and principled because of his background, and Enver was the enlightened one, educated and aware," says Shehu. His face betrays no emotion as the words slowly come together to form sentences. "If he knew which books to ban, it was because he'd read them all and he understood why they might be dangerous. I thought Albania was on the right path, I thought it was opening up. But in 1971, at my father's sixtieth birthday party, Hoxha made a speech. First, he listed my father's achievements, but then out of the blue he changed the subject and began talking about the situation in the country, saying that Albania was becoming too liberal. I spent the whole night awake, wondering what his words might mean. I suddenly realized it would only get worse, that we weren't safe, and that one day they might come for us, too. Censorship and a lack of freedom were at the heart of the regime. They weren't just a side effect of that political setup—they were its central aim."

Despite the signals, of which only the dictator's entourage was aware, in 1972, on the wave of liberalization, the first and last gala of its kind took place: the Eleventh Song Festival, which went down in history as the jolliest communist event with the ghastliest consequences. The singers performed in brightly colored miniskirts or showy hippy-style dresses, the hammer and sickle were missing from the geometric set design, and the winning song was called "When the Spring Comes." "A thaw, a thaw in Albania!" wrote the Yugoslav press—because the music was kind of

Italian, the singers looked a bit Western, and it made you tap your feet and swing your hips. The Italian journalists couldn't get over their surprise: "One big band, two smaller ones, a jury in the studio, juries in various cities—it's a small but charming copy of the Sanremo Festival!" So Italian tastes and flavors were even getting through to incarcerated Albania!

The Sigurimi had news for the leader that was so good it was bad: The festival had been a great success all over the country. People were playing the songs on tape recorders and singing them aloud in their homes. In communist Albania, they were singing at the top of their lungs, as if they were in a place like America! As if they had reasons to be cheerful! As if there were nothing to fear!

Not even the most tolerant dictator could put up with that. If the people felt free for a single moment, they'd soon want more. Soon, their minds would be clouded, they'd be like people in the West, they'd want clothes, entertainment, food—but what could skinny little Albania give them, surrounded on all sides by enemies, with its chronically inefficient agriculture and its dreams of industrial strength? Albania, whose scorn of the West increased with its fear? The economy was collapsing, the five-year plans were barely half-fulfilled, and China's fraternal friendship didn't include military aid. Besides, just a year earlier, Mao—Albania's only ally—had shaken the imperialist hand of Richard Nixon; Albanian propaganda hadn't breathed a word of that treacherous act. All this was weakening the dictator, who had had heart trouble for months. . . .

The iron fist came down. Nobody is going to sing in Albania, he decided. In Albania, everyone will be afraid. We may not have much food, but we have more than enough enemies. Seize your rifles! Everyone must be on their guard, ready to protect the fatherland!

Six months later, a plenum was held that targeted the harbingers of change. The dictatorship would not allow cosmopolitanism. It would not allow the foundations of socialism to be undermined. All enemies would be crushed. Not a stone would be left standing.

The plenum nodded and unanimously branded the festival a party organized by enemies of the people and a symbol of contempt for socialist ideals.

A major witch hunt began. Fadil Paçrami, the Party's ideological sec-retary who had gotten his ideologies confused; Todi Lubonja, the head of radio and television; and the singer Sherif Merdani all went to prison, followed by anyone who might pose the slightest threat, real or imagined.

The grand inquisition raged for two years, because the Party already knew; it had already identified the problem: "Under the guise of the struggle against conservatism, attempts are being made to open the door to liberalism, causing our literature and art to diverge from the path of socialism." The dictator put his foot down: There were arrests, intern-ments, and reprisals. Long prison sentences were handed down to the art-ists Edison Gjergo and Ali Oseku; to Todi's son, the writer and political analyst Fatos Lubonja; to the writer Zyhdi Morava; the poets Frederik Rreshpja and Visar Zhiti; the theater director Kujtim Spahivogli; and to hundreds of others. The most influential journalists, editors, and poets lost their jobs and some were interned. Hurricane Enver tore through the whole cultural establishment; only a few survivors, whom the leader hadn't noticed, remained on the battlefield.

––––––

"With each new wave of arrests there was fear," says Bashkim Shehu. "The desired reaction was hatred toward enemies of the people, but hid-den beneath it was terror for your own fate and, deeper down than that, a sense of guilt."

The more afraid Hoxha was of the enemy, the weaker and more isolated Albania became. China was eyeing it suspiciously, because although it had been pouring money into their great friendship for years, Albania was shrinking and declining. "Albania shows no promise," Mao's successor proclaimed and redirected their fraternal aid to Third World countries. He also showed a friendly face to Tito and Ceauşescu, who in turn were all smiles toward the United States. No one wanted anything to do with the iron leader of Albania.

Without Chinese equipment, tractors, and loans, Albania's "great industrial machine" was left gasping for breath. The system slowed down, choked, and stalled more and more often. Albania was alone and nobody was going to help it.

"We don't need any help!" was Hoxha's response. "But what if we do?" asked Mehmet Shehu, sowing seeds of doubt. Without foreign loans, imports, and aid, Albania would become a medieval feudal farm, if it hadn't already. With such differences in world outlook, Hoxha realized that Shehu was not fit to be his successor. Nexhmije, Enver's wife, had long held the view that Ramiz Alia, fourteen years younger than Shehu, was a stronger believer in communism, and he was also a member of the family: His niece was married to the Hoxhas' son, Ilir.

Now they just had to wait for the spark to ignite the fire. When Skënder Shehu, Mehmet's second son, announced his engagement to the volleyball player Silva Turdiu, there was nothing to herald a storm. Silva's father was a professor who had shown up in Blloku at various social events—meaning that, officially, he seemed to be "one of us," and that the authorities had turned a blind eye to his family connections with Arshi Pipa, the Albanian dissident who had been talking to the American press about Enver's crimes.

But now the eyes of power were open, and the veins on Hoxha's temples were starting to bulge. Why had Mehmet Shehu allowed his son to get engaged to a girl with a bad background? Was it an act of rebellion against his great friend, with whom he had served Albania for so many years?

Mehmet tried to put out the fire, and Skënder broke off his engagement, but it was too late. Number Two would have to be wiped out.

———

Rumors about Mehmet Shehu's suicide continued to do the rounds for many years. The dominant view is that the Sigurimi pulled the trigger. But Bashkim Shehu is sure that his father took his own life because he believed in communism to the bitter end.

"I had a farewell letter written in his handwriting, in his style, explaining the tragedy of the situation."

Did Mehmet Shehu commit suicide to prove his innocence to the dictator? Perhaps, but Enver Hoxha had his own truth: Shehu was a traitor, his family were enemies of the people, and everyone associated with him had to be destroyed.

Mehmet's wife, Fiqirete Shehu, a very old friend of the Hoxha household, was arrested and, after many days of torture, testified to the existence of a gang plotting against the dictator. She died in internal exile seven years later.

Shehu's oldest son, Vladimir, was interned and committed suicide six months later.

The middle son, Skënder, who had fallen in love with the wrong girl, was given ten years in prison.

The youngest son, Bashkim, was interned, and two years later, he was sentenced to eight years in prison, too.

Feçor Shehu, the notoriously cruel former head of the Sigurimi and later minister of the interior—and worst of all, the traitor's nephew—faced the firing squad in 1983. At his side stood Kadri Hazbiu, the long-term minister of the interior and defense minister—and worst of all, the traitor's brother-in-law. Both were killed for attempting to overthrow communism.

There was nobody left on the battlefield who could pose a threat to Enver and his new successor.

———

"Someone must have slandered Josef K., for one day he was arrested even though he had not done anything wrong."

"When the atmosphere around my father began to grow more tense, Vladimir told me he wouldn't testify against him, he wouldn't say what they told him to say. He kept repeating: 'I know what I'm going to do.' But many years later, I found out that after hours of interrogation, under the influence of torture, he did sign a statement forced on him by the Sigurimi. Perhaps he couldn't live with that knowledge afterward? He sent me a message from Gramsh, telling me that I had nothing to fear, because he hadn't said anything against me. Then the news came that Ladi had killed himself.

"I survived my time in prison and internal exile thanks to my good friends and prisoner solidarity. And because I read nonstop. I spent the few pennies we received for forced labor on nothing but books. Manuscripts and prison translations were also passed from cell to cell, Dostoevsky's *The House of the Dead*, for instance; Sophocles in French, which I copied into a notebook; Kant's *Critique of Pure Reason*; and *King Lear* and *Macbeth*.

"I often think of Ladi. For many years, I couldn't believe he was dead. I knew he had died, but something inside me couldn't accept it. When I was released from prison, I ended up alone, in a remote village, in exile, with no one around me. And that's when I realized he really was gone."

———

Everything has happened before. Everything has already been written down. Every incident that happens to us can be found in Greek mythology, in Shakespeare, in Dostoevsky; literature only differs from real life in a few trivial details.

Bashkim Shehu says that Kafka's parables offer the best explanations of what real life was like in Albania. They include three levels relating to the freedom of the individual: their attitude to their father, their country, and God.

"I think there are times when father, country, and God can be the same thing. And that in Kafka, the main character's isolation is just as important as his lack of freedom—his desperate attempts to find someone who might be able to reverse his fate, who might be able to help him, who might recognize the absurdity of the system and rebel against it. But sometimes that scenario simply isn't possible. The only things left are flashes of human kindness, a few lines in a banned book, a brief moment of understanding."

———

"His gaze alighted on the top floor of the building next to the quarry. Like a flash of light, a pair of windows flew open. A figure, feeble and thin at that distance and height, threw themselves forward and stretched their arms out even further. Who was it? A friend? A good person? Some-one who sympathized? Someone who wanted to help? Was it just one person? Was it all of them? Could there be any more help? Were there objections that had been forgotten? There must be. Although logic is unassailable, it is no match for a man who is determined to live. Where was the judge he had never seen? Where was the high court he had never reached? Raising his hands, he splayed all his fingers. But the hands of one of the men grabbed K.'s throat while the other man thrust the knife deep into his heart, twisting it twice. With fading eyesight K. saw the men, cheek-to-cheek and close up, observe the verdict. 'Like a dog,' he said; it was as if the shame were going to outlive him."

The Happiest People in the World

The wall of the building declares:
"The people's power was born at the end of a rifle barrel"

Onward marched the long line of brawny, menacing soldiers, still onward, their heavy boots thumping on the cobblestones of Gjirokastër, their movements stiff and their faces steely. They looked like giants as they climbed uphill, without a trace of fatigue, carrying rifles longer than the height of the children staring after them.

That day, four-year-old Stefan Arseni was roaming about the old market, near his father's shop. The first time he saw the Germans, he felt such great fear that throughout his entire life he has never forgotten it. No one will ever defeat those men, he thought.

Stefan smiles, and his fingers briskly tap along to the rhythm of his sentences. He's nearly eighty, though as I look at his slim, wiry figure, the spring in his step and the sparkle in his eyes, I forget how old he is. But his gentle smile is deceptive; Stefan decisively and unexpectedly cuts short each of our three meetings, nimbly avoids the questions he doesn't like, and keeps on returning to the same old stories. He's the one who sets the boundaries of each anecdote, and I am unable to cross them. Before me sits a man who has spent his entire life perfecting the art of avoiding trouble.

————

"My father was a pragmatic man," Stefan tells me with a wink. "When he met a German officer in the street, he invited him into our home. The German kept eyeing us and scrutinizing every corner of the room. He looked handsome and stern. My father fetched out the brandy, filled two crystal glasses, and looked straight at him. 'No,' said the German. 'You first.' And without batting an eyelid, my father emptied his glass. I was standing in a corner of the room, hidden in the shadows, and I couldn't stop staring at them."

————

A year and a half later, the victorious Albanian partisans marched through Gjirokastër and the people cheered. The terror only came when the blood of executed enemies of the people began flowing over the cobblestones: supporters of democracy, fascist collaborators, suspect intellectuals, and anyone who, for justified reasons or not, was considered a "dubious or unreliable element."

They had come knocking on Stefan's door when Albania was still one big battleground. His father had offered them some raki, but they had refused. They had placed a sheet of paper on the table, and next to it, a gun.

In the days of peaceful poverty, his father and brother used to buy marten and fox pelts from the areas surrounding Gjirokastër and Tepelenë, and sell them across the border in Ioannina to elegant Greek dressmakers, who made collars for overcoats out of them—the *dernier cri* in prewar fashion. When war broke out, the business waned; later on, partisans started coming down from the surrounding mountains to Gjirokastër.

"They showed my father a document stating that they were requisitioning all the pelts from his store. Three hundred items, our whole future. They assured him that after the war they would give him back the money. My father signed, with one eye on the gun, but the document soon turned out to be worth as much as the piece of paper it was written on. The communists didn't stand on ceremony with wealthy craftsmen and tradesmen—they fleeced them down to the last penny and gave the poor the most valuable thing on offer in Albania: land. Anyone who dared protest ended up in prison if they were lucky, and faced the firing squad if they were not."

All this had caused his father to fall sick. Stefan inherited an empty shop and a bad family background: the son of a furrier, and from the Greek minority, too. The spawn of the devil. In the best-case scenario, a suspect element—and in the worst, an enemy of the people.

————

A propaganda billboard in a city square:
"Albania has built everything on her own, by the sweat of her brow,
through the effort and knowledge of her sons and daughters"

With the support of the Yugoslav Communist Party, Enver Hoxha took control of a devastated country through which three professional armies and two underground ones had marched in the space of six years, and where the war had leveled a third of the houses and almost all the infrastructure. The new Albania was born out of ruins and mud.

So they rebuilt and repaired, laboring for free as a contribution to society, in toil and hardship. Brigades and battalions consisting of workers, soldiers, farmers, and students cleared the rubble, put up houses, and surfaced the roads. Every citizen, like it or not, took part in the collective crusade; the whole nation was building the future of a socialist country. As that country was going to become a paradise on Earth any day now, the population had to be trained to defend it—and so, every year, some of the Albanians reported to the "Zbor" (Yugoslav People's Movement), for military training that lasted from one to four weeks, where they learned how to defend the fatherland against the schemes of the enemy.

Little Albania was meant to become an industrial giant, with the Lenin Hydroelectric Power Plant, the sugar refinery in Maliq, the cement factory in Vlorë, and the textile plant in Tirana. The nation supported the

Party nonstop and under its leadership, redoubled their efforts for their socialist fatherland to flourish without cease.

But the more industry developed, the worse agriculture fared. Everything was in deficit: grain, tractors, sheep, bread, milk, and meat. Agriculture was primitive and inefficient, but the authorities kept telling the hungry Albanians that this was how steel was tempered.

In the early 1950s, smartly dressed gentlemen with notebooks started appearing in remote highland villages, where people slept on straw mattresses in thatched cottages.

"Do you have plates?" they asked.

The country folk shook their heads.

"What about cutlery?"

"Comrade, what are you on about?"

"Pillows? Bed linen?"

So the envoys made a note: "For this family: this many plates, this much cutlery, an eiderdown."

"Eat fruit and vegetables!" the smart gentlemen encouraged them, but the people just shrugged.

"Where are we supposed to get them?"

So the Party sent citizens from the south to the north, to teach them how to grow potatoes, tomatoes, and cucumbers in fields where until then they had only grown maize.

The smart gentlemen had a noticeboard put up in the village with slogans on it such as: WASH YOUR HANDS! USE CUTLERY!

The old people summoned the teacher to read out what it said, and to explain what the hell was happening to their country.

The teacher came along and declared: "What's happening is progress."

He said the village was going to be supplied with electricity, too.

The old people assured him they weren't afraid of anything.

A signpost in the middle of the street:
"Our people have freely chosen the path of development and
they don't have to justify it to anyone"

"At every step, I kept a close eye on my own shadow," says Stefan. "Whenever the state noticed something suspicious, it ordered arrests, and then the surface of the lake became smooth again. With a black mark in my family history, I had no hope of a scholarship, even though I studied day and night. Because of my father, they wouldn't let me go to university, and after I finished high school they sent me to work in a village in the south. I was to be a school teacher. I was so young that when they said they were moving me to Konispol, near the Greek border, I burst into tears. I was barely eighteen, and I didn't want to leave home. In the end, they sent me to a village near Sarandë, and there, alongside several other teachers who were just kids, like me, I taught Albanian and math, while I taught myself how to cook and clean. We had no idea about life, we only knew that we had to watch out for ourselves and others. If we made the slightest mistake, we'd be in big trouble."

———

Just like the other teachers, Stefan used to force his pupils to write out slogans on the hillsides using heavy stones:

MARX ENGELS LENIN STALIN

GLORY TO THE PARTY

LONG LIVE ENVER HOXHA

GLORY TO MARXISM AND LENINISM

They used the biggest stones they could find, beautifully whitewashed, guarded and tended, so that everyone would know, so that no one would dare to forget. Stefan did his best, remained dutiful and never doubted, until finally the Party appreciated his commitment and allowed him to go to university.

By consistently demonstrating the right attitude, after university, Stefan was put in charge of a library in Gjirokastër. If someone was arrested, he and his team had to roll up their sleeves and remove all references to the newly appointed enemy. The traitor's name was erased from books and magazines, and his face was scratched out; the enemy was deprived of his past and changed into a formless apparition, or else he disappeared completely, as if he had never existed.

Such was the will of the Party, and nobody dared challenge it. Stefan was all the more scrupulous because he knew a journalist from Tirana who had taken up writing poems. In one of them, he had compared the country to a cactus; he was soon obliged to bid farewell to Tirana and say hello to Gjirokastër instead. It gave Stefan food for thought.

There was a similar story involving his cousin, whom he had employed just to help a poor soul with a bad family background—his father had owned a factory in the days of King Zog. Everyone around him waited patiently for the cousin to say the words that would help destroy him.

One day, his colleagues at work were talking about alcohol, and the cousin said: "I've heard Metaxa isn't bad."

But that wasn't quite enough.

So when his workmates denounced him, they claimed: "He said Metaxa was much better than the Albanian brandies, and then he cried: 'If we take power, we'll hang all the communists!'"

Even the prosecutor knew they had added the communists for the purposes of the denunciation, but, as they had their orders, there was no harm in sending the cousin down.

"The poor guy spent seven years in prison," Stefan says, shaking his head. "From then on, I only visited his family at night. If someone had seen me entering their house, I'd have been in trouble."

———

A sign displayed on the balconies of a building:
"Albania—the invincible fortress of socialism"

Communism did nothing but keep building itself, through the physical labor of socialist man and the toil of political prisoners. In the late 1950s, Albania flourished, mainly thanks to money borrowed from the Soviet Union; there were new textile factories, new canneries, new hydroelectric power plants, and new Albanian strength. Enemies of the people atoned for their sins by draining swamps, and the authorities recorded major progress in the fight against the malarial mosquito. Areas formerly associated with disease and danger were transformed into cultivated fields, which were always in short supply in mountainous Albania. These were the great successes of a small, brave nation.

Those who did not have the Sigurimi knocking at their door believed communist rule was the best thing to have happened to their country. The landowners were rotting in jail, the land had been placed in the hands of the people, and as for the fact that collectivization had taken it back again—too bad, clearly that was for the right reasons. If anyone saw things differently, they should mind what they thought. Minor adversities such as food shortages, would eventually be overcome. The new man could read and write, and had read about the endless stream of successes in the newspapers.

Meanwhile, the authorities reported a wave of revisionism that was sweeping through the Soviet Union; under new leadership, Big Brother had lost faith in Stalin's wisdom and betrayed his ally and was now patting Albania's worst enemies on the back. Luckily, Albania had already opened its arms to accept China's fraternal embrace; China was a truly socialist country and it was generous with its aid. In the 1960s, cash began to pour in from the Marxist dragon, Albanian women used Chinese tractors to plough Albanian fields, Chinese workers hummed Albanian songs, and Chinese and Albanian hands were clasped together.

And while her Chinese brother was propping her up, Albania could stand straight, it was still possible to believe in communist progress, it was still possible to be happily deluded. But collectivization was already having hiccups, industrial production was stumbling, the economic indicators were in decline, and more and more creativity was required when writing out the statistics.

That is why fists were raised and shouts in praise of the nation grew ever louder, parades were on the march, successes were triumphantly exalted, mouths sang, children waved, old people wept, trumpets, thunderclaps, drum rolls, singing, and cheering resounded! How developed our fatherland is, how well educated our youth, how greatly everyone envies us! Who could fail to believe it? Who would dare wander from the Albanian path to happiness?

――――――

A toast for every occasion:
"The Party lives and will live for ever!"

"When I became the manager of a theater in Gjirokastër, I was sent to the morality front to teach people discipline in their private lives. One day, an old man and his little woman came to see me, complaining that one of the actors regularly beat their daughter, who was his wife, forcing her to flee to her parents' house. I gave the actor an earful, tore a strip off him, and taught him a lesson: 'Behave yourself or we'll kick you out!' Did he have any choice? He'd have struggled to find work if he were unemployed, he'd have ended up in prison, and there he wouldn't even have a mirror to shout at himself in. That's how the Party took care of public morality. We were truly grateful to it. We believed in socialism.

"At the table, the first toast was always: 'Long live the Party, and may it rule for ever!' Enver Hoxha looked down on households from a portrait in every home. I had not just a portrait, but also a bust of the leader. But when we regained freedom, I immediately destroyed them. Now I regret it—I'd have had an interesting souvenir of the past.

"In communist Albania, if a woman had a bun in the oven, sometimes she'd be asked: 'Would you rather have a boy or a girl?' And she'd reply: 'Whatever the Party sends!' Well, perhaps not everyone answered like that, but some of them did.

"Because the Party meant more than God. God did not exist. And even if he did, he was only almighty in theory, while the Party was almighty in practice. God couldn't destroy the Party, but the Party could destroy God. We had an icon of Jesus at home and sometimes we lit a candle before it, but in secret, because we knew that in this country even a father would inform on his son.

"Whenever we organized a folk music festival in Gjirokastër, we knew the first song always had to praise Enver Hoxha. And it had to be good! Tuneful and catchy, so it would delight our leader. Otherwise we'd be in trouble. On the radio we only listened to folk music, politicians' speeches, or classical music. Even if someone knew a thing or two about rock, they didn't brag about it, for fear of ruining their life.

"The first time I saw a television was in 1967, at the home of a friend whose family in Italy had provided this extraordinary gift. How amazing it was to see pictures and hear sounds coming from a square box for the first time in my life! I worked in the state sector, where every employee could be allocated either a fridge or a television, and when I got a TV set I was very happy.

"Every day, we watched programs showing that the Albanians were the happiest people in the world, and I believed them, even though the whole country was surrounded by barbed wire, and I needed a special permit to be able to travel to a village near the border. If anything shook the fence, a signal was sent straight to the nearest watchtower. The guards could shoot any fugitive in the back.

"We might not have had camps that turned people into soap, but we did have the best-guarded borders in the world."

Slogans on the cooperative wall:
"Long live communist chickens!"
"Long live communist cows!"

In 1978, after breaking ties with revisionist China, Enver Hoxha announced to his beloved people that there wasn't a country in the whole wide world with such a firm belief in communism as Albania. "The Tito-ists, the Soviet traitors, the countries of Eastern Europe and China all had a hidden, hostile objective—to enslave our country. We shall rip off their mask and tell them to their face that Albania can't be bought for a handful of rags, or for a few roubles, dinars, or yuan," the Supreme Comrade shouted to the crowd.

Albania was left alone on the battlefield for the only true socialism. "You must always be on the alert," the dear leader kept telling them, "because our country is surrounded on all sides by revisionist and imperialist states that will never stop trying to destroy us or do us harm. If we lower our guard for just a moment, if we relax our struggle, the enemy will strike at us immediately, like a snake that bites and injects its poison before you know it."

The authorities' mouths were full of platitudes, but meanwhile the shelves in the shops were empty. After thirty years, ration cards for food were back. Since 1982, the year of livestock collectivization, if the sign above the entrance to a shop read *Mish*, meaning "Meat," the shoppers could be sure they'd find a wide range of empty hooks inside.

The first ghostly figures would start to line up outside the shops at around four or five in the morning. Sometimes, to make their lives easier, people would leave an object in the queue and then go home to sleep for another hour or two. Occasionally, even four in the morning was too late to stand a chance of buying milk. What could you do, if there were twenty people in the queue and only ten bottles were delivered that day?

News that meat had appeared went round at the speed of light, and crowds soon gathered outside the shops. Knowing that deliveries prompted strong emotions and frail women could be injured in clashes with men, the authorities gave orders for equal rights to be observed and for the meat to be sold to a man and then a woman by turns. In a socialist society, respecting gender equality was a priority.

One day, the amazed citizens of Shkodër noticed a new, highly unusual shop on the high street, full of sweets, fruit, and treats they hadn't seen for years. A crowd quickly gathered, but the police ordered it to disperse, to make way for a beautifully dressed woman, who in a confident tone was saying into the lens of a camera: "You claim there's no food in Albania. Look at this, you liars! In Albania the shelves are full!" For the purposes of the report, three overjoyed individuals were allowed inside, after which the shop was shut and the crowd chased away.

A declaration on a fence in the capital city:
"We're heading for new victories on the road to building
and strengthening socialism"

"Whenever I received news from the committee that a foreign journalist was coming to Albania to write an article about the Greek minority, I immediately had to tell the members of the cooperative in the village he would visit to hang up some meat in the local shop. With my superiors' consent, I also fetched some coffee from the stockroom for the Greek families to offer to the journalist when he visited them. Because people only ever had enough meat and coffee for the first half of the month. But of course there was always some to be found behind the scenes for decorative purposes.

"In 1986, I was sent to Greece with a folk group from Gjirokastër. At the time, there wasn't even enough bread in the shops, and finding a tin of sardines was like a dream come true, and here were the Greeks asking us: 'Is there anything you need? Would you like a hair-dryer? Or a Dictaphone?' Of course, as far as I was concerned all these things were miraculous, but there was definitely more than one Sigurimi agent in the group, so I replied: 'No, thank you. In Albania we have everything we need.' We were allowed to walk around the town in groups of four, and we were allowed to go into shops, but I couldn't tell anyone what I'd seen.

"So later, when people kept asking me: 'Stefan, Stefan, how was it?,' I'd reply: 'Well . . . it was pretty good. But you know what, they've got an awful lot of flies over there!' If I had told the truth, that Greece was day and Albania was night, I'd have been in hot water.

"Once I'd seen Greece, I realized that capitalism was better than communism. Everyone could say what they liked there, and nobody walked with a shadow like we did. In Albania, it would never have occurred to anyone to sit and chat about politics over a cup of coffee—only prisoners could afford to do that! Telling the Greeks anything about our country would also have been suicide. When they asked how we were doing, I always replied: 'Life's great, we're very happy.'

"For years, we kept repeating: 'Albanians are the happiest people in the world,' and we believed it, because how were we to know otherwise? We only knew communism, nothing else, and for years we had nothing to compare our lives with. Happiness is a relative concept. In other countries, there were people who had more, for whom life was easier, but I didn't know about that. I had nothing to long for and no one to envy.

"It was only the trip to Greece that opened my eyes. And so what? Sometimes it really is better not to know, not to wonder, not to ask questions.

"Because before then, I genuinely thought I was happy."

Enver Is Forever in My Heart

AS THE RUSSIAN POET Vladimir Mayakovsky wrote:

> The Party and Lenin are like twin brothers,
> Who is more valued by history, their mother?
> When we say Lenin, it's the Party that we're naming,
> When we say the Party, it's Lenin we're proclaiming.

It's the same for me. When I say "the Party," I mean "Enver Hoxha."

My name is Nexhip Manga, I'm a stonemason and poet, and I believe that with Enver's death we lost the greatest Albanian in the history of our nation.

When he died—may I go blind if I'm lying!—for two months I couldn't find a hole in which to hide away and cry. I was embarrassed in front of people, because I was constantly on the edge of tears. Would anyone cry nowadays for Edi Rama or Sali Berisha? But back then, people wept so loud that even the birds in the sky could hear them.

Throughout his life, Enver Hoxha breathed the same air as the Albanians. He was also unusually well educated for those days. First, he studied in Korçë at the best high school in the country, and then he went to university in France, where he joined a group of French communists and saw for himself how odious capitalism is and what made the putrid West like that. During the Second World War, when Albania had to decide whether to support the capitalists or the communists, Enver chose the communists without hesitation, because he knew he must protect the country from capitalism.

He was the best leader in the world—wise, provident, and farsighted. As soon as he saw that a civil servant was pilfering, fiddling the books, or making a profit at the citizens' expense, he immediately exiled him to the provinces to teach him a lesson. He was sincere and just, full of love for his people.

Even now, I feel like crying at the thought that he's gone. But he lives on in our hearts. Oh yes, Enver's right here, in my heart. Nobody loved Albania as much as he did.

You ask me why I miss Enver when I'm so much better off now. Forgive me, I don't mean to offend you, but that's a stupid question. So what if we can sit on the sofa in front of a television set and eat cake, if we don't know what tomorrow will bring? So what if we can travel around the world, if we don't have peace in our hearts?

In the past, I used to get up in the morning, work for eight hours, and then sling my jacket over my shoulders and go home. I knew that next day, I'd go back to the factory, I'd have a nice time with my colleagues, and everything would be as it should. My mind was clear, my dreams were bright, my brow was smooth. But now I break my back every day and worry about what fate has in store for me. I'm seventy years old and I can't rest, I have to keep on working, while the country is sliding over a precipice.

Before Hoxha died, I didn't have a single picture of him at home, and I'd never read any of his books. It was only when he died and capitalism ran riot in Albania that I realized what wonderful times we'd lived in.

A journalist once asked Enver's wife, Nexhmije Hoxha: "Why was Albania so poor?" And Nexhmije replied: "We were poor, but everyone had what they needed to live, and they could sleep easy. We did our best to make sure everyone had the same as everyone else."

The manager of the factory where I worked earned maybe two thousand lek more than I did. I didn't mind—he was the boss. But there weren't such large differences as there are now, when the managers earn millions and never stop wanting more, when some people leave the bank with suitcases full of cash while others search for food in rubbish bins. And there were no drugs, we had no idea what drugs were, but nowadays there's marijuana growing all the way from Sarandë to Theth.

These days, the biggest millionaires are the political party bosses, who are selling off the country. And everyone's afraid of losing what they have. Since the early 1990s, someone has come to the stream behind my house every day to collect empty cans that they can sell. What kind of a life is that, where people have no dignity, where they can't be sure of anything?

These days, there are machines, modern factories, and all sorts of beautiful things. It's just as Marx said: In capitalism, development is paramount because it drives profit, and competition boosts quality, production, and income. Under communism we didn't have all those machines. I worked in a shoe factory, where I made wooden lasts. In those days, the ministry managed production at each site from the top down. Our comrades would call and say: "The factory in Gjirokastër has to produce this number of shoes of this kind," and all four shoe factories in Albania worked according to the plan, as in a clan where everyone has their duties and respects the head of the family because he gives the orders.

Centralization meant it didn't matter whether the shoes were well made or not. They were subjected to quality control, but who cared about quality? There were always enough shoes for everyone! It's not true that under Hoxha the children of people with bad family backgrounds went barefoot—who told you that? The system provided for everyone. Even if the quality was poor, not a single pair would be left in the warehouse because everyone wanted shoes and everyone took what they were given. There was no alternative, and nothing went to waste! But now, if one factory produces more at lower prices, the other factory goes bankrupt and the workers lose their jobs. Does anyone ever think of the workers nowadays?

We had ten factories around Gjirokastër, including one that made cigarettes, with two hundred employees. In the 1990s, the finance minister Genc Ruli closed it down and started importing truckloads of cigarettes from Greece. But ours were just as good! Partizani cigarettes, the ones they used to make in Gjirokastër, were the best in the world. But after the fall of communism, everyone lost their heads, and people were fooled by the colorful foreign packaging. Quality didn't count—all that mattered was that someone was smoking Western cigarettes. The factory closed down, and two hundred people went abroad in search of a living.

In the past, everyone went to school and then to work. Anyone who came out of prison had to accept a job at once and integrate into society. Even people with a bad family background could go to college. You don't believe me? Then I'll tell you the story of Neritan Ceka, the famous Albanian archaeologist, who told it to me himself. When he finished high school, the Party committee wouldn't let him go to university because he was the son of Hasan Ceka, an archaeologist who once wrote that Albania should unite with Yugoslavia, and that was that—his family was downgraded and its members recognized as enemies of the people. But Neritan wrote a letter to Hoxha in person. And Enver gave him permission to go to university.

Because he made sure Albania was a fair country. If the grants were mainly awarded to people with a good family background, the bureaucrats were to blame, not Enver. After all, it was the officials who decided who'd get a television, who'd get a fridge, and who would go to college. If Enver had known about the abuses, there wouldn't have been any!

After the October Revolution, Mayakovsky wrote that he'd be fighting the bureaucrats for the rest of his life, because even in a communist system there were always some black sheep. In the end, there were so many bureaucrats that they drove Mayakovsky to suicide. And they cut Enver off from the people like a wall.

His two greatest achievements were the creation of the education system and the reinforcement of the defense system. Because Enver always had the dignity of the Albanians in mind.

In the 1940s, after the liberation, everyone went to junior school for four years and that was it. People with higher education were extremely few and far between. My mother only went to school for five years, and she used to read the letters and newspapers for everyone in the district. Schools had to be created from almost nothing, but twenty years later not a single person in Albania was illiterate.

In the 1990s, my wife's relatives tried to arrange a marriage for their daughter with a boy from Ioannina. The girl's family went to meet him. While they were getting to know each other, the girl's father quoted some lines from the Iliad. "How on earth do you know Homer?" the Greeks asked in amazement. "Because we studied Homer at school!" he replied.

They couldn't believe it, because most of them had only had four years' education at junior school. What did the Greeks need school for, if they worked in factories or farmed the land? But in Albania, everyone who worked was educated. If a young man who didn't have an education came to work at our factory, the management set a condition: If you don't finish high school, you won't get a promotion. And a promotion meant a pay rise. So the young people had to study. Who would encourage a factory boy to study nowadays? He's only meant to be part of a cheap, mindless workforce and that's all.

And his second achievement: the defense of the country. Because all the countries around us were capitalist, and Yugoslavia was leaning toward a market economy. Nothing but enemies, all pushing for a change of system! But Enver always kept to the designated path, and preferred to be ready for an attack rather than submit to anyone else. In 1965, the United States started bombing Vietnam, and Albania was buzzing with reports about it. As a defense against the air raids, the Vietnamese built a network of bunkers and tunnels, and after each bombardment they emerged safe and sound from underground.

Hoxha had a choice: defend communism or surrender. But the Albanians are born with a sword in their hands. Yes! In 1913, our great politician Isa Boletini went to Great Britain to debate Albania's destiny. Before the meeting, the guards searched him and took away his pistols, but at the meeting one of the English lords made a joke: "Who'd have thought the British would manage to disarm an Albanian!" At which point Isa Boletini brought out another gun he had hidden under his clothes and said: "An Albanian never lets himself be fully disarmed!"

So Hoxha opted for the Vietnamese defense strategy and covered the whole of Albania with bunkers. When a delegation visited us from Greece, their jaws dropped. "What on earth is that?" And my uncle's cousin, who was the minister for trade in those days, replied: "These are our tanks. They can't actually attack you, but they won't give an inch if you come at us."

The Albanians took food from their own mouths to build the network of tunnels and bunkers. If the whole project hadn't happened, our lives would have been a lot easier, it's true. But it's a matter of give and take! If we were attacked, our defense infrastructure would have prevented the enemy from taking control of the country. "The capitalists are trying to bring us to our knees," Hoxha often said, "but if American ships were to enter our waters, we'd shower them in such a rain of bullets that they wouldn't stand a chance."

But when Albania collapsed in 1991, we were instantly down on our knees before the United States. And now we're like a little lapdog that happily wags its tail as soon as its master looks at it.

It all fell apart after Hoxha's death. His successor, Ramiz Alia, was the greatest traitor in the history of the Albanian nation. Before the tears on our faces had dried, he started closing factories and taking the bread out of our mouths. He was the first to make contact with the Americans, and he cynically condemned the country to bankruptcy. He destroyed the economy and closed down the factories, because he knew an impoverished Albania would have to turn to the West for aid. People began to hate communism and Enver Hoxha.

My brother was the commissar for an army corps in the south. He told me that Albania had such large food reserves that the people could have had enough to eat and drink without working for sixteen years. But when Hoxha died, the traitors to the nation threw the stocks of corn and wheat into the sea, to speed up the collapse of the system. So we'd starve to death like dogs. Ramiz Alia consciously and cynically wrecked the Albanian economy and the image of Enver Hoxha in the eyes of his compatriots. People thought it was Hoxha's fault that they'd ended up in extreme poverty, but it was foreign imperialism that ruined the Albanians! The fall of communism began in Poland, and then the floodgates opened: Czechoslovakia, Hungary, Romania, Bulgaria, until it reached Albania. The imperialists already had experience of destroying other societies.

In their blindness, people began toppling statues of Enver across the whole country. But so what if they pulled down a bronze statue? A monument is nothing—the real Enver lives on in our hearts.

I refuse to listen to complaints about crimes committed by the system. Stories were spread in the 1990s about Hoxha killing his high school classmates. The journalists wanted to make a monster of him at any price. But if Hoxha gave the orders for anyone to be killed, it was because he had a good reason to do so. Those who acted against the country had to be killed, just like all the dangerous intellectuals who studied abroad and were in touch with foreigners. Once dead or interned they couldn't make any more mistakes. The Ballists escaped from Albania and founded an association in the United States, they organized congresses and tried to bring down the system by sending saboteurs to Albania, but we had no idea it was happening! So no wonder Hoxha isolated the sons of the Ballists. They were the moles undermining the foundations of the system.

Maybe communism did kill a hundred or a thousand people, but they were all enemies of the regime. Nobody was killed or interned if they weren't guilty. It's nowadays that innocent people are locked in jail because there's no justice in this country, and anyone can buy himself freedom if he has the money. One day you're in prison—the next you're out. In Enver's day, if a doctor took the smallest bribe from a patient, he'd have been interned straightaway. But now, if you don't grease his palm, you could collapse in the waiting room and no one would cast you a second glance. In the past, there were rules in force that nobody dared break. Today there are no rules. The American secret service once sent a paid assassin to kill Enver, here, in Gjirokastër. But when the assassin saw how much the people loved Enver, how the children kissed his cheeks, how the adults wept with joy at the sight of their wonderful leader, he said: "How could I kill such a good man?" And he handed himself over to the Albanian police. Honestly!

There is no greater beauty in the world than the beauty of communism. Thanks to communism I had inner peace, as a man and as a citizen. I had no problems whatsoever. But today, the Albanian millionaires sleep with guns by their beds because they can't be sure of anything.

That's why I weep at the thought of Enver. And that's why I bought so many portraits of him in the 1990s. Go ahead and count them—there are six. I made a clock in my workshop with his picture on it and I set it for a quarter past two in the morning, because that's the time of Enver's death.

I've written poetry since I was sixteen, and I've published lots of collections of it. I wrote a long poem about the death of Enver, too, and in the early 1990s I wondered whether to include it in my new book. Should politics appear alongside love poems? But then it occurred to me that my poem about Enver was a love poem, too! After all, it describes the pain that comes with the death of a beloved leader.

> Dear Enver's life will never end
> Our broken hearts will never mend,
> We now declare our sworn endeavor,
> We stand with him now and for ever.

> For us his words are precious treasure,
> There's none to whom they don't bring pleasure,
> His name won't be besmirched with grime,
> Our leader till the end of time.

> Let April the eleventh not come back
> All Albania dressed in black,
> Enver died, the sky grew dim,
> The world won't see more men like him.

Enver died? That's a mistake!
That piece of news is simply fake,
That piece of news is like a toxin,
A son was taken from his kin.

In April, the eleventh day,
When death took that great man away,
Such floods of tears flowed from our pain,
That all through spring there was no rain.

———

While I was talking to Nexhip Manga, his eyes misted up time and again.

When I asked about Hoxha's crimes, he frowned in disbelief, as if my question caused him pain.

Nonetheless, toward the end of our meeting he took me to his library of several thousand books. From the top shelf, in a gold frame, Enver, with rosebud lips and gentle smile, gazed down benevolently at us. One of the six illustrious Envers reigning posthumously in this home.

Children of the Dictator

Dear Uncle Enver, you're so good
Your hands are full of honeyed food
One holds sugar, the other dates
The Party's in a happy state!

How many times have I heard this rhyme since coming to Albania?

My thirty-year-old boyfriend recites it with a laugh, but his sixty-year-old mother shakes her head.

"Believe me, there was no Albanian who didn't have those lines carved on his mind as if in stone."

Her ninety-year-old mother-in-law, the wife of a partisan and daughter of a kulak, who often forgets what I'm called and what I'm doing here, recites the poem faultlessly and sighs.

The dear old uncle of all Albanians knew what was good for each lamb in his flock. If you had the greatest luck possible and were given permission to go to university, you had to fill in a form. Box number one: the course of study the Party wanted you to take. Boxes two and three: the courses you would like to take. In exceptional circumstances, if you were born into the right family, the Party would agree to fulfill your dreams, but usually it chose your course for you, according to the needs of the country.

It's only after hearing my friends' stories about their parents that I realize how great an attack on personal liberty this was. "My mother is a lawyer, but she always wanted to work in a lab." "My father's a teacher, although his dream was to study geology." People's unfulfilled ambitions trail after them like shadows. The girl who wanted to be a doctor became an architect, even though she couldn't draw. The boy who dreamed of a career in soccer was assigned to philology. For your own good it was better to have pragmatic aims in life, of benefit to the country.

The Party chose your course of study, the Party sent you to live in the city or in the countryside, the Party gave its blessing to engaged couples, the Party broke up inappropriate relationships and ensured there would be no unsuitable marriages. The "bad guy" had to get the "good girl" out of his head. The "good girl" had to forget about the "bad guy" and take the "good one" offered her by the Party.

From morning to night, you heard that you lived in the best of all possible worlds, and that kindly Uncle Enver was watching over you. He drew the limits of your personal space and didn't let you stray, because you might get lost. You owed him an infinite debt of gratitude, because he knew best what you needed and how much—and that was exactly what he'd give you.

> *Dear Uncle Enver, you're so good*
> *Your hands are full of honeyed food*

I'm with the writer and journalist Fatos Lubonja, sitting in Iliria, the only bar to have kept its old appearance in the Blloku district, and I've just asked him about this rhyme. By now all the bars around here look as if they've been transplanted from Italy, London, or France: islands of hipster cool and garish bling among the small, crumbling apartment blocks and cracked sidewalks.

"Imre Kertész once said that dictatorship reduces people to the level of children who want to survive at any price, even if that means collaborating.

The Party and Enver were the Great Parents. Everyone had to think what Hoxha told them to think, work where the Party wanted them to work, and dress the way the authorities expected. When freedom came, the Albanians were like children who didn't know what responsibility was, because until then the government and the system had been responsible for everything. Suddenly they were given the right to grow up and start making their own decisions, but all anyone thought about was how to satisfy their own needs. The communist mentality merged with neoliberal ideology, which teaches that there is no such thing as society; there are only individuals, so I take care of myself and the market regulates it all. Some Albanians went abroad, but even there they didn't form a society. Why not? Because Albanian communism was opposed to the idea of society. Within a society, we create something together, voluntarily, whereas under communism, everything was imposed. And so we're still in that childlike state of regression, failing to learn how to take responsibility for each other. We'll spend our entire lives trying to grow up."

A photographer's workshop in Durrës, 1984.

PART TWO

MUD
SWEETER
THAN
HONEY

The Bad Boy

THE ONLY PARADISE ATTAINABLE was on Earth, and it was called Albania—the authorities would not consent to any other kind. You could only express a longing for God in the privacy of your own home, once you had veiled the eyes of the windows and plugged the ears of the walls. What did the Albanians need God for when they had Enver Hoxha, a smiling, earthly god who rewarded good and punished evil?

"Every night and every morn, some to misery are born." So here, in a small, barred, and bolted country and into a bad, unnecessary family, a child was born who would always have to carry the burden of his origins.

"Every morn and every night, some are born to sweet delight." So it was, is, and shall be in a paradise ruled by a ruthless god.

———

"Bad boy," the teacher barked at me on my first day at school. He grabbed my hand, pulled me after him, and dragged me into the middle of the classroom. There I cringed, while they didn't stop staring at me. Just the one of me and a hundred pairs of glaring eyes.

"Look!" cried the teacher. "This is a bad boy. You'd better keep your distance from him."

He put me on show, defenseless, for the little hyenas to devour, and gave them the signal: "Take him. Whatever you do to him, you have my blessing."

The children could smell blood, and they went for me over and over again, making the most of my helplessness. The teachers made sure that the boy with the bad background was always the worst off.

One time, a girl in my class copied my homework and took it with her to answer questions in front of the class. She got the top mark, a ten. Later on, the teacher summoned me to the blackboard.

I took the same answers with me and I got a four—in other words, a bad mark. I was speechless.

"But why?" I cried. "Blerta copied my answers and she just got the top mark!"

The teacher looked at me.

"It is your moral obligation to help her whenever she asks you to. Be pleased that a nobody like you is fit for anything at all."

I walked home alone, the tears pouring down my cheeks.

I have so much anger in me whenever I think of that small child, standing in the middle of the classroom unable to defend himself, as yet unaware of what lay in store for him, how much good, how much evil. I was so little. What had I done to anyone? Sometimes that pain comes back to me, and I feel the rage boiling up inside me.

In the 1990s, the people who hurt me when I was a child would put a hand on my shoulder and say: "Forgive us the bad things, that was the system." What am I supposed to make of their apologies? I was a human being just as they were, but they didn't treat me like one.

———

I was born in the village of Sinanaj. My father had said goodbye to Tirana when he had dared to say that collectivization would destroy Albania's already half-dead agriculture. The authorities had thanked him for expressing his opinion by exiling him and his wife to the countryside, so he could spend his time in the lap of nature and find out if life was really so bad there. And while they were about it, they hadn't failed to bring up the fact that my father's brother had been an officer in King Zog's army. As if that weren't enough, my mother's brother, who had fought as a partisan against the Germans, had had the nerve to declare after the war: "I didn't fight the enemy for communism to win, but to liberate the country. And that's why I want to be free now! I want to have the right to say what I like!"

And no sooner had he opened his mouth than he was in prison.

There were sixteen of us at home: my parents and fourteen children. Fourteen stomachs to be filled, fourteen little mouths crying out: "Food!," fourteen backs on which to lay a burden, fourteen pairs of hands that were soon accustomed to labor. For as long as I can remember, we were always hungry, and my only thought was of what to put in my mouth. We had a roof over our heads, it's true, but we didn't have a floor. Every day was a struggle against the lack of everything and against petty humiliations.

The countryside was much more familiar with hunger than the city. In the 1960s, all the rural families worked at cooperative farms, and they spent all day looking at food they could only dream of eating. All the potatoes, tomatoes, and cucumbers were exported or sent to the cities. To buy a bottle of milk involved a long walk into town. We drank it in tiny mugs because there was so little of it. Around us, state-owned chickens dug in the dirt and state-owned cows mooed, but we weren't allowed to touch them. The bravest people kept chickens in the cellar—secret, reactionary chickens that had never seen the sunlight and were strictly forbidden to cluck. I had no idea what a real shop looked like, not to mention a boutique, because I only knew the miserable tin shack in the village where you could buy bread, pasta, rice, jam, and oil so disgusting that it was only fit to be poured away.

One day my parents called me over and said: "Tomorrow your uncle's coming to take you away to Tirana."

When my eyes filled with tears, my mother hugged me and said: "Don't cry. Life at your uncle's place will be like paradise."

I didn't know what paradise was, because I was only five years old and I was a boisterous little tyke, the youngest of all fourteen. But I knew that somewhere, in a land far, far away, lived our uncle, my father's brother, who had a pretty good life. In fact, he'd had a bad life, because he'd spent twelve years in prison, but now, at least, he lived in the capital and not in the countryside like us. The authorities had been merciful and hadn't sent him to some hopeless backwater from which there was no way out, but had allowed him to return to Tirana, where he was from.

Our uncle knew we were languishing. When he came out of prison, it turned out he couldn't have children.

"You've got fourteen, but I don't have any. Give me one to bring up," he'd asked my father.

My father didn't take long to decide.

"I'll give you Yzeir, because he's the youngest and he's named after our father. Let him grow up to be a good person."

My parents were happy that at least one of us would manage to escape poverty. If you'd seen me as a child . . . I have hardly any photographs, because who could afford photos when they were that poor, but picture it like this—as a kid, I looked like my oldest son, Ruben: long eyelashes, large eyes, and big, red lips. I was a lovely, bright boy. I thought: "I'll have parents in two places, here and there."

The bus journey felt as long as if I were traveling to another country. The only thing I remember is the colors: the green of the fields and trees, and the blue sky above me.

My aunt and uncle were like a sunny day, always smiling. To say hello, they put a piece of chocolate in my hand. I didn't know what it was—it was the first time I'd had chocolate in my mouth. I couldn't believe there could be something in the world that tasted so good.

Then my aunt took out some small colored balls. "Sweets," she said. "Sweets," I repeated. I tried one. And again, I couldn't believe it. Where had something like this come from?

And later on, my aunt said: "Have some sponge cake." What's sponge cake? I put it in my mouth and closed my eyes. At home, on special occasions, we were sometimes given bread with sugar or a bit of jam on it.

On the second day, they took me to the puppet theater, and I didn't know how to contain my joy. I jumped up and down, shouted and wept, and my aunt and uncle laughed.

They gave me such beautiful shoes that I couldn't believe they were mine. I put them on and was afraid to take a step. Then they took me to the playground and I showed those shoes to all the children there. And I kept cuddling up to my aunt and uncle. I didn't want to let go of them at all.

My mother was right: I had landed in paradise.

But in Albania, the law was written by the devil. Seven days went by, and then they came for me. Large, stern, and furious. My uncle shrank before their shouting.

"You fetched yourself a little brat from the countryside without asking anyone for permission? Do you think we'd let a treacherous louse like you corrupt a child?"

And one of the men dragged me after him, as if trying to requisition me. I screamed. To him, I was just an object that gave him the chance to harass an enemy of the people. I remember how bitterly my parents wept when they saw me back at home after a week.

I had to return to that poverty, to that hunger and that mud. I have so much pain inside me. Sometimes I wonder what my life would have been like if the authorities hadn't wanted to deal my uncle another blow. Who would I be? What would I have achieved? I went to school: a small, snot-nosed enemy, without so much as a decent pair of shoes.

Equality in the communist system was a sham; society was divided into the good and the bad, the model workers and the parasites, the city-dwellers and the country bumpkins, those who had a little and those who had nothing. The model workers needed the reactionary parasites in order to oppress them. The good needed the bad in order to see themselves reflected in their eyes and feel superior.

If a person stood out, if they caught the eye of a Sigurimi agent, the search for dirt on them began, in order to destroy them. Conscientious, eager spies freely presented evidence of political agitation, both real and invented. Something could always be dug up. Every year, the system produced new enemies of the people because the dictatorship needed them just as much as it needed believers. We had to be alert and keep tabs on one another. The system fed off our terror, because people who are afraid applaud and bow their heads. And although, as a philosophy, communism seems far nobler and more humane to me than capitalism, in Albania the ideology put down its roots by feasting on the fear in our heads.

Anyone could fall from the mountaintop into the abyss. Even the most enlightened, most devoted admirer of communism. This mechanism for devouring the very best people changed my life.

———

I remember the first time he entered the classroom and sat down at his desk—the new headmaster, who'd come all the way from Tirana. He was tall and as straight as a pencil—strong, as if nobody could break him. Smartly dressed, with smoothly combed hair and calm eyes—completely different from everyone else.

"How handsome he is!" I thought. "The minister in person!"

Because just a few months earlier, our new headmaster, Thoma Deliana, had been minister of culture and education, and for the longest period in history—thirteen years. People said he was responsible for the reform of the Albanian language, and it was he who had founded the Academy of Sciences of Albania. We couldn't get our heads around the idea that such a learned man, who had studied philosophy in Moscow, had ended up in our village at the ass-end of nowhere.

Deliana was knocked off his pedestal for liberalism, or opportunism— in fact, for whatever; in 1976 he simply fell out of favor. That was the time when Hoxha's paranoia grew more intense, and so did the purges. According-ing to the whispered rumors, his life had been saved by a self-critical letter he'd sent the leader. His stay in Sinanaj was meant to help Deliana reconsider his reactionary attitude and draw conclusions for the future.

Thoma Deliana looked at us with a smile and asked each of us in turn to tell him our name. Finally, he reached the desk where I was sitting with my brother's daughter—you need to know that there were eleven of us at school with the surname Ceka, including my brothers, sisters, and cousins—a whole gang of Cekas.

"What's your name?" he asked my chubby classmate.

"Flutura Ceka."

"And what about you?" he asked me.

"Yzeir Ceka."

"Are you brother and sister?"

"No," replied Flutura, shaking her head solemnly. "He's my uncle."

And she pointed to skinny, scruffy, ten-year-old me.

Thoma burst out laughing, and he went on laughing as if he couldn't stop.

"What a jolly man," I thought, and smiled, too. We were more used to a teacher whacking our hands ten times with a ruler than smiling at us. But this teacher was nice and clean, and he liked to laugh. You could tell he was from somewhere else. The funny minister man.

I liked him at first sight.

———

Everyone knew that name: Thoma Deliana! The great minister from Tirana was now my neighbor. I couldn't take my eyes off him as he walked through the village, upright and dignified. He carried himself differently, he spoke differently, he behaved differently—as though he'd only come to us for a short while and would soon go back to his own world. Every day in the literature class he'd ask me something, as if testing to see if I had any curiosity. Of course I did! The more wretched we were at home, the more I thirsted for knowledge, for history, for pictures. Thoma noticed that I liked reading and had a talent for making up stories. One day, he asked me to bring him a parcel from school.

He lived next to us, though not in a miserable cottage, but in a lovely, grand house that he soon renovated to make even lovelier. The first time I visited him, I saw that he had a fridge and a television. There was also a shotgun hanging on the wall, which meant he could go hunting, and that was a great privilege. I'd never seen a shotgun like that, or that sort of television set before. The only television was in the village club room, and sometimes I hotfooted the three miles to be there at six o'clock for the three or four hours of stuff and nonsense they put on for us. When I was little, we didn't even have a radio at home. But Thoma Deliana had everything.

And he also had books. Two thousand books! He came to our village with a huge library, which took up three rooms in his house. I felt as if I'd stepped into a great canyon full of books. I looked at them, enchanted.

"Would you like one?" he asked.

I nodded, and he picked out a book of fairy tales and handed it to me. "But watch out, because I'll test you on it."

I ran home and immediately hid the book under my pillow; I was already aware by then that the less people knew about you, the better.

Thoma sometimes asked me if I liked the teachers and what I thought about them, but he didn't do it directly, because he knew there were no innocent questions in Albania. Whenever I went to visit him at home, he never expected me to repeat all those stupid slogans we were taught at school. He didn't want ideology from me, he wanted me to think. And in communist Albania, thinking was a rare and dangerous thing to do. People who thought had to be particularly on their guard.

———

A year of peace and quiet went by, but then everything came to an end. An order came from Tirana to cut short the regime of that bloodsucker, Deliana, and send him to do a job suited to an enemy of the people. And so the headmaster, the former minister of culture and education, became a cowherd. "People like him should get the punishment they deserve," declared the representative of the Central Committee, standing in the middle of the village. The authorities encouraged people to stigmatize the traitor, the bourgeois, the fraud.

Thoma and his wife had to move into a shack, which he couldn't even renovate. He was only allowed to put in a door and windows. And he was past fifty; easy things—fetching water, lighting the stove—were becoming harder and harder for him.

And so the minister who had studied in the Soviet Union was ordered to graze cows. They threw him down to the lowest depths. But Thoma knew that in Albania things could always be worse, which was why he trembled with fear for the fate of his sons, who were studying in Tirana. For his wife, who had been a university lecturer, life in the village was torment, and when they were moved to the shack, she broke down completely. Thoma tried to rescue her at any price.

"If you want to save our family," he said, "you have to do the same thing to me as the Party has done."

A few days later, the petrified residents of Sinanaj watched a scene many of the men would never forget for the rest of their lives. In the middle of the village, Virgjini, Thoma's wife, raised her hand to him, while screaming: "I hate you!"

The countryfolk had never seen anything like it: a wife hitting her husband! My father came home in shock.

"Well, I'll be damned!" he cried as he came in. "You won't believe what I just saw," and he called for my mother to pour him some raki, because you can't tell a good story without a strong drink.

I knew Thoma loved his wife and I knew that over the past year he'd come to understand the village mentality. People began to gossip about him, and the rumours quickly reached his intended target. Perhaps the only thing Thoma hadn't expected was that when his wife raised her hand to him, the people around them started to cheer her on and shout: "Hurrah!"

A few days later, Virgjini was granted permission to return to Tirana, to their sons, and her husband's life became torture.

At seven o'clock every morning, Thoma had to report to the local police and sign a register: "I, an enemy of the people, am here." He wasn't allowed to leave the village. He was watched closely, to see who he met with and what he talked about, and the denunciations were zealously laid on the altar of the Sigurimi.

When Thoma said: "Good morning," he was met with silence. Only the children who remembered him as their headteacher sometimes greeted him first. Nobody else. Crude village vulgarity and fear took revenge on civilized behavior. After a year of this life, the minister looked worse than we did. Everyone around him was working hard to destroy him.

One time, I saw Thoma's two sons heading for their father's house under the cover of night. Thoma was standing in the doorway, and he saw them and me at the same time.

"Don't tell anyone," he said, as if in passing, the next day.

How could I have informed on him? I already knew by then that I had to protect him.

But Thoma didn't trust anyone, not even me, the bad boy. Another time, when I asked him why he had a portrait of Enver Hoxha in his house, he looked at me for a long time, as though attempting to figure out if I was trying to provoke him.

"Don't ask," he said at last.

The worse life became for Thoma, the more often I went to see him. In the school library I could only find communist propaganda: Marx, Engels, Stalin, our gracious leader, and some math and biology textbooks. Other than that, there were a few books by native writers, including Ismail Kadare and Dritëro Agolli, and classics such as Shakespeare and Gorky. Nothing else—everything in line with the spirit of the Party. But at home, Thoma had a collection three times the size of our school library, because, amazingly, they hadn't confiscated his books. He even had a copy of Freud in German hidden away! Sometimes he talked to me about it, and for a sixteen-year-old from the Albanian provinces, Freud's books were more interesting than the Bible is to a priest.

Thoma also gave me popular romance novels; there was one, for instance, about a rich man who had lots of women falling in love with him. He said even trashy books like that could teach me something about life.

"Your imagination has to work," he kept saying. "Here, in Albania, you don't even know what you can aspire to, because you've never seen anything else. But a book transports you through time and space like a flying carpet: You're sitting under the persimmon tree, the cows are milling about you, and you know you'll never get out of here, but in your thoughts you can be anywhere. It's as if you are constantly opening new windows and seeing new places and unfamiliar faces."

After three years, they finally transferred Thoma to a job on a cooperative farm. It was hard, physical labor, but much better than grazing cows. Over time, Thoma started to regain respect, too, because he knew more than others did. People came to him for a recipe for soup or jam, or they asked him to write a letter to the Party for them. He was also familiar with all the medicinal plants and could give advice about various ailments.

I well remember the time in the summer of 1983 when we went into the hills together to gather herbs. When we sat down on the hillside, I asked him again: "Thoma, why do you have a photo of Hoxha in your house?"

But Thoma said nothing. He was afraid to reply. Anyone could go running to the Sigurimi, even me. I'd been arrested a few months earlier, as he was well aware. There was nothing simpler than making a spy out of a little shit like me.

"So why don't you tell me why they picked you up?"

"You know it was about the book you gave me."

"You mean the one that was stolen from me?"

We burst out laughing. That was the official version we had to stick to.

But I knew Thoma still didn't trust me. I looked him straight in the eye.

"Do you think if I'd turned you in when I was at the police station, they'd let you pick herbs with me now, as if nothing had happened?"

Thoma looked at me and laughed out loud, just like the first time I ever saw him, and then he began to cry. He cried without making a sound. As though the strings that were keeping him upright had suddenly snapped.

"Why do we live in a country that's run by a cannibal?"

That's exactly what he said. A cannibal. Because Enver fed off us, off our pain and our terror.

"Don't you understand why I have to keep a photograph of that monster in my house? It protects me from death. If I didn't have a portrait of the cannibal at home, I'd be the next to be devoured."

And then they came for us.

There were three of us who read Thoma's books: me, my friend, and a soldier from a nearby army base. Whenever I had the time, I'd go to the hideout we'd made among some bushes. There, in an agreed spot, a book was always waiting for us. The soldier used to come at night and read by candlelight while he was meant to be on duty. One time he said: "Never leave a book at home, no matter what, because one day they'll come and search the place and you'll be in trouble."

At first I didn't believe him, but I talked to my friend whose father had spent sixteen years in prison, and we reached the conclusion that we had to be more careful.

But even so, eventually someone spotted our hideout, went to check what we were doing there, found a book, and took it to the police. Sometimes I wonder who ratted on us. In our village, even the trees had eyes.

They took the soldier in for interrogation. A friend of his came running to me with a message: "Keep your mouth shut—they're about to come for you."

But I was already adept at the art of lying, so I just said: "I don't know what you're talking about."

I was still taken to the police station. I entered the room, and there on the table was the book we'd been reading, *And Quiet Flows the Don*, part two. The policeman looked at me and waited: Would I be afraid or not? But I didn't react. I remained stony-faced. I looked at the book, then out of the window. I looked at the policeman, as if to say: I don't know what this is about. He asked me my name, where my family was from, and how I was doing at school.

"Not too badly," I said.

"How do you know the soldier?"

"I know lots of soldiers."

"I mean the soldier you're friends with!"

"I'm friends with lots of soldiers."

"Do you like literature?" he asked innocently.

"Yes, I do," I replied, but I didn't even glance at our book. I fixed my eyes on the policeman, as if nothing was up.

"And what do you have to say about this book, *And Quiet Flows the Don*?"

"I haven't read it."

"Haven't you?" he asked, and pointed at it, lying on the table.

I reached out a hand, as if seeing the book for the first time and wanting to take a look at it. Then the interrogator rapped on the desktop, and at this signal two guards appeared.

"This is your book," said the policeman. "And you are an enemy of the people."

"No," I replied.

I could see that the policeman was hesitating. He wasn't entirely sure I was mixed up in this, because he knew someone had broken into Thoma's house a few weeks earlier and stolen lots of things, including books. Every one of Thoma's books had a bookplate, so when they found *And Quiet Flows the Don*, they knew straightaway that it belonged to him. I could have got it from him and read it in secret, but it could just as well have been discarded after that burglary.

The policeman looked closely at me.

"Tell us the truth. Who gave you this book? If you've read it, we'll turn a blind eye—just tell us who gave it to you. Thoma Deliana? You're a good boy, why would you have anything to hide from us?"

I didn't answer, so the policeman signaled to the guards and the beating began. They hit me on the belly, hands, and calves, then finally punched me in the face until I was covered in blood. Then they gave me a wet rag to wipe myself.

I didn't know that in the next room they were beating up the soldier, too. But the soldier was strong and didn't let them break him. He answered every question with "I don't know," just as I had.

It turned out the beating was just a preventive, cautionary one.

They couldn't arrest me, because, apart from the denunciation, they had no evidence.

"What's happened here," said the policeman with a smile, "will remain between us. Don't you dare mention it at home."

Mention it at home? Never in my life. Nobody knew I read Thoma's books. But when I got home, my nerves were jangling, and finally I confided in my brother, who had spent time in prison.

"What the hell have you done?" said my brother, bursting into tears. "You're going to ruin the lot of us!"

We didn't talk about it again. And I never told anyone else what had happened to me. I was afraid one of my relatives might be cooperating with the Sigurimi.

———

Finally, even our immortal leader died, and I wept. To me, Hoxha was like a prophet, Jesus Christ, God. I remember my father asking me: "Have you lost your mind?" But I was sixteen years old and I thought that without Hoxha, Albania was finished. Any day now the Americans, Italians, or Germans would come and kill us all. I had a simple division in my head between us good Albanians and the bourgeois criminals over the border.

After Hoxha's death, Thoma said: "You must watch out and stay alert. The system will soon collapse, but it'll be a long time before we get it out of our heads."

I couldn't believe my own ears! Communism was going to collapse? That was beyond anyone's dreams.

Thoma had never criticized communism before. He thought it was the only legitimate system. It was just Hoxha and the people around him whom he hated with all his heart.

"Hoxha wasn't God. The real God is immortal!"

I was dumbstruck.

"The real God?"

"God, who exists, and is eternal."

"But religion is the opium of the masses!" I cried out.

"Do you really think everyone who lived before us was wrong?"

Thoma went into the other room and brought back a faded old Bible from 1938, when King Zog was still in power. I had no idea what it was. But Thoma started telling me about Adam and Eve, about the prodigal son and the good Samaritan, the most beautiful stories I could imagine.

And then he looked at me and slapped me in the face.

"What was that for?" I cried, holding my cheek.

"To make sure you remember for the rest of your life that God exists. To make sure you never forget!"

Thoma showed me another world, another way of thinking. I liked it best when he told me about life in Europe.

"Did you know that in Europe women are allowed to choose their own partners?"

"No way! But that's madness!"

Although Hoxha had banned the age-old Albanian tradition of arranging marriages in the cradle, in the provinces, families still made this sort of mutual agreement. The authorities turned a blind eye, because what actually mattered most was for real communists to marry real communists.

"But it's true!" Thoma would say. "And in France and Germany, people choose their presidents in free elections."

"Impossible!" I would cry.

"On the contrary!"

And he explained to me what democracy really was and how it had nothing in common with the system governing Albania.

After Hoxha's death, people started to invite Thoma into their homes again. A few months later, he was finally allowed to return to his hometown of Elbasan. His eight-year exile in the countryside was at an end.

When we saw each other again in 1992, after the fall of communism, Thoma hugged me like a son, and then his eyes glazed with tears.

"You must never believe in totalitarianism again! All those years we believed in that cannibal's system . . . Never again!" he said, taking a swing as if he wanted to hit me.

"No, you don't need to remind me," I said, laughing. "God exists, I know."

We were free. He, the enemy of the people, and me, the bad boy. From then on, we could write our own life stories, knowing that God exists, that paradise is somewhere else, and that we can leave Albania at any time if there's no place for us here.

Have you got any books in English for me?

———

Thoma Deliana, born in 1925 in Elbasan, was Communist Party first secretary for the Elbasan district and minister of education and culture from 1963 to 1976. From 1977 to 1985, he was exiled to the Lopësi region, then transferred to Elbasan. He died in 2014.

Mud Sweeter than Honey

WE FOUGHT FOR THIS LAND to the last drop of our blood, we wrenched it from the hands of the Germans and the Italians, we farm it, sparing no physical effort, and the land is good to us, bearing a bountiful harvest. And for us it has produced the potato. The potato is not just a vegetable, the potato is our bread and meat! Eat a potato and your belly's full from dawn to dusk—there's no greater enemy of hunger than the potato. Words cannot describe our joy when we see the potatoes growing under Albania's socialist sun, to the glory of the nation.

Long live the Albanian soil that bears our potatoes!

Long live the Albanian soil!

Eternal life to the Party!

Eternal life to the Party!

In our land, where the mud is sweeter than honey!

Albania's soil is bountiful! Let every Albanian make a gift to the soil of his own waste material! That's why at today's meeting we're issuing the following order: From now on, as a donation to Mother Earth, every morning, each person is required to gather their daily waste in a bucket and deliver it without delay to a collection point. From there, the communal waste will be transferred by the appropriate means of transport . . .

By shitmobile . . .

. . . and then it will go to the Albanian fields and the Albanian hills, where it will be presented to the soil in gratitude. Such is the great national need.

In a socialist society, wastefulness is not tolerated. From tomorrow, schooled by the experience of our Chinese brothers, we commit ourselves to adding our own personal brick to the construction of the socialist fortress wall, to make it grow higher and higher, separating us from the threats of the imperialist world. The successes we've already achieved bring joy to every worker at the cooperative, because there's less and less starvation and our harvests are more and more plentiful. We have created a healthy foundation for further growth, and now the growth will grow even more when, by the sweat of our brows, we fertilize it with the product of our own bowels. The members of our cooperative are people with thorough political awareness, who will give everything they have to offer.

Yes, in a bucket. The collection point has been established outside the village.

Our strength is organization, knowledge, and experience! The fatherland is striding down the paths of progress!

The soil is generous, so let us be generous to it, too. The soil is good, and it will be even better, thanks to the people who don't spare their blood, their sweat, and the yield of their bodies. Never again should anyone say impurities are impure! For our harvests to be more plentiful, for our potatoes to grow stronger, for our corn to grow higher, we give the soil everything we have! Dear Party, dear Enver, we are always ready!

In one hand, a pickax, in the other a shotgun, and in the third a bucket! Does anyone have any questions? Does anyone have anything to say?

Albanian shit ain't worth a shit!

Who said that?

A starving man's shit is worth nothing. . . .

Italian Songs

IMAGINE ALL YOU EVER HEAR IS: "Be grateful to Enver because he is the best leader in the world." "Don't eat so much, overeating is bad for your health." "Thanks to socialism, Albania is at the highest level of development."

The system thinks for you; it tells you how to live, what views to hold, whom to love. The authorities fill every hour of your life for you: get up at six, send the children to school, go to the factory, fulfill your work-norm . . . The regime dictates the rhythm so there's never a single moment to stop and wonder: "Who are we? What are we doing?"

And now try saying out loud: "I don't like the way we live in Albania." Go on, dare to confess to someone: "This isn't the life we wanted." Try it and see what happens, see who comes knocking on your door the following day.

———

My name is Mari Kitty Harapi, which under communism meant: daughter of Simon Harapi, enemy of the people; niece of a member of Balli Kombëtar, traitor to the nation; niece of a minister during the fascist occupation; and niece of the Albanian ambassador in imperialist France.

The whole family was educated abroad, in Padua, in Venice, in Florence—in other words, the worst, most abominable bourgeoisie. In the eyes of the communists, I couldn't have been more of a nobody.

My father ended up in prison for five years because his brother informed on him: One brother publicly accused another of criticizing the regime. My uncles, the minister and the ambassador, were going to be shot, but the system showed how merciful it was and condemned them to a mere hundred years in prison—one hundred years . . . One of them served twenty-seven years, the other seventeen, until they were at last released so they could die in their own beds. Their bodies were ruined, their eyes were vacant, and their minds were destroyed, as if they were already on the other side. They took live human beings from their homes, but sent them back as shadows.

My father came home from prison a changed man. He never talked about the torture, but one day when I was walking around the flat humming an Italian song, he grabbed me by the arm and, looking to one side, he said: "Kitty, that's the last time you sing in Italian. If you want to sing, do it in the bathroom, the walls are thicker there. You mustn't do it in here."

I never dared to hum at home again.

Sometimes, we listened in secret to Voice of America or the Vatican Radio. When the program ended, my mother would ask: "So what's new?"

"Nothing," my father would mutter.

"Really?" she'd ask.

"Really," he'd repeat.

His brother's betrayal meant he no longer trusted anyone, not even his own wife. There was no hope for us.

———

A woman with a family history like mine could only become a common laborer, not even at a factory at first—that would have been too great a privilege. They sent me to a collective farm, to do a tough physical job, to lift and carry, to break my back, to be worked into the ground. I had excellent grades at high school, but going to college was for good communists,

not for good students with a bad family background. And even if I had
got a university degree, I'd probably have had to go to the countryside
anyway—the city was for people with a good family background.

Not a word! Don't say a single word!—that was how I survived communism, that was my strategy for getting through it. If you're born into a bad
family, one day you realize that there's no one to support you. Whenever
someone came to the house, I never knew if they wanted to borrow something or to spy on us. If a friend complained: "We're only entitled to a half
pound of coffee a month," I had to say: "What do you mean? We're entitled to plenty of coffee!" With every word I spoke, with every step I took,
I protected myself against others. There was always a transparent wall
between me and the world. Whenever I left the house I did my best to
disappear. I'd walk down the street imagining I wasn't there. Just as long
as nobody took any notice of me. As long as nothing brought me down.

It was four of my old friends who informed on me; when I saw my file,
I wasn't at all surprised.

———

I was the one who had to visit my uncles in prison, maybe because I was
the youngest and the strongest, and in my badly damaged family I had
suffered the least harm. The buses only ran a short stretch of the way, so
beyond that I would wait for a truck with a driver compassionate enough
to be willing to give me a lift without asking questions, and I covered the
last part on foot, feeling the stones through the thin soles of my shoes.
And so, many hours later, I would reach the camp near a town named
Laç, where both my uncles, educated at the best universities in Europe,
did physical labor like slaves.

There would be the dark shape of the massive prison building, then
the bloated warder and his two overfed dogs. Puckering with disgust, the
warder would stick his big, fat fingers into the pies, jam, and cakes I had
brought and obdurately poke around in them with a scowl on his face,
then offer the dogs his dirty fingers to lick. Their big, red tongues would
slaver over them, while their greedy gaze followed every movement. A

mechanized system of shame and humiliation, to show that the prisoners were less than dogs.

I trembled with fear as the guards glared at me. Without taking their eyes off me, they would open an iron barred gate, then I would enter the visiting room and sit down in front of another set of iron bars. I would look at my uncles' faces, scored with wrinkles, burned by the sun, their skin peeling: a gray, weary shadow. I'd press my cheek to the bars and feel their chill, and right after that, a pair of chapped lips on my skin.

And in those five minutes we had to tell each other all our news—but of course, we couldn't say a thing.

How are you? You don't look bad . . . Do you need anything? Please get me a pair of shoes, please get me two towels. How's your mother? How's grandma? Come here, let me give you a kiss.

And that was it. Our five minutes were over in a flash, even though the journey there had taken all those wasted hours.

Then my uncles' letters to my mother would arrive: "It was so wonderful to see Kitty and her beautiful face. We're cut off, completely alone. Seeing her is the greatest joy."

My darling brother Angelini was also sent to prison. When I arrived with food for him, the guard scowled at me, then shrugged.

"What have you come for? We shot him ages ago!"

I staggered, doubled up and burst into sobs. The guard slapped his thigh.

"Why are you crying, you fool?! That was a joke! A joke, you hear me? Hand over the food."

He just wanted to make fun of me . . .

Many years later, when my brother came out of prison, he'd sit at the table and talk about it: "I knew they were taking me away, so I hid behind a column, and the guard sneaks up behind me, quiet as a mouse, but I don't react, and then *wham!*, he whacks me on the back with his truncheon, and I go: 'Aaaargh!'"

We used to laugh so hard we nearly fell off our chairs. "What a joker my brother is!" I'd think, and it was only years later that I realized it was his way of coping with the cruelty he'd encountered, the bestial fear and daily degradation. He laughed, and we laughed with him, because we had no alternative, because it was better to laugh than cry, it was better to be alive than dead. But our hilarity, frightened and pitiful, had nothing in common with genuine laughter.

We were all bound by a chain of fear. Ultimately, we understood that nothing was the way the propaganda presented it, that we were working as slaves, that the authorities knew all about us, that the nomenklatura had things that were beyond our dreams. But even they, the "red pashas," watched their own shadows, because at any moment the system could knock them off their pedestals, press them to the ground and wipe them out. In communist Albania, nobody fell asleep assuming that they'd wake up in their bed.

Our whole family was persecuted, and yet my mother would try to comfort me: "Others have really suffered! At least we were lucky—none of us died under torture."

We knew that some people were hung upside down and left without food or water, in the cold, that they hung like that for hours, days, waiting for death to finish them off. There was never a shortage of pain; there was always more of it to inflict. Some people were interned; others died slowly in a pool of blood.

———

There were better and worse years. Until 1960, while Albania was fraternizing with the Soviet Union, we could bake cakes, we ate sweets, and everything was more easily available because we were rescued by imports from Russia. But we still didn't need fridges, because there was never enough food for any of it to go bad. Then we caught our breath for a while in the late 1960s, when the system relaxed its grip, but everything changed around 1973, when we got our own taste of the Chinese Cultural Revolution in its Albanian version.

That was the end of watching French films at the cinema; we weren't allowed to look at Brigitte Bardot's face or Alain Delon's suits anymore, or those beautiful coats, hairstyles, and cars . . . No more listening to Italian operas on the radio. No more smart clothes sent from abroad, no more songs from another world. The system had declared war on everything that was beautiful, and it nurtured our terror. Professors and intellectuals who had been educated abroad ended up behind bars, so it was people who had only just finished high school who became the teachers.

The Chinese came to Shkodër and brought new customs with them, such as half an hour of gymnastics: A crowd of tired people in a factory would leap up and down, doing star jumps. As if we didn't have enough Albanian nonsense, they had to import it from China, too! The bolder people told jokes about it.

But telling a joke could change your whole life. Up to ten years for political agitation—that's how the system cured the Albanians of their sense of humor.

"Why did you end up in prison?"

"Oh, it was just a little thing."

"Such as?"

"I'd failed to put a good lock on the door."

If the Sigurimi had you on their list, that kind of joke was perfect for them.

But in 1978, Albania broke ties even with China. Even diehard China wasn't socialist enough! Now we were supposed to become completely self-sufficient, and that meant one thing only: poverty. The authorities gave you oil but no potatoes, so people were always finding ways to make do or swapping food. We baked the simplest, plainest Regina cake: two tablespoons of baking soda, a little flour, olive oil, butter, sugar, and water instead of milk. For the major holidays we sometimes managed to bake baklava, but we had to get several people to help us gather all the ingredients.

We were all poor. We ate nothing but bread with oil and cheese, and if anyone had more they were seen as the lucky ones. When our mother wanted to treat us, on Saturdays she'd bake fresh bread, our greatest luxury. Sometimes we'd get sweets in parcels from our relatives in Italy, but we ate them at home, in secret, to avoid making anyone jealous. Once I dropped a sweet wrapper on the pavement outside our house and I saw the little boy next door pick it up avidly, turn it over, give it a sniff, and then lick it. He'd never had any sweets.

Hoxha shouted from the tribunes: "Never for a moment will we close our eyes, we will always be alert, the walls of our fortress are made of granite!" Proud, alert, and forgotten. Even if small sparks of resistance were flickering somewhere in Albania, we didn't know about them. And in the rest of Europe, nobody realized how much we were suffering. Foreign delegations would arrive in Durrës, where there was music playing and the tables were groaning under the weight of food, and nobody had any idea that Albania was hungry. Those who came to write about us didn't get anywhere near the truth: that society was extremely divided between the well-educated people with a bad family background and the model citizens, suitably terrified and docile—the ideal material from which to mold the new Albanian man, unconditionally devoted to the Party. In the countryside, people had always slept on dirt floors, on straw mattresses, and then suddenly the system would allocate them a bed, a pillow, some forks. Or they were given a job in a factory, or an apartment—for them, the regime meant great social advancement, a better life.

The credit for everything was due to the system, even the fact that one plus one equals two. Newspaper headlines cried: EINSTEIN MADE GREAT DISCOVERIES AS AN ARDENT COMMUNIST. In a world of lies, nobody could be themselves. Our children didn't belong to us. My son was not my son; his mother was the Party. If the Party said: "It's time for you to get married," he had to get married. I had no influence on his life. I wasn't even a number. I was nothing.

And nothing was mine—the only thing that was mine was fear. Had I done something wrong? Beautiful women had to sleep with Sigurimi men to avoid going to prison. The Party needed children—future workers and soldiers, so abortion and contraception were banned. Not even our bodies belonged to us—the Party was lurking even inside our bodies.

———

Both my mother and my father had studied in Italy, so life in communist Albania was more painful for them than it was for me, because they still had images in their heads of another world, but the door to it had been slammed shut in their faces.

That's why, in 1972, we jointly agreed to do whatever it took to buy a television, which at the time cost forty thousand leks, the equivalent of eight months' wages. To make this dream come true, we had to sell everything we could: the sewing machine, an old mirror, and my father's beloved books. But he didn't complain—he kept saying that the television would be our window onto the world.

Then came all sorts of monkey business with aerials to get just a brief flash of reception from Yugoslavia or Italy. Until then, we'd listened to music on the radio, but suddenly, amid the buzzing, flickering, and crackling, we heard songs from the Sanremo festival. We knew the names of the Italian singers better than the Italians did, we knew every piece of music and the words to every song . . . Sometimes I felt as if we were watching a dream.

That little box in the sitting room shattered the myth of Albania's great power. My father would whisper: "Good Lord, we believe in lies, pure lies."

But if we tried asking him to tell us more, he'd raise a finger and say: "The less we talk, the better."

I loved music and ballet, I adored the singer Adriano Celentano, but I had to lock all my love of music in my head. I couldn't say to a friend: "Demis Roussos is so wonderful! Mina looks so beautiful on stage!" I hadn't forgotten that the Greek singer Demis could get you three years, and Mina, the Italian one, twice as much.

———

The dresses were all the same, the shoes were all the same, whatever flat you went into, everything looked the same. "Thank God that at least the wives can look different from one another," joked my father.

In 1945 my mother's sister had married an Italian, so three times a year we'd receive a parcel from her. If our aunt sent us something particularly nice, the customs inspector would confiscate it and leave a note saying: "Not appropriate for Albanian reality." In Albania there was no room for beautiful things, at least not for people like us. Or else they'd claim we had to pay twenty thousand leks to receive the parcel. That was four months' wages, an impossible sum for a normal family! So we'd band together with our neighbors—one would give three thousand, another four thousand, and then we'd share the things out. But all it took was for a secretary in the personnel department to say: "Oh, what a lovely dress you're wearing," and you had to exclaim: "Please, take it, if you like it!" The secretary would pretend to have scruples: "But how could I, without paying?" But if you tried saying she should pay for it, the next day her husband would hiss in your ear: "You Italian imperialist, so you like slutty dresses, do you? Maybe exile would knock some sense into you." As a punishment for having bourgeois tastes, you had to tidy up the entire neighborhood, in rain or snow, in shoes that leaked. If I was given that punishment, I put on thick socks and wrapped my feet in cellophane to avoid catching a cold. And so we only wore the prettier things at home, because if somebody took against you, they could always dig up some dirt on you.

Once I asked my aunt to send me some shoes. And, wanting to make me happy, she found me something special: some orange pumps. When I opened the parcel, I was so amazed I had to sit down. My darling, naive auntie, she really had no idea about life in Albania! Everything around us was the color of dust, dirt, and grime, while that orange color was a challenge to the predators: "Go get her!" In Albania, those shoes were more conspicuous than a pair of martians would have been, but I didn't have any others, so I had to wear them. They instantly caught the eye of the shift manager at the factory. She hinted that she could really do with a pair of shoes like those, but I pretended not to understand what she was talking about. The next day she fired me for imperialistic extravagance in the way I dressed! In place of the factory, I was sent to work at the market, alongside the Albanian gypsies.

Yes, opening those parcels from Italy gave us brief moments of happiness. Happiness was also eating something other than bread and cheese.

Happiness was going to the beach and bathing in Lake Shkodër. We needed special documents to do that, and the inspectors always ransacked our baskets, prodding every tomato and fingering the cheese. We only had fifteen days' leave a year and we went on holiday when the state decided we could: once in May, once in September, and once in February. Holidays were a privilege and a reward: for the workers, for the administration, and for the Sigurimi. The deserving few had their own holiday resorts. We spent our time at workers' holiday camps or in a tent.

———

Here in Shkodër there were constant rumors that Hoxha, the Red Pharaoh, was growing weaker, and when he died, the bolder people among us joked: "There's so little meat they've probably sliced him up for cold cuts by now."

"At least that's one communist fewer," we sighed.

Something did change. At last the authorities began to worry that the people wouldn't put up with the poverty anymore and would finally rebel, so they loosened their grip.

More and more people came out of prison, and it was easier and easier to go to college. The terror lessened, but the hunger grew. We made everything ourselves—cheese, bread, butter—because at the market you could only buy chives. People became obsessed with food, and didn't think twice about stealing. In those days I was working at a state-owned florist's, and time and again I managed to swap an illicit bouquet for a piece of cheese . . .

Sometimes I thought Albania had gone and that the country had collapsed, but some evil people who wanted to cling onto power at any cost were trying to convince us that the state still existed. Once, when I was on my way home along the road by the lake, I saw something floating on the surface of the water. I went closer. They were books—books by our beloved leader, the dead yet immortal Enver Hoxha! I looked around anxiously. I was afraid something bad might happen to me, so to be on the safe side, I went to see the factory manager.

"Comrade Manager, I saw the works of our Supreme Comrade thrown into a lake!"

But the manager merely said: "I see. Go back to work."

He didn't ask where or when, what books or which lake. I thought I saw the faintest hint of a smile on his face. And then I understood: Albania as we knew it was at an end.

Finally, on September 27, 1990, I went abroad for the first time in my life, to Venice, to visit our dear aunt who had saved us with her parcels for all those years. The ship was beautiful, clean, and luxurious, but the people on board were from another world—all they had with them was bread, cheese, and tomatoes. The man next to me trembled throughout the journey.

"You don't realize," he whispered, "but they can turn us back at any moment."

When an Italian sailor said: "Have a good trip," I muttered: "Go to hell!"—because the only thought in the back of my mind was that a man in uniform means violence and trouble.

Physically, my mother lived in Shkodër, but mentally she spent her whole life in Venice. When I went there, I felt as if I were returning to a familiar city, because my mother had told me about every building, every square and alleyway, every trip in a gondola; I had always dreamed of ending up in the land of her stories.

And it came true. With the fall of communism, I regained control of my life. I could sing Italian songs whenever I wanted.

———

And yet . . . So many years have gone by, but my terror is still lurking in the background. When we came in here, to this café, I looked around, and I was pleased to see we were alone. I picked the most secluded table, and then I took a good look at your clothes: Where might you have a bug hidden? Even though you told me you'd be recording. I laid out these books about communism in front you and I thought: "It's lucky no one can see us." So many years have passed, and my thinking is still guided by terror; it's still there inside me.

Once, in 1992, I went to a government office and accidentally found myself in an empty room, where there were stacks of official files and piles of documents lying on the floor. I picked up one of them: *In Koplik, sixteen people are painting eggs red for Easter.* Neat, rounded letters . . . A message from a bygone world.

Lots of people will tell you that communism in Albania hasn't ended, because the same characters are still in power and nobody has really been punished. What is democracy? Voting should be free, shouldn't it? And yet people here vote because someone from a particular party got them a job, because someone gave them fifty euros, or because there's something in it for them. Nowadays anyone can get away from here, but where are they going to go? Nobody wants Albanians in their country.

In the past, if you held your tongue, you were safe. These days you can scream, but no one will hear you.

How We Used to Vote
Bright and Early

HAJDE, HAJDE—COME ON, PEOPLE, come on, folks, get up, get on the job, look lively! Give each other a shake, wash that face, scrub those mitts, slick down your hair! The rooster's crowing, the sun's scrambling into the sky, and we're off, in our finest shoes, our cleanest shirts and embroidered skirts, whoever's got something nice to wear, now's the time to put it on. Today the authorities will kindly turn a blind eye to any fancy frills, because today's a great occasion, *hajde, hajde!*

The villagers are gathering, the people are climbing the hill, smartly dressed and smiling, hair combed and faces washed, delighted by the rewarding opportunity, here and now, this very minute, to say what they think, to show how much they love the Party, they're going to cast their vote and joyfully declare that the Party is their cherished mother, the Party is fire into which they'll boldly leap, one after another! So off they go, all bright and shiny, with a spring in their step, greeting each other, *mirë, shumë mire*, it's good, very good, this life of ours, and so they form a big crowd, and down the hill they go in a black, gray, and blue flock, buzzing away, looking swell, they climb the narrow lanes again to reach the spot where the band's playing, where there's dancing and prancing, where the joy of the worker greets the joy of the farmer with a handshake, and then they raise their arms and clench their fists.

Suddenly the rooster crows, the clock strikes six, and a stern-looking man opens the gate. *Hajde, hajde*, everyone to the ballot box! The great election is declared open, whoever wants to vote can do so! Because in Albania, communism is democratic, today everyone can say if they're in favor of the government of our graciously ruling Party under the leadership of our dear uncle Enver, or if perhaps they're against it. Maybe there's a fool out there who's not happy about something? You can vote yes, you can vote no, you can do anything you like, you can live with dignity and die in agony.

So the musicians lead a lively dance, and the people race to the polling station, there's a bit of shouting, a bit of sparring, someone snatches someone else's voting paper, one man gives another a shove, everyone wants to have their say as fast as possible—yes or no? In communist Albania, you can think various things, that's why there's a special voting booth with a curtain, anyone who wants can go inside, they're free to! But so far no willing taker has appeared. People say: "He's voting behind the curtain—he's got something to hide, he doesn't like our legitimate, gracious Party, he doesn't like our beloved Enver."

So everyone's off at a brisk and festive pace to cast their vote under the watchful eye of the committee—their wise and fitting vote. Here's old Rrumbulaku cackling with joy, there's the Markaj boy twirling the girls about in a dance, the band's playing, and the committee's looking at the people's nice clean hands.

And now the radio's blasting away, it's bringing news: The Dibra constituency finished voting at eight this morning, the turnout was 100 percent, 100 percent say "yes" to our beloved Party! A little worse in Tepelenë district—the voting finished at nine, the turnout was 96 percent, alas, someone chose not to perform their civic duty, someone has let down the Party disgracefully today. In the decent constituencies, voting begins at six and is over by seven; in the decent constituencies, only madmen and internees don't vote, because nobody cares what they think.

And what about here in Gjirokastër, is everyone present? Oh no, look, old Bani must have gone mad—people, look at him climbing that hill with his flock of stupid sheep, what a scoundrel! What a lousy swine! What a putrid saboteur!

The committee members exchange glances and frown. It's almost ten o'clock. Ten o'clock isn't noon, but still, it's brutally late, horribly late. How do you explain a turnout below 100 percent? Old Karajova hasn't trudged up here to grace us with her presence, either—she says the grim reaper's already staring her in the face, the lazy old hag, lounging on her deathbed! Who's going to explain that to the Party? Beads of sweat appear on the committee members' brows. They're wavering, stammering, this is very bad. They'll have to make a report, look for an explanation—but there's no possible explanation for this, is there?

And so two of the committee members jump to their feet and set off down the cobbled streets, over the grass, across the meadows, in pursuit of the shepherd, the vile traitor, unwashed and unkempt, subversively herding his sheep! They race across the fields, ties flapping in the wind, as the band's merry tune rises to the top of the hills. The shepherd sees the black figures, alarmed and sweating, in the distance—he sees them and his lips curl into a very faint smile. He turns his back on the town and walks into the forest.

By the Light of
the Paraffin Lamp

AT THE TOP OF THE MINARET, a man fires a rifle.

The dogs raise their slender muzzles and listen; earlier they had sat, patient and impassive, as little Fatbardha Mulleti laid her hand on their wet noses. Sometimes, when they stretched out on the rug, she'd rest her head on their firm bellies. They made fine dogs: smooth, gray coats and calm temperaments, warm tongues and trusting natures. But then the men had come, with their black boots and black rifles. Carefully taking aim at the dogs' backs, they pulled the triggers.

It was all over.

Gone was the crystal glassware, the latest luxury item in the apartments of the Albanian upper class.

Gone were the curtains beneath which the dogs used to sleep, the marble staircase, the red-brick fireplace, the guest room with gilded furniture and the crimson-upholstered armchairs.

The huge table in the dining room, under which little Fatbardha sometimes used to hide.

When Haki Mulleti, a civil servant and owner of all these goods, was studying in Vienna in the 1930s, he didn't waste any thought on communism. Now it was communism that was taking away his beloved house, his shops, and his garden full of peaches, grapes, and figs.

When the new authorities forced their way to power, his paintings were lost, too: a portrait of the national hero Skanderbeg, a portrait of Grandma Mulleti, and portraits of the Mulleti sisters. The older one was solemn and intense, her face fading into darkness on the canvas; the younger one glowed in the light, bright and cheerful. The artist's brush had foreseen their destinies: The older one died of meningitis at the age of eighteen, and the younger one lived to a great age.

————

At Haki's trial, the crowd roared: "Death to enemies of the people! Hang them!" Their cries thundered in little Fatbardha's ears.

Civil servants, especially those educated abroad, were the first to face the gallows or the firing squad. Haki was sentenced to five years in prison, but the communists confiscated everything he owned.

Haki considered himself extremely lucky.

His wife promised herself she'd survive it all.

Little Fatbardha didn't know what to think. She missed the dogs.

Haki ended up in a dark prison cell, while his wife and five children were sent to live in a basement in the little town of Kavajë; the gloom was dispelled by narrow streaks of light from the windows just below the ceiling. The communists had let them take nothing but a sprung bed frame—the only piece of furniture in the dark basement, an incredible luxury in a hopeless void. Instead of chairs, they sat on cushions stuffed with fleeces.

"Our dining room table would take up this entire space, so maybe it's a good thing we haven't got it," their mother joked.

Now she faced a backbreaking task: to feed all five of them amid daily starvation. In these conditions, people start to realize how tough they are. Their mother clenched her fists and turned to stone.

"The colder a stone, the harder it becomes," said people in the village.

Their mother got up early in the morning and went to gather wild plants that they could eat. She made tea from herbs, darned their clothes, fetched water in buckets, and never stopped for a moment. She had to give her children hope—that a new day would dawn, and that life would carry on.

When Haki came home from prison, he told them stories about children who had lost their homes but were still very happy because they had their parents with them.

"Learn to pray," he would say, "because soon the system will take God away from us, too."

Fatbardha would go outside and dance and dance and dance, but just beyond the fence, another world began. A world of bodies turning blue as they hung from the mulberry tree, bodies wrapped in white sheets with the word "enemy" written on them in red paint, bodies blackening in ditches. Corpses were loaded onto carts and left by the entrance to her school, so that everyone could see what the authorities did to those who failed to believe in communism.

———

Every night the Sigurimi took her father away, and in the harsh lamplight he made statements.

"Has your brother, Qazim Mulleti, returned to the country yet?"

"Qazim will never come back here," Haki kept saying.

Every day as she left for school, Fatbardha prayed that, during her absence, the Sigurimi, that monster with a million tentacles, would return her father to her.

And at school she was met with laughter: "Look, the prefect's niece!"

The niece of Qazim Mulleti, Albania's most famous enemy of the people! Fatbardha's uncle had been prefect of Tirana for three years, its wartime mayor who had collaborated with the Italian government. When the scales of victory started to tip in favor of the communists and Qazim realized he was high on the list of people to be shot, he fled the country, leaving behind his whole family. That was in 1944.

Five years later Qazim Mulleti became the main character in a stage play, *The Prefect*, which ran nonstop for the next forty years. Superstitious and autocratic, and as smart as a stack of bricks, the prefect was the laughingstock of all Albania, a symbol of what communism was arduously battling day after day. The citizens of old, fascist Tirana who made up the prefect's entourage held the most idiotic, irrational beliefs and would have sold their own mothers for a handful of wheat. The gallery of morons, idlers, and boors won the hearts of the entire Albanian nation. *The Prefect* was broadcast on Radio Tirana, and in the early 1970s, when Albania discovered television, a screen version of the comedy was made with Robert Ndrenika in the starring role, which was as popular as Monty Python in the West.

As soon as *The Prefect* appeared on stage, the life of the real prefect's family turned into a nightmare. His wife, Hajrie, represented in the play as a repulsive, arrogant goose, was interned, along with their fifteen-year-old son, Reshit, in Tepelenë, where the most horrific of all the prison camps was located.

Life in Tepelenë was hell. Day after day, the men chopped wood; day after day, the women hauled it back from the forest, and the slightest misdeed was punished by being made to spend hours standing waist-deep in ice-cold water. For many, this punishment was a death sentence, because there was never enough food, and the people were suffering from malnourishment and illnesses. During a typhus epidemic, thirty children died in a single night.

Reshit had to bury the bodies. In the course of five years he buried two hundred small children. And hundreds of adults, men and women, people who only recently had said good day to him. After three years, the camp commandant decided that the dead had to be dug up and moved to another spot. So Reshit exhumed the children's little bodies and the adults' bigger bodies, and once again said good day to death hundreds of times over.

On the one hand, there was hatred—on the other, contempt and mockery. Young master Reshit, the camp's gravedigger, was, after all, the son of that dolt, the prefect, whom everyone could despise as much as they liked. Sometimes Reshit snapped back: "So you think you could govern Tirana then, you village idiot?"

But he still heard snickering behind his back every day.

"I've always been a laughingstock," he told Fatbardha toward the end of his life. "I have suffered from early childhood to old age. I've never known a moment's respite."

Fatbardha loved Reshit like a brother.

"He was a beautiful, sensitive man, subtle and aware of his situation, which is why he never married. He couldn't imagine building a family that he'd inevitably burden with his suffering."

Whenever the authorities planned to open a new camp, Reshit was summoned and sent to work there, and so he spent his entire life living in tents. After five years in Tepelenë, he was transferred to the Myzeqe marshes, where he had to report twice a day and couldn't go anywhere without permission. But even so he considered himself lucky—in Tepelenë, a five-person family was allotted twenty-one square feet, so they all slept like sardines, gasping for air. In Myzeqe, two families lived in a single hut. Over here, people were to work and live—over there, they were to starve and die.

One day a letter arrived: "Dearest Fatbardha, I'm writing to you by candlelight. We're building a camp, it's dreadfully cold, but I'd like you to come and visit us. I know you haven't any money, but don't worry, I'll pay for your journey."

"When I visited Reshit in 1956, I realized they were so isolated there that they were still singing songs from 1945. We spent all night long talking about books, and about what was going on in the country, because they were in total ignorance. They had no access to the radio or the newspapers. They lived in their own world, in their own time, in an enclosed space. In spite of appearances, life was easier in an internment camp than in a village. No one lived in the camps but enemies of the people, so they were all equal, they shared the same suffering. But in the villages, there were people with good family backgrounds, too, whom the authorities encouraged to intensify the suffering of the exiles."

Reshit and his mother were tossed around the entire country—to villages in the Savër district, then Gradishtë, then Grabian. In every single place they were traitors, surrounded by good citizens who obeyed the regime. In Gradishtë there was no water, so whenever the water truck arrived the villagers formed a queue, but the enemies of the people were always the last in line. Sometimes they were refused water, sometimes their jugs were smashed. Class war engulfed the whole of Albania, splitting the country into two castes, one of which felt duty-bound to stigmatize the other.

Reshit spent his entire life in internal exile; forty-six years, as many as communism lasted. And when the system collapsed, Reshit behaved as if he were dead. Suffering had sucked all the joy out of him. The man who walked the streets of free Tirana was just a dried-out husk.

"He died of a heart attack," Fatbardha says. "Maybe his heart broke from grief after all those years of suffering?"

———

Fatbardha read in a history textbook that on February 4, 1944, the Germans carried out a massacre in Tirana, for which her uncle Qazim was partly responsible.

"That stupid traitor, the prefect!" roared the children.

"If only I could dig myself a hole to hide in," thought Fatbardha.

Fortunately, one of her teachers, Zoi Xoxa, was a friend of her father's, exiled here from Tirana as a punishment just as they had been. He called Fatbardha *kokrra e grurit*, "little grain of wheat," because she was tiny, with hair as fair as flax.

Zoi Xoxa used to be a journalist, and he'd built himself a house in the heart of Tirana—right where the communists decided to establish their enclosed private district, Blloku. Anyone who had previously studied abroad and who owned a house there was dispossessed of it. Xoxa's house was allocated to country folk from the Skrapar area who provided security for Enver and his entourage. On the day the Sigurimi came knocking at his door, Xoxa's oldest child, a boy of seventeen, had died of meningitis.

"Please, at least allow me to bury him," Xoxa begged.

"No," replied the men in gray coats. "Your whole family is to be interned, including your son's body."

They packed some furniture, a rug, a lamp, and the coffin onto a cart, and off they went, from Tirana to Kavajë, in a slow funeral procession.

The teacher belonged to Fatbardha's world: the world of intense suffering, where every day could bring yet more pain. Sometimes he told the children a story about an old oak tree, and Fatbardha was sure he was telling it especially for her.

"Once upon a time there was an old oak tree—tall, wide, and beautiful, but the people decided its time had come, and they swung their axes at the trunk, once, twice, three times, then chopped the tree to pieces and lit a bonfire. As the flames soared high and the people warmed themselves in the heat, they heard the voice of the oak tree's ghost, telling them about the days when it was a young tree, growing in the sunshine and providing shade for everyone."

Fatbardha understood that the teacher was talking about himself—he was someone who'd worked to build Albania, and although he was someone whom society had cut down, he was still giving people warmth by working as a teacher. That was when she decided she would become a teacher, too.

———

But the authorities had no easy scenario in mind for the niece of Qazim Mulleti. Fatbardha was denied the right to go to college, but she was allowed to move to her grandmother's home in Shkodër to finish high school.

"What have you brought her here for?" her grandmother asked. "She could die, too."

A year earlier, meningitis had carried off Fatbardha's sister, whom the artist had immortalized in the painting, plunged in darkness. Fatbardha took over her desk. And she studied from morning to night, if only to prove to the authorities that she should be given a chance.

"Does not qualify for teacher training," she read in the official letter. But they allowed her to become a teacher in the Lezhë area.

"We know who you are," said the head teacher as soon as they met. "We'll give you six months and then we'll try to think what to do with you."

And so Fatbardha ended up in the village of Kallmet, not far from Lezhë at the foot of Velë mountain, amid boundless green fields, and brooks that became streams after the rain.

Fatbardha found out that, as a teacher, she had the right to continue her studies by taking a correspondence course. The officials in Lezhë advised her to specialize in biology, geography, and chemistry.

"I would sit down to study at seven in the evening and stop at two in the morning, all by the light of a paraffin lamp, because in those days my village didn't have electricity. First, there were three years of general studies, then five years specializing in chemistry, and I did all the work sitting at the same table, completely alone—just once every three months I had contact with another living being, when I took my exams.

"I was about to take my final biology exam when rain began to bucket from the sky. All the bridges were flooded, and the only route out of the village was over a concrete dam . . . I walked across that dam to the other side, in torrential rain, over a rushing river.

"I sat down in front of the professor and answered the first question. I could feel the water dripping off my hair and trickling down my back. The professor looked at me and asked: 'How did you manage to get here, my good girl?' I sat there speechless, not knowing how to reply. No one had ever called me a 'good girl' before. Me, an enemy of the people, a good girl? 'How on earth did you get here, putting your life at risk?' insisted the professor.

"I hung my head. I couldn't tell him I'd only received a permit to leave the village for that one day, and I wasn't sure I'd get another one because of the flood. I couldn't tell him that whenever I lit the paraffin lamp, I finally felt happy, and that the light kept me company every night, giving me the strength to keep working . . . I wanted to study so much that if I'd stopped, I'd have died . . . It was only thanks to my studies that I could bounce back from the very bottom.

"'Good girl.' Those words kept coming back to me for many, many years. In some other world, in another reality, I was a good girl."

———

"In 1967, when I was working in a village called Manati, a coarse, fat man with a nasty look in his eye came up to me and said that on Tuesday at ten o'clock I was to report to the Department of Internal Affairs in Lezhë.

"He turned on his heel and left. I thought about my father, who was taken away from us every night by the Sigurimi, and how I used to wait for him to return, the joy I felt when I came home from school to find him lying in bed, and the fear that the next day they'd take him away again, perhaps forever . . . Our beloved father with eyes as black as olives . . .

"At the department they told me: 'Someone with as bad a family background as yours can only erase their guilt by means of cooperation.' 'I have no friends,' I replied. 'There's no one I could persuade to confide in me. People run away at the sight of me. I want nothing to do with politics.' The head of the department, the local Sigurimi chief, a small, pig-headed man with a puffy face, turned purple on the instant. He pointed a stubby finger at me and said: 'We gave you a chance, even though you're from a lousy family, we let you study, we let you work, the state has been extremely generous to you, and this is how you repay it?'

"I didn't hang my head, I just kept looking straight in front of me, as solid as a rock, like my mother all those years ago—I didn't blink, I just stared into space above the Sigurimi chief's head, above his wide, red face. And I did the same thing at the next meeting, and the one after that—the Sigurimi was talking to a rock. Finally the chief surrendered, but his fists were still clenched as he told me: 'You'll sign a declaration that you refused to cooperate. And if you tell anyone about it, we'll lock you up for agitation and propaganda.'

"I leaned over the piece of paper, which said: *I, the undersigned, Fatbardha Mulleti, have refused* . . .

"I felt as if I were signing my own deferred death sentence. I knew that at a trial people you'd never met testified against you as eyewitnesses to a crime you hadn't committed. As soon as the Sigurimi wanted to do so, it activated a vast machine that had only one purpose: to crush you.

"From then on, I had to build a wall between myself and the world. After something like that, how could I get close to people? How could I trust anyone? I loved books, but I never discussed them with anyone . . . I adored classical music; for me, the concerts by the Vienna Philharmonic that were broadcast on the radio were like a glass of water in the desert, but I never talked to anyone about them. I couldn't allow myself to fall in love. But signing that declaration was the most glorious moment in my life, and, paradoxically, it set me free. A few years ago I received a medal and a certificate from the president: survived communism with dignity. Me, the bad girl . . ."

———

In 1975, Enver Hoxha thundered: "There are reactionaries hiding among the teachers." This speech by the enlightened dictator, who had tightened his grip on his people's throats once more, was the start of a great purge within the schools. After seventeen years as a teacher, yet again Fatbardha Mulleti lost everything.

"In my file they wrote: 'Not fit for the teaching profession.' I had to go back to my family, in Kavajë . . . But I loved teaching so much . . . All those years I'd been the most devoted, exemplary teacher because I'd wanted to prove they'd been right to give me a second chance. Night after sleepless night I went back over every detail of those seventeen years— who was the best student, who sat at which desk, who was the best singer . . . To be on the safe side, I destroyed the diaries I'd written over the years, so they wouldn't fall into anyone else's hands.

"At last, after three years of unemployment, after three years of having door after door slammed in my face, I found a job at a clothespin factory in Shkodër. I had to twist the metal springs that connected the pieces of wood. Look at my hands . . . But I met some wonderful women at the factory, decent, warm, and compassionate. The people there weren't as cruel and vindictive as in the countryside.

"And finally, at the age of forty, I met my future husband, who also carried the burden of a bad family background, so it was easier for him to understand who I was . . . But this time it was his family that stood in the way—I was Muslim, he was Catholic. On the day of our wedding, my husband's family broke off contact with him.

"I spent ten wonderful years with him, full of love and happiness, because my husband was a true gentleman, as well as being extremely witty—he could sweeten the bitterest moments with laughter. He loved performing on stage—he came first at every amateur stand-up contest. He used to joke that it was me who brought him good luck—me, the prefect's niece. He died of a heart attack in 1990, the day before the storming of the embassies, when the regime began to come apart at the seams. Piter, our little boy, was only six years old. And today he's a lecturer at the university in Shkodër. Thanks to him, my story had a happy ending."

———

I'm gazing at seventy-eight-year-old Fatbardha: She looks great, in a green dress, with a string of large wooden beads adorning her tanned neck. Time hasn't taken away her charms; on the contrary, it has sharpened the beauty of her subtle, classical features. For Fatbardha, the past is happening now; thanks to the present, she's adding a new dimension to bygone days. Between us on the table there are three books, for which she started collecting the material as soon as the system collapsed: detailed accounts of the lives of women who suffered just as she did.

"Do you know why I wrote them? First of all, to set the record straight on fifty years of Albanian glory. Secondly, because I once met a man who said: 'Under communism, nobody went to prison without a reason.' Really? I was five years old when my family lost everything, I was stigmatized for half my life, I saw children dying of malnutrition, writers put in prison, poets hanging on the gallows, young people shot in the back as they tried to escape . . . And yet there are still people alive who claim the system was valid. That we suffered legitimately, the right amount, just as much as we deserved for our innocence.

"In the comedy *The Prefect*, the actor playing my uncle was always saying: 'You'll see what communism brings us, you'll see what happens to us,' and people roared with laughter, but in time the snickers died on their lips. Anyone who wanted to jeer at Qazim Mulleti could do so, but it was my uncle's ghost who had the last laugh at all of us."

Beauty Will Always Find a Way

"A" IS FOR *ATJE*—THERE . . .

"B" is for *bir*—son . . .

My father writes the letters on a sheet of paper, then his lips pronounce the sounds—round "a"s, brash "b"s—and then they form a smile.

Or I'm trying to pedal, but my legs are like two wooden planks, they can't get the hang of the bike. I can hear the crunch of sand under the wheels and my father calling: "Look where you're going!"

Or I'm watching his tanned body immersed in water, his strong worker's back, his hand waving to call me over: "Jump, don't be afraid, it's deep!"

It was my father who taught me to read when I was barely five years old, and to this day my gaze sometimes pauses on the words and I think of him with gratitude. My name is Ridvan Dibra, my father was a worker, but I am a writer and college lecturer, and that's partly thanks to him. Sometimes I used to watch him studying Italian in the evenings, by the light of a paraffin lamp. Even in those circumstances a beautiful bond was formed between us . . . The system wasn't capable of destroying everyday beauty. And that was our salvation. Beauty always found a way around the system.

I think the time I spent in internal exile actually saved me. Internment was supposed to be the end of me, it was meant to crush me, but instead I learned something from it that I wouldn't have understood if I'd been stuck in the bubble of the urban socialist world. Our life was exhausting, but if something good happened, we savored it to the full; beauty pervaded us through and through. Everything brought joy: the view of the mountains, the sunset . . . A courgette flower looked wonderful. If I'd lived in Shkodër, I wouldn't have noticed all those things. I'd probably have joined some organization and got into trouble straightaway. Internment in the countryside protected me from much greater misfortune.

Sometimes I tell my son about the past, but he doesn't believe me. Maybe he has no need for those stories—after all, he's living in a completely different world. Nowadays that old capacity to experience pleasure has gone. Nothing can fully gratify modern man any more—he always feels unsatisfied.

All my life I've been an avid reader and have written with ease, but it was only out there in the countryside, at the back of beyond, that the writer in me was born.

———

Whenever I held the pen in my left hand, the teacher would come up behind me and whack my knuckles with a ruler as hard as he could. I'd be sent to the headmaster, and he'd bellow: "Writing with your left hand is improper!" They'd have loved to chop off that hand to force me to write with the right one, but I never gave in. My aching hand gave me my first lesson in what an authoritarian system was.

The left hand was for holding a hefty textbook full of propaganda. With fire in our eyes, we declaimed deplorable poems glorifying the Party and Hoxha. Soon I started writing the same kind of mediocre, formulaic stuff myself, praising the development of the beautiful Albanian countryside, even though the countryside was sinking further and further into poverty, and I wrote about the partisans, although I was clueless about war. At the age of ten, I won a prize for my wonderful patriotic poetry, but it soon began to dawn on me that there was something not quite right about our great Albanian literature.

My eyes were fully opened much later, when, as a high school student, I went to do manual labor among the working class. That's how the system planned it, to make sure a future stuck-up member of the intelligentsia came face-to-face with real life and didn't get too attached to the idea that he was an intelligent. I'd arrive at the brick factory and from dawn onward I'd hear: "To hell and damnation with this job!" "For fuck's sake, it's all falling apart!" Because conditions at the factory were medieval—we made the bricks by hand, willy-nilly. It was hell, both Albania and that job—a hell that teaches you to drink, smoke, and swear, but also opens your eyes. Just as Eve's eyes opened when she ate the fruit of the forbidden tree.

Around that time, I took several dozen poems to the board of censors and awaited the verdict—was my poetry acceptable or not?

"Why haven't you written anything about tractors?" the censor asked anxiously. "The tractor symbolizes the development of agriculture, doesn't it? Why does your poetry so ostentatiously ignore tractors? I'm sorry, but I just can't imagine this collection being published without a major poem about a tractor . . ."

So I composed the required epic. The censor cast an eye over it, then smiled.

"You know what? We were within a hair's breadth of overlooking something extremely important! You've forgotten to include an extended poem in praise of the Party!"

What a monstrous oversight! The collection was finally published, but it wasn't my book, it was the authorities' book, perfectly meeting the requirements of the times, as crude as if I'd composed the poems out of bricks. Our eyes had to be firmly shut, our minds empty. I felt dirty.

But by then I knew I was very keen to study literature, and that literature would allow me to survive. Meanwhile the committee ruled that, in my case, the fatherland was more in need of a soldier than a writer. Me, a soldier? Fortunately, the Shkodër League of Writers came to my aid and secured me a place at university.

But when I got there, it was all just a lot of hot air about propaganda literature. What's more, the indomitable authors wrote books that were as long as they were earnest, a thousand pages each—evidently, they never suffered from writer's block. We devoted a lot of our attention to classical literature and realism by the likes of Balzac and Stendhal, but not a word was said to us about Sartre or Camus. Luckily, after some time we realized that by turning criticism of modernist literature on its head we could learn some sort of truth about the world.

But during my third year, I hit a crisis point. I already knew that socialist realism had nothing to do with reality, but was a surreal per-version of it. Nothing in the books tallied with the world around us. Only in Kadare's work could I perceive some muted traces of resistance, a feeble light in the tunnel. The atmosphere at university was like tossing around a deflated balloon, and on top of that, I'd realized by now there were narcs among us. I couldn't compare the situation in Albania with life in Eastern Europe, but it looked as if we'd be suffering for decades to come. How can you build a life if you can't trust anyone? I managed very well at university, I published articles in literary journals, and I got good results. What's more, I came from a poor and simple family, so there was everything to imply that I'd stay on at the university. And yet suicidal thoughts kept returning, like splinters under a fingernail, telling me that the system was a disaster, and that living amid lies was a worthless form of existence.

One day, in 1981, I was sitting in the Grand Café with friends. I'd had a drink or two, and I got into a discussion about literature. It came around to the works of Gjergj Fishta, a Franciscan priest from Shkodër—nowadays regarded as one of Albania's leading poets, but back then he was an unmentionable enemy of the people, someone the authorities wanted to sink into oblivion. My friends were criticizing him according to the Party line, but emboldened by the raki, I said that no, it wasn't true, Fishta deserved to be our national poet.

"How exactly do you know that?" asked one of my friends, because Fishta's work was banned.

"I've read extracts."

Silence fell, and my friends stared pensively out of the window; suddenly they found the view outside fascinating. On the way home, I continued to feel anger, and something like relief. But I didn't expect any consequences—after all, I'd been drinking with my closest friends.

I was summoned to appear before the Party committee immediately, the very next day. I went with my father, and all the way there I could hear his calm, steady voice, as if he were teaching me the alphabet again: "Everything's going to be fine."

By way of welcome, the Party secretary stabbed his finger in the air at me and cried: "You enemy of the people!"

At once a chorus of judges chimed in: "We'll break you, you traitor! We'll break you, and your father, for bringing you up a traitor!"

Out of the corner of my eye I could see my beloved father trembling like a leaf.

"Either you can go to prison now, or you can finish your studies and then we'll send you to the bottom."

There was no need to think twice. My studies became a nightmare, a string of humiliations and petty injustices. At every meeting they discussed my attitude, calling me a traitor in disguise. When I took my exams, the professor failed me in philosophy, my favorite subject, though formerly I'd been one of the best students. I felt as if I were shrinking. Soon the splinters were back, the suicidal thoughts.

They exiled me to a village so small and remote that it didn't have a name, it was simply called the Village. Getting there was a real communist odyssey. The Village was eight hours on foot from Kukës, and no buses went there. At the bus stop, someone cheered me up by saying there was a shorter route through Buzëmadhe. In the end I managed to hitch a ride, but eventually the driver set me down at a crossroads and said: "Now you can just ask the way." I was carrying a heavy suitcase, into which I'd packed my entire life to date. Before I reached the Village, I stopped at the house of a man, who in bygone, better times, had been a

Bektashi "baba," a spiritual leader in a branch of Islam that was popular in Albania. I greeted him. He said nothing. He looked at me and said nothing. Finally, he set off down the road with me.

Only later on did I learn that people used to come to him for healing, because they believed he had special powers. One time, one of my colleagues went to see him and started calling him a charlatan.

"If you're so special, make a wolf appear right now!"

"There is a wolf here," replied the baba.

But that came later. First, in the holy man's silent company, I reached the Village. My first impression was so bad that I put down my suitcase, sat on it, and thought I would never move again. Very thin, very shabbily dressed people, crumbling stone houses, clouds of dust hanging over the road. It was a highland village. People had lived there for centuries thanks to their animals, but in the early 1980s, yet another of the hundreds of idiotic reforms had taken away all their livestock except for cows. The wretched Village had been half starved to death.

"You'll rot here," the school secretary said to me in welcome.

I felt as if she were putting a curse on me. Several of the teachers had been sent to the Village on a mandatory placement, but others had been sent there as a punishment.

"Eight years, Gjirokastër," a young man greeted me.

I studied their faces: gaunt, tired, some marked by signs of mental illness, suffering, and isolation. I looked at them and thought: "That's my fate. If I give up, I'll be like them. They're me, in five, eight, ten years' time. Watch out."

And I promised myself I wouldn't give in to the curse—the Village wouldn't break me.

Rumors quickly spread that I'd done something truly abysmal in Shkodër, though nobody was entirely sure what, but to be on the safe side, the headmaster decided to punish me. He gave me the task of tidying up the large school library. The glint in his eyes said: "So you won't have it too easy."

It was my salvation: that extraordinary library. Whoever had taken care of it earlier on had put together a wonderful collection—the complete works of Shakespeare, the complete works of Balzac, and all the Greek classics. Knowledge was supposed to have reached the most backward corners of Albania, but the Village's isolation brought another surprise— here on the shelves I found banned books that had been removed from circulation in Shkodër long ago: the works of Petro Marko, Dritëro Agolli, and Ismail Kadare. Clearly, the Party's orders hadn't reached the periphery. That library saved me. Here I was on a desert island where I could educate myself all over again.

Feeling heartened, I went to visit the baba. He was sitting in his gloomy cottage under a thick rug.

"How long will I stay here?" I asked.

"Five years," he replied.

And he was absolutely right.

But I could have been there much longer, considering what happened to me. One day in April, I was returning from Kukës to the Village, just a little tipsy, and somewhere along the way I saw a car from the cooperative. I piled in, but my traveling companions seemed even more morose and gloomy than usual.

"Why are you so sad, my friends? Perhaps I should sing you a song!" I said, because after a drink or two, I'm usually quite the optimist.

But when after two verses nobody joined in, I stopped. When we reached the Village, I saw people sniffling and wiping their eyes. "Oh dear, the head of the cooperative must have died," I thought. "But is that really worth crying about?"

When I entered the teachers' hostel, I heard sobbing. And as I walked past the room of my colleagues from Gjirokastër, I heard heartrending wails. I knocked.

"Our Supreme Comrade is dead," my colleagues stammered.

"What am I supposed to feel now?" I wondered. "Will anything change?"

In some ways, the government of Ramiz Alia was even more abhorrent. The iron grip relaxed, but we were still on a short lead, not knowing what to expect. No longer on a chain, but still in a cage. Two of my friends were killed on the border trying to escape. That winter, news got out that two of the teachers—a quiet, retiring couple—had disappeared. Four versions of what had happened to them went around: Either they'd been shot, or arrested, or eaten by wolves, and only one guy insisted they'd managed to escape. Just a few months ago they sent me a friend request on Facebook. They live in the United States and they're doing very well.

The Village was a very far cry from Facebook—worlds apart. I remember how happy I was when they finally installed a telephone in the Village and I could speak to my fiancée in Shkodër. The connection was always breaking off, we both had to shout over the interference, and we'd wait for hours to hear a voice at the other end. Or how much joy I felt when I could watch an entire soccer match without any power cuts. Or when they cleared the snow off the roads before New Year's Eve and I could go to Shkodër to see my family.

But I know that by isolating me from Albania, the Village protected me from greater misfortunes. There was nothing going on around me, so I'd go to the library to read. I kept my distance from the local notables, but with my friends, I could be sincere. People showed me great generosity. They were poor but honest; they didn't have much, but they shared everything. Deep down, people are more alike than we think. Essentially, they're all the same: They try to avoid evil and they respond to good with good. I've always done my best to make friends with people, counting on the fact that they're naturally good. If the system wants to bring out the evil in someone, it won't have any trouble, but if someone tries to bring out the good in a person, they'll find more than enough of it.

My friends were far more worn out than I was, because they'd spent far longer in internal exile. We'd head out together to arrange stones into absurd political slogans that stretched across the steep hillsides. Whenever the Party celebrated the anniversary of the 1941 uprising, we'd stand in line like soldiers and sing idiotic songs from the past. At meetings of the collective we used to discuss issues of vital importance for our community, such as why teacher Dibra wrote with his left hand. The collective declared its expectation that I would demonstrate a constructive attitude and start writing with my right one.

"After thirty years of activity by the left hand, the right one has lost its capacity to assume the functions of the left," I would explain in deadly earnest.

To avoid a breakdown, some of my colleagues were never sober, and came to their classes drunk—anything to avoid seeing things in focus, anything to fence themselves off from the system. Some committed suicide, others found refuge in insanity. It took great strength not to go mad.

––––––

The winter of my first year in the Village was very harsh. The snow enveloped every detail; the landscape was smooth, without color or contour, as though hidden under a layer of magma. It occurred to me that this was the epitome of communism: conformism and monotony. Only Gjalica, the highest peak in the Kukës region, stood out on the horizon, clear and pointed—that was Enver Hoxha. Everything else had disappeared under the snow.

Enver towered over us and made all the decisions. He knew exactly what he was doing, and he consciously deformed communism in order to create his own system. He was in love with himself, but he also had a paranoid love for Albania and regarded it as his own property. The regime demanded passivity and uniformity, and because it was merciless, it met with no resistance. The Sigurimi's files are locked away to this day, which could be proof that a major part of the Albanian elite sold out to the authorities. For years I was pressured to become an informer, too. That was the most dreadful thing about the regime: how easily it corrupted people, how easily it could make them betray the trust of their closest friends.

Enver Hoxha tried at all costs to create a new Albanian man, but he created a monster who, after Hoxha's death, let himself be swept up by capitalism, flouting all the rules, ready for anything as long as it made him rich as fast as possible. Drugs, racketeering, prostitution. The shortest path to the goal. Enver Hoxha created a weak failure of a man, with no knowledge of the world, no institutions to back him up, and no support within the government.

Capitalism brought chaos, a lack of security, and inequality, and the more difficult life became, the more the myth of communism as an era of justice was reinforced. Our social and political transformation has been dragging on for an eternity, it's cruel and ruthless for the weak, and it has given rise to a nostalgia for communism—a new cancer that's consuming Albanian society.

A Tale About Shoes

ALBANIAN SHOES HAD A HARD TIME with everything—their thin soles struggled along the metaled roads or got bogged down in the mud. Sometimes the shoes managed to run away and see the world of their most ardent dreams. They only had to keep going for long enough across the high mountains on the frontier, along winding paths and through narrow passes. But usually they came to a sudden stop when the borderland silence was pierced by gunfire. The border guards would remove the shoes from the stiffening feet, because although the corpse wouldn't be of use anymore, its shoes were sure to come in handy.

Once upon a time, there was a pair of shoes that wanted to be sneakers—every day they ran at the stadium in Shkodër, come rain or snow or sunshine. People watched the owner of the speeding shoes. He's crazy—but why shouldn't he run? Where's he going to run to? He's only going to ruin his sneakers, because Albania only sent its sportsmen abroad to countries that were its allies. But as the years went by, fewer and fewer states were willing to be friends with it. Except that one day, the man disappeared. Only when his family was interned did the news go around that the runner who was always training and never grew weary had swum across a lake on the Yugoslav border and vanished into thin, foreign air.

His worn-out shoes had stayed behind on the lakeshore—they hadn't the strength to swim.

The shoes told each other this story and couldn't get over their surprise: Where on earth had that pair come from? For the length and breadth of Albania, all the shoes were identical: black and gray, with thin soles, produced in four domestic factories. Only occasionally were there better models—tough, leather ones—for the system's administrators and the "red pashas." But the other shoes didn't envy them. They knew that even if those better shoes ended up on the feet of people who'd reached high places, it would only take a moment for those soles to bid farewell to the marble flooring and say hello to the mud of a remote village. In Albania, fate was fickle, so all the shoes did their best to tread as quietly as they could.

It's important to have good shoes, so your feet don't freeze and aren't bothered by pain. For decades, people dreamed of good shoes because there weren't any, and the shoes that there were spoke of falling into line and feeling fear: a thorough polishing first thing every morning, and then walking on tiptoes to spare the soles.

Today, long-legged girls totter down the potholed sidewalks in their high heels, their slender, willowy bodies tilting gently as they try to keep their balance. The older women's shabby slip-ons shuffle heavily as they slide along, barely lifting their feet from the ground. The aging men don cheap loafers with long pointed tips and soles cracked from poverty. The young men wear sneakers covered in a thick layer of mud and dust, evidence of the winding paths of life.

Albania hasn't forgotten the humiliations of the 1990s: the worn-out shoes from Italian humanitarian aid, the new trainers stolen from a Greek shop, the stilettos that helped to earn a shameful living, the loafers in exchange for wartime fuel sold to the Serbs during the embargo. That's why nowadays Albanian shoes pretend they've seen Venice and have been to the carnival in Rio—they're colorful, shiny, covered in glitter and lacquered gold. "We may have got carried away, we may be over the top," they cry, "but look how far we've come! No more poverty, never again, no more bare, frozen feet, no more feet in shoes that let them get soaking wet, no more stones sticking into thin, leaking soles."

A young boy stands in front of a skip, holding a pair of blue trainers he has found in the rubbish. He gives them a careful inspection, puts his hand in them, and tests the insides with a finger. They're excellent shoes. He spends a long while admiring them, taking his time on purpose. There's another kid standing near him with arms akimbo. He's pleased, too.

Dust settles on the shoes of those who have very little and are fighting for a tiny bit more, as they stand at the side of the busy streets, at round-abouts and junctions, next to their spades and toolboxes: a sign that they're prepared to work, but are waiting for someone to hire them. Their shoes are as tired as they are; they look as if they're about to fall apart. The men stare at the ground, and in animated moments they spit underfoot. Here they stand, they're free, the state will give them nothing, their fate lies in their own work-worn hands. Being free means being able to do what you want and say what you want, it means standing in the street, waiting for someone to hire you, as you repeat to yourself how much you hate this lousy country, and that once upon a time it was better—when was that?

Men at a hunting club in Shkodër, 1984.

PART THREE

CIRCLES

In a Whisper

YOU'LL NEVER UNDERSTAND what Albanian communism was like. Somewhere on the edge of Europe, there was a North Korea, a bunker state, a fortress state. People sometimes say that our form of communism was like a minor Holocaust. Just as you can't describe the Holocaust, you can't describe life in a country that was a prison. You can quote the facts and present the personal stories, but you'll never come close to our suffering.

In communist Albania, the pain and trauma were mixed with a sense of the absurd. Fate meant nothing. Logic meant nothing. Every day, something that had a fixed meaning could become another thing entirely.

As you walked down the street you couldn't be sure the ground was the ground. You couldn't be sure you'd reach your destination. You couldn't be sure the people you were talking to were the people they claimed to be. You couldn't be sure that words meant what they were supposed to mean.

My cousin got two years in prison because during a West Germany–Albania soccer match he said: "That Beckenbauer is a great player!" He was at the community center in a group of several dozen people—moments later someone whistled, someone shouted, someone leaped up to cry: "Goaaal!" Just as if nothing were wrong.

The sentence was appropriately severe, said the judge. After all, by praising a German footballer, the defendant had insulted the Albanian players—he'd trampled on their dignity, which the justice system priced at two years. They soon took the trouble to find more dirt on him: Apparently, he had complained about being in prison. Having a bad time in an Albanian prison, was he? Eight years. He came out after ten. He was a wreck.

What did his life matter? What did his suffering matter, when everyone else was suffering, too?

You could get a few years if the tomatoes at the market weren't to your liking. If you'd complained they were watery, it meant you'd insulted the fruits of the Albanian soil. The stall holder might not be offended by that, but the guy standing behind you certainly was. He felt hurt on behalf of the Party, so he informed on you, for which he received some galoshes or three packets of cigarettes, while you wasted away in prison. By now you'd entirely lost your sense of taste.

Or perhaps at the bakery you said: "Your bread is getting worse and worse, it's rather hard and stodgy"—agitation and propaganda. Two years, if you were lucky. If you were unlucky, you spent ten years gnawing thin, dry slices of prison bread, while fondly remembering the kind you hadn't liked.

Whenever someone from abroad asks me about modern Albania, I say that 1997, when the country was on the brink of civil war, was a slap in the face. But in the communist era you felt as if you were being raped on a daily basis. Every single day you lost your sense of security and dignity. If you were born among the socially degraded, every single day you prepared for the worst.

My name is Gentian Shkurti and I'm an artist. I can tell you my family's story but it still won't explain anything to you, because what does our suffering mean compared to the suffering of others? That's what Albania is like—you can always find a more horrific story. What form did our suffering take? The fact that three cousins were murdered by the Party and seven spent half their lives in prison because their grandfather belonged to Balli Kombëtar? And that's just on my father's side. There's also the suffering on my mother's side . . .

My father spent years on end trying not to cast a shadow. Whatever he'd said, he'd have ended up behind bars—with that kind of family background, one careless word would have got him twenty years. So in order to survive, he taught himself not to speak. Even now, when he speaks to me, he leans very close and whispers in my ear so that no one else can hear. Sometimes when he's hanging over me I say: "Dad, communism's gone, speak up, no one's going to inform on you!" He gets a grip on himself and says: "You're right, son, you're right." And after a while he leans forward and starts whispering again. He'll whisper like that for the rest of his life. He'll never raise his voice, he'll never shout. That whisper is all he has left. He has to whisper to avoid being afraid.

For decades we've been living in a normality that's pure absurdity. In a world that's pure chaos, where the rules change every day. It's as if we've stepped straight out of Sartre: We struggle, we suffer, and then we die somewhere on the margins of the world.

You want me to tell you in detail how my uncles were tortured? You want to hear about the hunger and the beatings?

No one talks about it because no one wants to see themselves as a victim.

My father will refuse to talk to you.

Go to North Korea and you'll see what Albanian communism was like. When the language lies and the words are lies, nothing is true. You listen to the children singing that Enver Hoxha's hands are full of sugar, and you eat bread with sugar because there's nothing else.

Why do you really want to know?

Even so, you'll never be able to describe Albanian communism.

The Enemies' Revolt

THE SNOW FELL QUIETLY and without cease, all night it fell, steadily and ruthlessly. The ground was frozen solid. In the mountains, the cold bites into your body more acutely, every movement is painful, your fingers, feet, and cheeks sting, the blood flowing in your veins stings. Night fades slowly, unhurriedly. You're surrounded by high, almost vertical walls of rock that lock the area tight—the ossified earth and a gray patch of sky.

The men, who were standing in a row, were quiet, silenced by the frost, as still as statues of ice. The guard counted them slowly, one after another. And then they marched out: to the mine, up a narrow path, along passages between the steely cliffs. The tails of their prison coats flapped in the wind.

"What have you got there?" came a shout.

The march stopped. A guard went up to Pal Zefi, a nurse from the Durrës area, and pushed him, but the man didn't react; he was frozen stiff and snow-blind.

Then the guard tore off his prison coat and everyone saw what Pal Zefi was hiding underneath it: a red, woolen scarf with white stripes. Against the white snow, the gray sky, and the black rocks, amid the motionless, dark brown shadows, the red fabric whirled in the wind.

"Take it off," barked the guard.

But Pal Zefi refused. Six guards lunged toward him and dragged him to the isolation cell, while without a word, the prisoners moved uphill toward the mine, in a sluggish, steady procession.

———

That, according to a prisoner named Neim Pasha, is how the revolt at Spaç began in 1973: with a woolen scarf and the incarceration of Pal Zefi in the isolation cell, where he remained for the next three months. There were more than a thousand witnesses to these events, but each one remembers them slightly differently.

Did the red scarf really exist? Time erases the evidence, suggests cinematic scenarios, and looks for symbols. One thing's for sure: Pal Zefi did end up in solitary confinement and spent far longer there than the maximum thirty days stipulated by the prison regulations. According to Mina Kota, an imprisoned brigadier, Pal was confined in February, when he refused to go underground and demanded a job on the surface. And as he continued to resist, the authorities sentenced him to further months in isolation, to dry bread and piercing cold, because in winter the temperature fell to 14°F at night, and ice would creep across the walls of the isolation cell.

Pal Zefi gradually changed into a gaunt specter, his nose sharpened by hunger and his eyes shining anxiously from a face scarred by vertical furrows. One day, when the guard opened the door to bring him breakfast, Pal Zefi pushed him aside and ran off. Half crazed with anger and despair, he grabbed an iron bar, headed for the area where roll-calls took place, and froze there, like an animal in a trap.

"Don't come near me! Don't come near!" he shouted at the guards.

According to another version, as he ran out Pal Zefi managed to punch one of the officers in the face; the petrified prisoners saw the officer's cap go flying into the air, and then, by force of gravity, slowly fall to the floor during the longest seconds of their life.

One fact is beyond doubt: Pal Zefi stopped opposite the guards, who flew at him and knocked him to the ground. Then the silence was broken by a shout: "They're murdering our friend while we just stand and do nothing?" And about fifteen prisoners leaped up and attacked the hellhounds.

Both sides knew all about torture—on one side were the executioners, on the other, the victims, and their roles had been assigned once and for all. The victims, tied up with wire, would be covered in blood, in so much pain that they gasped for breath, lost consciousness, and with it, hope, while their tormentors hit them with planks, crushed them underfoot, stunned them with electric shocks, and knocked out their teeth, meticulously, methodically, and not without pleasure. *They* weren't the tormentors—it was the authorities, they were the ones who administered the suffering. And suddenly, for the first time in the history of Albania, the prisoners were paying the guards back for years of torture: The victims were standing up to their oppressors and striking back.

The guards scattered in all directions. The prisoners were left alone, bleeding and furious, at the very center of the prison, on the battlefield.

A few hours later, Sulejman Manoku, the head of the prison system, arrived.

"Go to work as scheduled," he called out. "We'll see to this matter. What you've done is unacceptable. The state has you in mind. It wants what's good for you."

Some of the prisoners obeyed, and some stayed put. But when the guards came for Pal Zefi, he simply trailed after them, although his fellow prisoners tried to stop him, knowing he was heading to his death.

Soon after, the guards came back.

"Where's the man who shouted that they were murdering your friend?"

The answer was silence.

"Come and get him, if you're brave enough," someone said from the crowd.

And then the prisoners were left alone again, and for the first time they felt free. And they believed in their freedom, because time and again someone cried: "Down with the dictatorship!" "Down with Enver!" "Guards, don't shoot!" The prison's main courtyard was filled with people.

The young prisoner Dervish Bejko was a wise man, so he was always careful to keep his emotions in check. But that day his jaw was clenched with emotion as he carried his friend Skënder Daja on his shoulders, a twenty-year-old with a calm but stern expression.

"We're innocent!" Skënder was shouting.

Everyone was listening to him—the prisoners gathered around him, and the guards crowded in the building opposite.

"You've locked us up without cause! You've made our mothers wear mourning dress. You killed my father, after groundlessly accusing him of taking part in the attack on the Soviet embassy! You call us enemies, but we're not the enemy! We love our country just as much as you do. We work in the mine like slaves. Set us free!"

"Down with communism!" someone shouted.

"We're innocent!" cried someone else.

"Criminals!"

The hatred that had been building up in the prisoners came bursting from their throats.

Almost all of them were there because they'd said something that had been their undoing, because they'd dared to complain, because they'd tried to escape, because they hadn't painted the way the dictator wanted, because they'd written poems that were too pessimistic, or because they'd said out loud: "Communism is Albania's ruin." That day, they could all shout whatever they wanted.

And when the speeches were over, the prisoners went for the cabinets where the names of the brave model workers and the miserable shirkers were displayed, they went for the propaganda wall, the *fletë-rrufe*, on which the Party's punishing hand separated the good from the bad. The glass shattered, and the posters and portraits went up in flames. Someone wrote: "Down with communism," and someone else wrote: "Enough is enough!"

But there were also those who lay down in their beds and kept still under the blankets, so they could later tell the authorities: "It wasn't us!" No one went near them.

———

What does a man do when he's free? What does a man do when his freedom can be taken from him at any moment?

"We're not enemies of the people!" shouted the prisoners. "We love our country!"

Who was the first to cry that they should raise the Albanian flag? Years on, it's impossible to establish the facts, because at least five prisoners in various interviews have claimed the idea as their own, each providing a different list of members of the "flag group."

One thing's for sure: Someone found a red blanket, someone else found a five-liter bottle of black ink for writing propaganda slogans, and someone sent for Mersin Vlashi, a young painter from Burrel, who was the best qualified to paint an eagle. An old man from Mirdita, the brave Ndrec Çoku, glanced at the prisoners with a twinkle in his eye as he mixed the dried-out ink with water.

"Here's a fine pudding for Enver Hoxha," he said with a snicker.

Mersin painted an eagle, a large, strong, black, two-headed eagle, and as soon as the flag was raised, total silence fell on the other side. But it was soon shattered by the boom of a rifle—a soldier opposite had opened fire. He missed.

The prisoners gathered around the flag. One of them, Bedri Çoku from Fier, declared: "Friends, this is the flag of freedom! This is the true Albanian flag, steeped for centuries in Albanian blood!"

Neim Pasha's voice cracks as he remembers that moment.

"Until then, all we had ever heard was: 'You've betrayed your country, you've betrayed your families, you have no right to call yourselves Albanians.' That gesture had great significance for us, because for a while, it gave us the illusion of being free. On our flag there was no star, the international symbol of communism. The revolt stopped being a crude scuffle and became a political act. Mussolini had added two fasces to the Albanian flag, and the communists had replaced them with a star. But our flag was the real Albanian one. Whoever imposes foreign symbols on a nation is stifling and oppressing it. We responded with dignity to all the abuse the authorities hurled at us, but we paid a high price for it."

According to one of the prisoners, the flag flew for two hours until it was taken down by those who feared revenge. But others say it survived the two days and two nights of the revolt.

A forest of sinister figures sprang up around the prison. Soldiers, officers, policemen, investigators, judges, prosecutors—successive levels of authority—and beyond them, the lowest one: the local people, who watched in silence. And finally, the special task force who deployed chemical weapons around the camp. A total of four thousand men against six hundred rebel prisoners.

By the evening of May 21, the water supply had been cut off; the prisoners didn't want to storm the food stores, but they were conferring in corners, asking each other: "What should we do? Should we negotiate? Must we surrender?"

Early on the morning of May 23, the head of the national police force, Kasëm Kaçi, declared through loudspeakers: "Anyone who's willing to go to work should come out into the main yard. Anyone who's not can stay in the camp."

Each man acted according to his own free will; each man made a decision according to his own conscience. And that was freedom—the chance to decide about your own life or your own death. Those who chose to leave were met in the yard by guards with heavy chains. The rebels were bound in pairs and ordered to sit on the ground, side by side, in silence.

But then the soldiers stormed the building, and the silence was shattered by the screams of those who had stayed inside. The authorities slaughtered them with wild, ruthless fury, finally taking their revenge and reestablishing who was the victim and who the executioner.

Half an hour later, the screaming stopped. A group of guards ran inside carrying stretchers. They came out very slowly, so that nothing would escape anyone's notice. Mutilated bodies, stretchers instantly soaked with blood, blood dripping onto the floor. The sickly-sweet odor of suffering.

When the prisoners went back inside, not a single object was in its right place. Deputy Minister Feçor Shehu, who the day before had got into an argument with one of the prisoners, Hajri Pasha, came back. Now, standing before the group of chained men, he simply asked: "Where is Hajri Pasha?" And was told that the guards had dragged him off to the military police. Hajri's howling could be heard throughout the entire camp.

An inquiry was launched immediately. One hundred and twenty prisoners were transported to Tirana.

"Did you take part in the revolt?"

"No."

"Who organized the revolt?"

"I don't know."

"Who raised the flag?"

"I don't know."

The prisoners were dragged into the courtroom because they hadn't the strength to walk. Four were shot dead that very day, May 23:

Skënder Daja, who had made a passionate speech and dared to shout: "We're innocent!"

Dervish Bejko, who had carried him on his shoulders, and then also taken the floor in praise of freedom.

Hajri Pasha, who had presumed to argue with Feçor Shehu.

And Pal Zefi, with whom it all started.

Sixty-six rebels were sentenced to an additional ten to twenty-five years in prison.

———

Mersin Vlashi, the thirty-five-year-old artist who painted the eagle on the red blanket without painting a star, was given a new sentence and was not released until 1991. In total he spent thirty-one years in prison. He died in 2010.

Mehmet Shehu, the prime minister and defense minister who had made the decision to establish a prison and labor camp in a narrow cleft in the mountains, shot himself in 1981 after being accused of treason.

Feçor Shehu, who so brutally suppressed the rebellion at Spaç, was shot ten years later on the orders of Enver Hoxha.

In 2017, Kasem Kaçi, the chief of police who was partly responsible for the massacre, was due to be decorated by the then–interior minister, Saimir Tahiri, for his decades of impressive work in the service of his country. But at the award ceremony he refused to accept the medal and gave this explanation: "Post-communist Albania has recognized those who fought against the dictatorship, so there's no need to reward me and my colleagues, who served it, and who suppressed the revolt at Spaç on the dictator's orders." There's no need. That's what he said.

Until the Bird Returns

I'M EXHAUSTED BY ILLNESS . . . Every morning I buy a new day of life, but there comes a time when each new day is nothing but torment, and when you say to God: "Enough." And yet you keep on living and you keep on fighting. Why do we cling to life so doggedly? You see this mark on my forehead? It's from being beaten up. I spent twenty-one years and four days in prison, and I'm still carrying that time here, on my back.

My name is Neim Pasha, and I was nineteen years old when they arrested me . . . What did I know? I didn't realize the world is so badly covered in mud and that it sticks to everything. When you're young, you want to explore everything, try everything, but you know and understand nothing. At school I recited black-and-white poems about love for the fatherland and enemies of the nation. When I ended up in prison myself as the worst kind of enemy, and the first time I was tortured, I still didn't understand what politics was, what the authorities were, or the Party. I had no idea about anything.

It was only in prison that I came to hate the system. It was only in prison that I learned: Cursed be the first man to have stuck a stick in the ground, drawn a circle around it, and said: "This is mine." Cursed be the man who says: "I'll kill anyone who enters my circle."

I matured in prison, thanks to books and people who knew more than I did. Extreme conditions sharpen the senses; a person only has to appear before you and you instantly know who he is. My prison friends gave me great solace and support—it was their kindness that kept me alive. We survived thanks to each other. It's a good thing you've come to see me. Writers are guides—by showing us the paths that others have taken, they help us to understand ourselves.

———

I was thirteen when my mother died. She left a great void, not just because a mother is irreplaceable; death changes everything, it rips a hole in a child's heart. Throughout my adult life I've been sure that losing my mother was the root cause of the misfortunes I suffered.

My father was a stern man who spent all his time working, so I transferred my vast reserves of affection to my uncle, my mother's brother. When my uncle was a teenager, Hysni Kapo, who was then one of the partisan leaders and later the third most important man in the country after Enver and Mehmet Shehu, had marched his brigade through the village. My uncle had leaped forward and called out: "Take me with you!" but the soldiers had shooed him away, saying: "Get lost, kid, you're barely knee-high!" But my uncle was determined, and he followed them until they accepted him. After the war he was a division commander in Shkodër, and there he fell into a trap: He was accused of collaborating with the Yugoslav secret service and sentenced to death. If his comrades hadn't spoken up for him, he'd have got a bullet in the chest. He was given a life sentence.

I didn't know that my affection for my uncle could put me in danger. I didn't know that in Albania convicts suffered not just during their years in prison, but for their entire life, because the regime followed their every move, and tried to scent out any weakness. I didn't know that under this system, the evil turned wider and wider circles until it affected everyone.

I never once stopped to wonder if life in Albania was good or bad.

In the 1950s, the Party gave each of us a monthly sack of corn, which enabled us to survive. We'd take it to the mill and be given seven or sometimes eight pounds of flour. Then we'd bake bread with it. We all rejoiced as we bit into the warm bread.

To begin with, the Party used to say: "Soon you'll be eating with golden spoons," and we believed it.

Later Hoxha was shouting to the crowd: "We'll eat grass before we bow to pressure from foreign powers," and so we ate grass. Children would go into the woods to pick wild herbs, then their mothers would mix them with corn flour and bake flatbreads. We drank watery soup with wooden spoons and ate flatbreads made with grass . . .

I was a simple village boy; I never thought of fleeing the country and I never asked questions. I was given a job at a coal mine in Memaliaj, so that's where I worked. Just like everyone around me, I was used to living without hope and without dreams.

———

How would my life have turned out if I hadn't gone to my grandfather's house that day? Seven of us met there: three of my mother's brothers, two of her brothers-in-law, my younger cousin, and me. My uncles said they wanted to escape over the border to Greece, and they set the date: May 15. We went back to our homes, each bearing the secret like a stone hung around our necks.

On the appointed day, a workmate came up to me and whispered: "The police are asking for you."

They took me to the police station. There I stood before a man whom I knew to be omnipotent.

"Your uncles have been arrested," he said. "Tell us what the plan was."

At the first punch I said: "I don't know," at the next one I said: "I don't know." I was soon choking on my own blood, but I kept repeating: "I don't know," until I wasn't capable of speaking anymore. My mind was racing with the thought: "The system got in between us. Who was the informer?"

I was forbidden to leave the town, but they let me return to the workers' hostel. One of the men living there had spent many years in prison; he was quiet and intelligent. I plucked up the courage to tell him what had happened.

"I'll give you some advice," he said. "Never ask anyone for advice, don't talk to anyone, never tell anyone anything. Destiny will do its work whatever happens, so hold your tongue and don't make your situation any worse."

I was arrested on June 4, 1966. At the same time, I found out that on May 15, two of my uncles had escaped from Albania. The others were still in the country—and so was every other member of the family, all of whom were to bear the consequences.

In love, it's the heart that does the talking; in wisdom, it's the mind; and in suffering, it's the body. Suffering makes the body scream. They tortured me inhumanely, but my answer to every question was still: "I don't know." In the courtroom I stood eye to eye with my uncle's wife, who was a witness for the prosecution. Could I have held that against her? She had a very small child, she'd been left on her own, she had to save herself. It's easier to break a woman than a man—how was she going to live from then on?

"I left the house to cook outside," said my aunt, staring straight ahead of her, into the void. "When I opened the window a little to get the salt from the sill, I heard Neim saying: 'Let's go, or the police will come and arrest us.'"

It had been raining that day, she hadn't done any cooking outside, she'd been sitting next to us. Her entire statement had been prepared in advance; none of it was true. My aunt's face was stony and her eyes were blank—she played her role like a puppet on strings. I had tears in my eyes.

I was sentenced to twelve years in prison. My uncle got six years, one of my mother's brothers-in-law got three years, and the other was interned. My cousin, the thirteen-year-old, was left in peace.

I'll never stop wondering who informed on us.

———

They took me into custody straight from the mine, but they wouldn't let me wash, neither there nor before the trial. When I ended up in prison in Tirana, my heart was set on just one thing: to scrape myself clean of the stink of pain and fear.

The first person I met in prison was from Tepelenë, just like me.

"I hope you're lucky and won't have to stay here too long," he said.

He gave me soap and a towel, so I washed in cold water and laundered my underwear. There were twenty prisoners in the cell, who greeted me with a kind word and a cigarette. I fell asleep immediately, like a stone dropped into a well.

Next morning the prisoners were woken by screams of "Get up! Get up!" but I couldn't hear anything, or see anything, or feel anything—I'd sunk into a lethargy similar to a coma. The guard stood over me shouting, slapping my face, and shaking me, but I was unable to move, and I couldn't open my eyes. They took me to the hospital unconscious.

I was given a series of injections. The blood was barely flowing in my veins, but slowly, day by day, my sight, consciousness, and memory returned. Finally I crossed the prison threshold a second time, once again closer to death than life, and once again the first person I met was the man who'd given me the soap. He brought me some yogurt he'd made out of prison milk.

"Fucking Hoxha, to hell with him!" he muttered under his breath when he saw that I hadn't even the strength to eat. "What's he doing to us, that damned son of a bitch?"

It was like a wake-up call. So it was possible to say something bad about our leader? I was too young to know the difference between love of the Party and hatred of Hoxha.

Gradually my strength returned, my eyes regained focus, and I began to understand that the people suffering around me were innocent. In our cell there was a war veteran from Kosovo who'd lost both his legs in battle. He'd been withering away in bed for twelve years and could hardly move at all. You might have said he was vegetating, but he was a person, just like us. "I don't know when it's summer or when it's winter," he'd say, "but every day I wait for a bird to come back and perch on the windowsill. That is my only joy. If the bird is late, I immediately start to worry . . . My heart beats for nothing but that bird."

———

Each of us needed a thought to keep him alive, but in those days I wasn't yet aware of that. I spent my twentieth birthday in prison in Laç, where I was pals with three guys of my own age. The first was Naum Kondakçi, brother of the famous singer Liljana; he'd been a student in the USSR until it turned out the Russkies weren't communist enough for Albania. The authorities had ordered him to come back, but he knew he'd suffocate here. Someone had reported that the young Kondakçi was looking to the West. Off to jail. The second was Murad Martha from Librazhd, a good mate and a real live wire—he had fire in his heart. And the third was Sazan Haderi from Gjirokastër, nephew of the high-ranking official Shefqet Peçi—he was the one I knew best.

On December 6, 1966, we didn't go to work because it was pouring with rain. I was sitting in the corridor with Sazan, who kept going outside the building and staring at the clouds. He'd crane his neck, stand like that for a moment, and come back.

"The bloody rain won't stop."

"Does it bother you?"

"My wife and daughter are due to visit. When they arrested me, Alma was only six months old."

His eyes filled with tears. I felt sorry for him.

"Don't worry, the guards will call you when your girls get here."

"I know . . . I'd just like the weather to be nice."

And then we heard a strange rumble. Sazan leaped to his feet. I ran after him, with no idea what was going on, but suddenly he turned around and pushed me as hard as he could into the three-foot-deep ditch that extended the length of the prison building. Once I'd managed to clamber out, I saw Sazan jumping into the back of a truck, falling flat, and disappearing from view, and then the truck drove off with a screech, smashed the prison gate, and they were gone. I was speechless. Volleys of rifle shots tore through the air; the camp thundered with shouts and gunfire. They immediately held a roll call: Naum, Sazan, and Murad were missing. I stood there in the downpour, the rain washing away my tears, as I longed for them to succeed.

They were full of courage but short on luck. A mile or two away from the prison, on the main road from Tirana to Shkodër, a bus driver heard the roar of the rifles and blocked the road ahead of the speeding truck. My three friends jumped out of the vehicle and ran off into the forest. Inside the prison the rain continued to drum against the windows, while outside it cooled their brows and washed away their footprints.

At midnight they dragged Murad and Sazan back to the camp, tied up with barbed wire. They woke us, stood us in line, and threw their bleeding quarry at our feet.

"Look at them!" shouted the prison governor. "That's what traitors to the fatherland look like! There they are, lying before you! Never forget this sight."

Next morning, before the usual wake-up call, my bunkmate went out to the bathroom, and when he returned, he had a strange look on his face.

"They've brought back a body."

In the corridor, where the food trolleys usually stood, lay Naum—dead. They'd thrown his body there for us to see. So that we'd always think of it whenever we stood in line to wait for our food. And so that we'd always have that image before us as we ate.

It was the first time I'd ever seen the corpse of someone who'd been murdered. The dead face of a person I cared about.

When I saw his mutilated feet, I took the towel I had thrown over my shoulder and carefully wrapped them in it. But then my gaze fell on his stomach, torn open by bullets. I took the towel from his feet, gathered up his ripped-out innards, put them back inside, and covered them. An hour later, the prison governor summoned me.

"Who was Naum to you?"

"A cellmate."

"A cousin?"

"No."

"So why did you do it?"

"I felt sorry for him."

The governor stared hard at me.

"Take him away."

They took me to the isolation cell, threw me to the ground, and seized some blocks of wood. At that point I didn't yet know I'd be beaten so often I'd end up losing count of how many times it happened.

At the time, locked in a concrete cage measuring six-and-a-half by four feet, I realized that life in prison wasn't just isolation—it was also endless suffering, the torture and death of those closest to you, and a sense of helplessness worse than death.

I went through prisons in Tirana, Laç, Elbasan, and Reps, but the greatest suffering lay ahead of me, in Spaç. It was there that I acquired a conscience, and it was there that my second sentence crushed me. I got it for taking part in the revolt—another sixteen years.

———

The Spaç revolt was something that had never happened in Albania before, something unthinkable. People were sent to jail for saying they didn't like the bread, and suddenly several hundred prisoners had dared take a stand against the authorities. A rebellion within the context of the most dreadful terror imaginable. The authorities had to understand how it was possible for someone to slip out of their viselike grip.

I confessed to taking part in the rebellion because I couldn't endure the beating. They tortured me deliberately, strategically; torture isn't very tiring for the torturer, and when he gets tired, he can rest. The victim never gets a moment's respite from the pain. The authorities watched my suffering closely and drew conclusions from it. Many times during the interrogations I thought I was dying. But I didn't die.

Communism was a beautiful edifice full of dark, decaying rooms. That's what the prisoners used to say, old and new, because more people were constantly brought in, especially members of the nomenklatura sentenced as a result of Hoxha's rising paranoia. They understood very well what communism was and why they'd become victims. In Tepelenë 260 people were sent to prison, seventy of whom were former war heroes, partisans, the pride of Albania. They thought that, as they'd risked their lives for their country, they had the right to criticize the Party, because they'd fought for paradise on earth but were forced to live in hell.

But in a totalitarian system, no one has the right to speak the truth. No past service to your nation can protect you. That system fed on the blood of the Albanians—it was a bloodthirsty monster, so it was constantly on the hunt for human flesh. But as it became weaker from year to year, it needed more and more of that blood, and it sucked it from ever-younger people. The older ones who stood up to the regime at the very start were immediately shot or simply disappeared.

What harm could I do to the system, a nineteen-year-old who'd heard that his relatives wanted to escape? The system wanted blood in order to survive; it needed our terror.

When they dragged me to the interrogation room after the events at Spaç, through the window I saw some soldiers playing volleyball, I saw their healthy, lithe bodies in brightly colored shirts, and I heard their happy voices. The guards noticed that I was looking out and slammed the shutters closed. I got a punch in the face.

It took the investigators a few days to realize that I had been in the group responsible for raising the flag, and that's when their fury exploded. Every time I fainted, they revived me with water, but then the pain returned and I'd faint again. That's why I can't remember much about it. I didn't have a watch—in the torture room there was no such thing as time. I only realized later that on the first day, they tortured me for eight hours. By midnight I was unable to walk or talk. Two policemen dragged my body back to the cell.

There were four interrogators: They'd come in, beat me, shout at me, and then go into the next room to torture someone else. The screams could be heard from all directions; they carried down the corridor and escaped through closed windows. At one point I was left alone in the room with a female secretary and the fourth interrogator, a guy from Tepelenë.

When I looked at him, he came up to me, and without a word he loosened my handcuffs. He probably thought he was bringing me relief, but he didn't know that when your circulation is cut off and then the blood starts flowing again, the pain is so excruciating it can make you faint.

"We'll soon find out what you have to say. Start writing," he said to the secretary. "On May 28, I, Ministry of the Interior investigator Skënder Qerimi . . ."

He stopped. He was sitting on a chair with his head bowed. Suddenly he looked up and our eyes met. I knew I had a cousin who worked for the Ministry of the Interior, but I'd never met him. I only knew his name: Skënder Qerimi.

He asked questions, I answered them, and the typewriter tapped away steadily. "We're of the same flesh and blood," I kept thinking. They took me back to the cell.

A few days later Skënder sent for me.

"Don't you feel sorry for yourself?"

"You're the one who made me into an enemy," I said.

He offered me some food but I shook my head.

"Do you hate me, too?" he snapped.

We sat in silence. We both hung our heads. Me and my cousin, the enemy of the people and the people's darling.

"If I manage to save you," he said, "that's your good luck, but if I fail, it won't be my fault."

A few days later I was summoned for another interrogation. The investigator from Gjirokastër sat facing me.

"Get up," he said. "Come here."

And he struck my head a mighty blow, so hard that I fell to the floor and began pouring with blood.

"And now," he said, extremely pleased with himself, "you must thank our dear leader who has decided to spare all of you, even though you should be shot like dogs."

A few days later they took me to the interrogation room again. On the table lay a sheet of paper and a pen, and there were men standing all around. When I sat down, each of them shook my hand in turn. I looked at their clean-shaven, smiling faces, as one by one, they came closer to me and then withdrew.

"You're so young . . . your family's looking forward to seeing you . . . they were never enemies of the fatherland . . . a family of true patriots . . . we know all about you . . . your grandfather died at Ioannina . . ."

"Where is Comrade Ylli?" someone asked.

"In the next room. He'll be here soon," replied another voice.

And in came Comrade Ylli—which means "star" in Albanian—the investigating officer for the Spaç revolt, as handsome as if he'd stepped off a propaganda poster. Everybody stood up and saluted. Ylli smiled faintly. He was thirty years old, with smooth skin, and he smelled of cologne. A communist star in a dark-red suit and a white shirt.

"You're Neim?" he asked me. "We've heard you're a good boy. We're going to give you a chance, and you're going to tell us who's an enemy of the people."

My body hadn't forgotten any of the torture. I was so exhausted. I was desperate for some peace. So after a pause I asked: "Do you want me to spy at Spaç or outside?"

"At Spaç," Ylli said.

I'd spent seven years there. Seven years, during which I'd reached adulthood. I knew all the prisoners, and they knew me.

"You turned my family into enemies of the people," I said, "and now you want me to become a rat?"

I knew this was how they wanted to punish not just me but all the prisoners, because they'd have demonstrated that the authorities could break anyone.

The court session took place on June 20. In the declaration presented to the judge, my words weren't quoted. That was as much as Skënder could do for me.

But my statement began with the sentence: "I took part in the Spaç revolt, which I regret." That was as much as I could do for myself. I was twenty-seven years old.

————

After serving their time, many people were sent back to prison again. It only took two or three months. We'd ask them: "How did you end up in here again?" They'd reply: "My family rejected me."

I shuddered whenever I heard those words, because what I feared more than anything else was going back to life under the watchful eye of the

Sigurimi, and returning to my relatives, who would resent me for all those years, for all the pain they'd suffered because of me. I'd left my father and three brothers on the other side. Every day, each of them had to cope with the suffering I had caused.

I was afraid of going back to prison, and I was afraid of coming out of it. I was frightened of the world outside. I was nineteen when I was sent to prison and forty when I left—I didn't know real life and I didn't know what lay in store for me. I knew that soon after being released some prisoners committed suicide. They drowned or hanged themselves at the first opportunity. If they had no one and nothing to go back to, in the communist reality, their life had no meaning.

In its benevolence, the Party took a few years off my sentence, and so on June 8, 1987, I stood outside the prison gates—a free man. I looked at the world and I couldn't believe it. There was so much space around me, endless space . . . I had so much pain inside me, I'd been broken in so many ways, but the outside world had gone on existing; the trees had continued to bear fruit, while the flowers went on blooming and the hillsides turned green. So much suffering occurred amid all this beauty.

About fifty yards from the gate there was a stream. I dipped my hand into the water and felt its cool chill on my fingers. But when I stood up and stepped onto the bridge, I saw the prison governor. I had the gate behind me and the rest of my life ahead of me, and there he was, standing in the middle of the road. He looked at me and held out his hand. "What a civilized gesture," I thought, "I'm a human being again," and held out my hand, too, but instead of shaking it, he grabbed me by the arms and forced me to turn and face the prison. "Look!" he hissed. "Take a really good look."

It crossed my mind that the man wanted to arrest me again. So many people went back to prison!

"Never forget this sight. If you ever come back, I promise we'll torture you to death. We'll make sure you suffer more than Taras Agolli."

We all knew what had happened to Taras Agolli: targeted torture. When he came back to prison, the guards tortured him for three months under the supervision of an experienced doctor. Whenever Taras was on the brink of death, the torture stopped. He was taken to the hospital and given treatment, while they waited patiently for him to recover his strength. Once he was back on his feet, the torture would start again. And so it continued, without end.

The governor left me alone on the bridge. That was the image I took away with me from prison.

When I crossed the threshold of my family home, my brothers and father just hugged me, as if I were still the boy who'd left the house to go to work twenty-one years ago. From the moment I returned, without saying much, without any declarations, they created a protective shield around me so that nothing else could happen to me. I didn't have to say anything or do any complaining—they knew everything. Never in any way did they make me feel that they resented me.

But life was still very hard for me. For three months I couldn't find a job, and in communist Albania, parasites ended up in prison. I repeatedly went back to the mine where I'd worked in the past and asked them to take me on again, but every time I was told: "No." The punishment would never end.

Finally, when I heard yet another "No," I realized that the authorities would do anything to destroy me. One of my brothers was with me at the time.

"Give me one last hug, because this is the end of me," I said.

And something inside me snapped, as if I had nothing to lose, as if I'd lost everything by now. Or perhaps in that moment I simply lost my mind? It was finally clear to me: In prison or outside, I would never be free again. The authorities would always have me in handcuffs. And as if out of spite, in a sort of bizarre act of despair, I started to scream. I walked straight ahead of me, shouting: "Drop dead, the lot of you! I hate you! To hell with you!"

I screamed out all the pain I'd amassed in the past twenty years.

At first my brother was dumbstruck, but then he raced up to me and covered my mouth. His fingers dug into my lips. He pulled me toward him.

"Shut up," he whispered.

I was trembling all over.

"If you have no pity for yourself, have some for us!"

I clung to him, shaking, and he held me in his arms without a word until I'd calmed down. Until my body was still again. That was the most awful moment. In all those years, that was the most awful moment.

And yet my life got back on track and kept rolling onward, day after day. I found a job, then I met my future wife, and our three children were born. My parents gave me life, and I gave life, too—I became a father. I'll never forget how my brother saved me. In an extraordinary surge of humanity, he gave me more at that moment than anyone else in my entire life.

But in the new era, we could barely make ends meet; the children were growing up, there was no work, and a friend told me he had a job for me. I was to become a prison guard, me . . . I thought about my life, I thought about my children, and I felt that, once again, fate was giving me no alternative. The worst moment was when I put on the uniform. Everything came flooding back.

———

I thought we'd succeeded in replacing the dreadful, flawed system with a new and better one and that, if God couldn't punish the people who had harmed others, then the state would—the new, democratic Albania.

To heal the wounds, I joined an association of former political prisoners. At first I played a very active role in it, but I soon realized that nobody was particularly concerned about punishing anyone or about compensating us for our suffering. We were given a paltry sum of money and a pat on the back, some vague promises were made, and we were sent home.

But the representatives of the old system were never punished—the men who spilled all that blood were never held responsible for their actions. So many people suffered every single day, so many people died with an empty stomach, so many perished performing hard labor for which they were never paid. They hoped that when the system that had cheated them finally fell, a new and better system would condemn the crimes of the old one, and Albania would finally be democratic.

But that didn't happen. The system didn't change, only the form of it. The people in power are the same as before, they just talk in a new language. There's no real democracy.

The young people need to learn about the crimes of communism, but as no one has been punished, what kind of lesson are they gaining from the past? Sometimes I give talks in schools about what it was like in prison, but the kids just shake their heads and say: "No, that's impossible." Nowadays, people only go to prison if they commit a serious crime, so the young people can't conceive of someone being convicted without being guilty. And rather than condemning the old system, the state is only interested in how to get rich.

Corruption is rife, there are no principles, and without principles, there's no true freedom. My daughter had brilliant results at high school, but for her to graduate, I still had to pay bribes. The children of rich families study abroad; they pay for university with their fathers' stolen money. So where is freedom? Where is equality? Where is truth? Where is the dream of democracy?

We're disappointed and exhausted. We've become beggars steeped in suffering. Twenty-six years have gone by since the fall of communism, laws have been passed that promised compensation for the years of prison labor, but we've never received a penny. It'll only turn up when we're all dead.

In the new Albania, the truth doesn't count. What use is it to anyone? You can't sell it or buy it. People have stopped hoping that the truth will bring liberation, that it will cleanse Albania. The world is still covered in mud.

I don't want to take that mud with me to the grave.

———

Neim Pasha died on March 9, 2018.

How a Child Prodigy
Was Diminished

"YES, THAT'S RIGHT . . . How about twelve times twenty-nine?"

The little boy touched the tip of his nose, scratched it, opened his eyes wide, and then his face lit up.

"Three hundred and forty . . . umm . . . eight."

At the same time the teacher was nervously multiplying the numbers on a piece of paper. Just a moment . . . and . . . yes . . . hmm . . .

"Very good . . . sit down," he stammered, sat down, too, and then for quite some time didn't say a word.

The young man who had slumped onto his chair, crushed by the weight of his discovery, was called Gjeto Vocaj. The boy he was staring at had only recently turned six and his name was Nika. As they looked at each other on that morning in 1962, in the cold, modest school building in the remote village of Palaj in northern Albania, neither of them knew that fate had just united them forever.

Nor that it would bring Gjeto great joy in spite of the pain, and Nika, a brief moment of fame, followed by disappointment and despair. Nor that, in the eightieth spring of Gjeto's life, he'd tell the story of the genius from the Dukagjini region, while sitting in the center of Shkodër on the terrace of a smart restaurant belonging to that same one-time wunderkind, who is now his sixty-two-year old friend.

———

Here we see the young Nika Marashi: He has a round face, a little snub nose and shining eyes, and he's wearing his only pair of trousers, made by his mother, as he poses for a photograph with his beloved teacher. He's boisterous and curious, so when someone says that up in the mountains they've seen some mysterious lights sparkling in the distance, he joins the other villagers on an arduous hour-and-a-half climb to the very summit to see what on earth it could be. He looks out, and moments later he's told it's Albanian progress twinkling down below in Shkodër—the new system will dispel the medieval darkness once and for all. But the communist light hasn't reached Palaj yet. There's no radio or telephone, money is hardly used at all, and there isn't even a school. As soon as the kids are big enough, they're sent out to graze the cows and goats, and woe betide the child who loses a single one of them.

Nika would also be destined to trudge after the goats if not for the fact that in 1962, communism has finally come knocking in Palaj, too, and a teacher has arrived in the village. All the children from the ages of six to ten are now gathered into a single class and are gazing hesitantly at the twentysomething-year-old who has just left college, and is also looking around uncertainly.

The youngest child, the one who can't sit still, is Nika, but Gjeto hasn't noticed him yet.

It takes a few weeks for him to realize that, in a village where no one has ever seen a car, a boy has been born with a calculator in his head.

———

"Meet little Nika," begins Gjeto's article about the small, fine-featured boy who is leagues ahead of all the children he has ever known. The text, published in a journal called *The Teacher*, is handed around the length and breadth of the country, until someone from the nomenklatura deems it appropriate to leave a copy on their beloved leader's desk. And so the leader straightens his glasses and settles down to read.

A delegation is sent to see the boy and make an assessment: Indeed, he is a genius! He can solve logic problems with the analytical power of a little philosopher. What should be done with him so he doesn't go to waste?

The young teacher walks down the endless corridors of the Central Committee building, trembling with fear in the company of a taciturn secretary and Ramiz Alia. They come to a satin-upholstered padded door—then a deep breath in, a hand on the doorknob, a deep breath out . . .

And there he is: Comrade Enver Hoxha, unassuming and unwavering, pragmatic in his cordiality and his cruelty. As befits an absolute ruler in a poor socialist kingdom, he sits on a podium at a table covered in papers, surrounded by shelves full of books, and at the sight of his visitors he curls his lips into the smile known to every single citizen, the smile of the leader who can praise and then kill.

"And does this young genius already know the names of every member of the Politburo?" asks the leader. The answer wipes the smile from his face.

"Before you start teaching him that the Earth orbits the Sun, make sure he knows what Marxism-Leninism is!"

Albania's most extraordinary schoolboy is to be given a special teaching program: lessons in the fresh air, a broad but flexible range of material adapted to the boy's talents, with no consideration of his age. The system wants to turn the young genius into a brilliant academic, but to make sure the boy doesn't feel exceptional, he'll go on living with his ten siblings in his godforsaken village.

"Arrogance is a disease that ruins everyone it affects," declares the beloved leader, and those assembled in the office piously nod their heads.

Gjeto is to be the boy's personal tutor, and is to work with him for as long as possible.

The Sigurimi is to open a file on Gjeto right away, and is to keep a particularly close eye on the young teacher. The system simply waits: One careless meeting, a few words to the wrong person, one coincidence, and the crushing machine will be set in motion.

———

Meanwhile, everyone in the region knows by now that their soil has produced a genius. Everyone who meets him pinches his cheek and comes up with a mathematical problem to see if the boy really is as exceptional as they say. Nika likes these puzzles, he finds math simple and obvious, whatever he hears he immediately memorizes, and he can recall facts easily.

"How does it work?" people ask him.

"Just like that," says Nika with a shrug.

He's also grown used to being quizzed. Every few weeks he's taken for tests, now to Tirana, now Shkodër; the expectations surrounding him continue to rise. Let the young prodigy demonstrate his genius!

The middle-aged man who used to be this wunderkind, and who is now drinking coffee with me, smiles bitterly at his memories.

"An actor plays a role, steps off the stage, and goes back to normal life. A sportsman leaves the pitch and barely anyone can tell that that particular person has just won a major competition. But I had to keep meeting other people's expectations, constantly playing the part of a genius and solving problem after problem, to prove I really was as gifted as they said. Mathematics, which I used to love, became an ordeal for me. Sometimes on their way into the factory people would sing about how great it was to go to work, because later they could clock off and go home, but it felt as if my job—being a great talent—would never end."

———

The brilliant student and his teacher have work conditions like no one else in Albania. They travel to Durrës, where they lie on the beach while Nika solves the problems that Gjeto thinks up for him. By Lake Shkodër, they stretch out on rugs to discuss geometry and the concept of infinity.

After some time, the pair are transferred to Shkodër, where they quickly become famous, too. Everyone who sees Nika in the street says: "Oh, you're Gjeto's student!" And everyone who sees Gjeto says: "Ah, you're Nika's teacher!"

"Gjeto was a friend, teacher, and father to me," says Nika, smiling. "There were times when I felt as if we were one person, like Siamese twins. We'd lie in our beds and talk until three in the morning, not just about math but also about Stalin, Hoxha's policies, and freedom. We trusted each other completely. Gjeto is an exceptional person—in those days few people were as bighearted as that."

––––––––

Gjeto's heart beats fast as he shakes the hand of a friend from work who that same day is going to throw himself into the Buna river in the hope that, rather than drowning him, the current will carry him off to a new life in Yugoslavia. Neither of them knows if the escape attempt will succeed, or how this last encounter is going to affect their lives. Gjeto simply wishes his friend good luck.

Seven years go by, car horns are blaring, the sidewalk shudders above a subway tunnel, somewhere in the distance a siren wails, and in a small, shabby café in Manhattan, a group of Albanian émigrés try to outshout each other as they idly fill their glasses with raki. Yes, gentlemen, who would have thought we'd be doing so well? Us, the ones who escaped before the drawbridge was raised and the fortress gate locked shut, the ones who sneaked our way over the wall? We are the survivors, the luckiest people in Manhattan. A toast to those who escaped Albania! Death to Enver!

Death to Enver!

And then come the reminiscences: This guy fled through Peshkopi, that guy got to Greece through the forest; someone sailed from Himara to Corfu on a homemade raft! What a list of miracles!

"As for me," says one of them, "I escaped down the Buna to Ulcinj and nobody, absolutely nobody, knew about it, except for my one and only friend, a wonderful man named Gjeto Vocaj, who never let me down! Just as I'm sitting here with you now, I sat with him on the last day before I escaped, and then I shook his hand . . . Long live Gjeto!"

"Long live Gjeto!" they cry, then raise their glasses and smile—everyone's smiling at the thought of their luck, and only one of them is smiling at the thought of those details, too.

A name, a surname, the place and date of the meeting, the route—we've all got to make a living somehow, haven't we . . .?

———

Nika Marashi, the Albanian child prodigy, becomes a high school student and shines like the brightest star of communist education. It's a beautiful star, of course, but the teachers don't really know what to do with it. Apparently, various kinds of computer are being built somewhere in the world outside, but few people in Albania can imagine them. Nika more and more often spends his evenings reading books; math is becoming a bore and a source of stress for him, so he avoids it as much as possible. School has its own pace, but Nika's brain works on a different frequency. The system is giving him everything it can, but in communist Albania, that's still not enough.

But as anticipated, Nika does go to study math at university in Tirana, except that he can barely make ends meet: Thanks to a scholarship, he has just enough for food and a roof over his head, but he can't afford to buy soap or clothes. Supposedly he's privileged, and yet he wears the same pair of trousers in August as in January, and more and more often he skips lectures to go to drama classes at the Cultural Institute. The tutor appreciates both Nika's imagination and the dramatic expression of a young girl from Fier, whose name is Lili. Nika can't take his eyes off her.

———

Name by name, detail by detail, for years, the Sigurimi patiently and methodically collect the stones they will hang around Gjeto's neck before throwing him into the water.

"What do we have?"

"Gjeto Vocaj, from a socially downgraded family, worked as a teacher in villages in the north. His grandfather was a member of Balli Kombëtar and was executed; his family was interned in Tepelenë, and their house was burned down. The spawn of traitors! And someone like that stood in front of our leader . . ."

"He failed to denounce the son of a bitch who escaped in 1971, seven years ago! He just sat there, chirping away like a canary, gorging himself on our grain—we even sent him to Shkodër along the way. That's how we rewarded him for teaching that little brat from Dukagjini!"

"We can't use the statement from America or we'll expose our spy. So what else do we have?"

"We've got a brother-in-law, an uncle, a best friend, two work colleagues, a professor who taught him. He didn't like the fact that after university he was sent to the provinces. He listened to Vatican Radio and Voice of America. He kept saying it was better in the West, that Albania isn't developing, that you can't even buy cheese in this country . . ."

"Good. That's the perfect recipe for ten years."

———

After class, Nika sometimes chats to Lili, and there's no doubt he's found the woman of his dreams, though she's completely different from him: calm, sensible, meticulous. So he can't believe it when, in answer to his marriage proposal, Lili solemnly nods her head.

Except that he comes from the Catholic north, and she's a Muslim from the south. Nika's parents will get over their disappointment somehow, but Lili's father, a proud resident of Fier, refuses to hear of it: His daughter is not going to marry a ragamuffin from the mountains, an uncivilized savage.

But Nika has a plan: He and Lili will elope! Then, in keeping with Albanian tradition, their parents will have nothing to say on the matter. Sensible Lili finds this idea romantic and, above all, effective.

And so they carry out their resolution. When Nika appears at the door of his family home with his new wife, his father sighs, then puts on his best clothes and goes to Fier to see Lili's parents.

"My son didn't tell me what he was going to do, just as your daughter hid the whole plan from you, too. Neither of them asked us for our opinion."

Lili's father says nothing, but in the end he nods.

"It seems we have nothing more to say."

And a year later, when Lili and Nika's first son is born, the brand-new grandfather trails along endless potholed roads from Fier to the detested north, and leans over the baby in the cradle.

"What am I to do with you? I'll just have to be your grandfather, won't I?"

———

At about the same time, a stranger knocks at Gjeto Vocaj's door. The man, who has a handsome yet joyless face, tells him he is required immediately at the Department for Internal Affairs. What can the authorities want with this quiet, model citizen of communist Albania? Gjeto carries out a rapid examination of his conscience, but he can't find any sins. He glances at the coatrack in the hall but soon changes his mind; outside, the sun is shining.

"Take your coat, comrade," advises the Sigurimi agent.

Gjeto is an optimist by nature, an endlessly cheerful person, who wants to see the best in every situation. He decides he isn't going to need his coat. When they leave the house, the agent stops at a kiosk and buys a packet of cigarettes. Without a word, he puts it in Gjeto's breast pocket.

Briefly their eyes meet, and then they both look away. Now Gjeto understands.

———

The witness enters the interrogation room and Gjeto recognizes him immediately. It's his drunkard neighbor, who once knocked at his door and asked to borrow a plate for his cousin, a long-awaited guest from Yugoslavia. Then he dropped by to return the plate, and stopped for a chat in the doorway. Another time he asked how his dear neighbor got such a nice couch, sat down on it, and shared his thoughts about the excellent couches they made across the Yugoslav border, and what a great life they had there in general. And Gjeto understood: The Sigurimi was speaking through his neighbor. He immediately showed him the door.

He didn't yet know that a small device had been stuck to the outside of the window frame and was recording all the complaints, grumbles, and sighs, all the banned broadcasts, all the foreign songs, all the discussions about the future in a country without hope.

"The man who has just come in has two signs, one on his back and one on his chest," said Gjeto, pointing to his neighbor.

"What signs?" asked the investigator in surprise.

"He has a sign on his back saying 'Spy' and one on his chest saying 'False witness.'"

His neighbor was seething with rage. He was swaying on his chair; ratting on people was a tough job, so before the interrogation he'd had a few drinks for Dutch courage.

"Revered comrade," he cried, "the man sitting there, that rogue Gjeto Vocaj, he sometimes shouts such loud abuse at the authorities in his house that I can hear him through the walls! He says Enver Hoxha's a bastard, we've nothing to eat, he can't go on like this, so tomorrow he'll flee the country! Sometimes he even stands at the window as if he wants the people outside to hear him—he stirs up others, too!"

The investigator looked crestfallen.

"You said something different earlier, comrade. You said you went to the suspect's home because he invited you in for coffee, and—"

Gjeto interrupted. "You're feeding him the answers like a teacher who wants to bump up a weak pupil's grade to a pass! I won't sign any statement you've prompted him to make!"

They handcuffed Gjeto; the interrogation was over.

———

As a recently qualified teacher, Nika looks around the classroom where his new, slightly frightened pupils are sitting. Just as long as there aren't any geniuses among them . . .

He and Lili have been sent to work in Theth, even farther north than Nika's home village.

"Theth was infinitely beautiful, and that did sweeten our life a bit, but then they moved us to Pult, where we felt completely cut off from the world. Except that everyone was struggling just as much, so there was no one to envy. We only discussed our theater course in Tirana occasionally. The fact that'd we'd met in a place like that seemed impossible . . .

"At night I'd go outside and look at the sky. There was darkness and silence all around, as if we were living in a total void. I wondered if we were in for the standard five-year teaching assignment, or if the authorities would show their claws and we'd get ten, like some of the others."

––––––––

In the cramped prison cell, instead of silence, there's a din. The man staring at Gjeto has a skinny body and a round face. Sometimes the words flow from his mouth like a river after a storm, and sometimes they trickle like a dried-up stream.

"Aren't you surprised I always have cigarettes but you haven't had a single packet from your family?"

"No," Gjeto says.

The two slim, stooping figures bow their heads.

"Every day they take five days off my sentence. If I find out something interesting, they'll cut my sentence in half . . . That's how it is. I'm sorry . . ."

"That's how it is," says Gjeto.

"I've read your file. Your brother-in-law informed on you. So did your uncle, and your best friend . . . What a fucked-up country."

Gjeto bows his head. So that's how the system works? Is it really so ruthless? Is it really so effective? Is it really so inhuman? Does it change friends into traitors, and spies into comforters?

––––––––

In the café in downtown Shkodër, the adult Nika nods.

"Gjeto was like someone from a different world—even in communist Albania no one had a bad word to say about him. When the news of his arrest got out, I went to Shkodër and I could see that, although people were trying to hold their tongues, many of them were outraged. Because why on earth had Gjeto been arrested, of all people? No one had any idea about his friend who'd escaped, which made it even harder to understand."

———

The trials of enemies of the people always take place in packed courtrooms, so that the general public can get a view of the infallibility of the system, but the indictment against Gjeto is so poorly cobbled together that the authorities decide to revel in their own efficiency behind closed doors. The public in Shkodër sometimes shows unusual courage, and when the lies exceed the limit to which they are all accustomed, they come out in defense of the accused. But before the trial has started, Gjeto hears banging at the courtroom door.

There in the doorway stands a woman with fiery eyes and an ashen face, small and shriveled, with sunken cheeks.

"Another false witness?" is Gjeto's immediate thought, before he hears the woman's loud, ringing voice: "I have a right to be here!"

It's Liliana, his wife, whom he hasn't seen for six months. Strong, cheerful Liliana, who now looks like a skeleton draped in skin. Only her voice hasn't changed—it's the same familiar, powerful voice in a completely alien body. Years later, Gjeto will recall that seeing his wife like that was a far greater blow than the interrogation and the trial put together. What the suffering had done to his beloved Liliana . . .

When another of the witnesses has finished speaking—a female neighbor from their apartment block—Liliana asks to take the floor.

"That shameless woman, with whom none of us has ever spoken, is a member of the Party. What reward are you expecting to give her for making a false statement?"

"You'll leave here in handcuffs, comrade!" cries the prosecutor.

But Liliana is in a frenzy, and instead of keeping quiet, she holds out her hands and says: "Go on, then, handcuff me, don't be afraid. Since you're convicting my husband on the basis of lies, you'll have no trouble with me, but you'll never shake off the shame!"

Gjeto goes weak at the knees. Liliana has gone mad. What will happen to the children? He watches as the guard escorts his wife out, and another witness enters the room, his head drooping. It's his best friend.

"He never spoke badly of the Party . . . But he did say that exiling him to the countryside was unfair."

The judge clears his throat.

"Thank you. I can see that the defendant disagrees with the Party's policies. That's enough for us."

The court rules: seven years for agitation and propaganda, to the disappointment of the prosecutor who has demanded ten.

"Only seven years!" Gjeto, who isn't known as an optimist for nothing, thinks happily. His best friend, head bowed, stands in the witness box in despair, inspiring pity rather than anger. The community policewoman, Belkize Mjeda, who's been summoned to court, has been bold enough to say that Gjeto Vocaj is the noblest person she knows. And they haven't arrested Liliana . . .

––––––––––

The adult Nika raises a finger.

"Collective guilt was at the heart of Albanian communism. Whatever you'd done wrong, all your loved ones had to suffer. You might not have been in touch with your brother for years, but if he suddenly felt like fleeing the country, they exiled you to a village at the end of the world. That's what communist justice was like. When Gjeto landed behind bars, the authorities came knocking on Liliana's door, too. She and the children were interned in the village of Pistull near Shkodër, and were ordered to work on a cooperative farm. They could hardly afford to buy bread. That's what life was like in communist Albania. There was no alternative."

––––––––––

The men under the tarpaulin are handcuffed and tied together with wire so tightly that if one of them makes a careless movement it causes another one pain. They even dig into the skin every time the truck bounces over a pothole.

"Bloody Albanian junk, these handcuffs!" moans one of the prisoners.

"Look at these! Mine don't hurt."

"That's because yours are German, the luxury kind!"

"Anyone who gets German handcuffs is a Soviet spy!"

The men burst out laughing.

"Don't fall about like that, it hurts!" groans someone sitting in the middle.

They're crowded together, the handcuffs cutting into their wrists until they bleed, and there's no air under the low tarpaulin, but Gjeto laughs so hard his belly aches. When they let their heads droop, they're nothing but prisoners, but when they laugh, they are people again.

The truck driving along those winding, potholed roads is taking them to Spaç. There the enemies' broken spines will be straightened by slave labor and torture.

———

The tiny figures in gray prison garb roam around the gray earth amid the gray mountains that enclose the camp in their tight grip.

Before the revolt, conditions at Spaç are inhuman. Only after it will they introduce one day a week that's free of work, and the guards will stop torturing the prisoners who haven't the strength to meet the work-norm. But the dead will still be buried on a hillside near the camp, as if the system wants to show that not even death can wipe out their sins. Mothers and fathers will only learn of their sons' deaths when they come to visit, exhausted and overburdened. The guards will just shrug and say: "One less enemy of the people!"

And as the great leader is always telling his flock: "No concessions, no mercy for the enemy, and no fear of mistakes. Nobody who shows hostility to an enemy of the people is making an error."

Gjeto Vocaj only spends three months in Spaç, because his cousin is one of the prison guards. The authorities magnanimously regard this as a conflict of interest, and Gjeto thanks his lucky stars. Three months in Spaç are like three years in any other prison.

―――――

"When they arrested Gjeto, I was devastated, as if they'd taken my father," recalls Nika. "Prison was a tragedy, but when I thought of Gjeto, I sometimes wondered if our life was any better. After hard, exhausting work we returned to homes that were like prisons, too. They were built so low you only had to raise a hand to touch the ceiling. All to make sure we had no sense of space and couldn't catch our breath. We were meant to feel weak and incarcerated. The system made a constant effort to diminish us, our homes, and our lives."

―――――

From afar, the prison in Ballsh looks just as miserable as the one in Spaç, and the prisoners seem just as emaciated, but here, no one is expected to perform slave labor, and the convicts can read and do what they like, even learn languages. This is where the top brass are sent, fueling the ranks of the "revisionist unit" composed of former ambassadors, ministers, officers, and diplomats: the system's elite, who've lost their jobs and freedom mainly because of Hoxha's growing paranoia. Mehmet Shehu's personal tailor is sent here for sewing treacherous coats, and so is the dictator's photographer, who worked day and night retouching his face in official photographs so that it always looked kind and cheerful.

Many of these people are convicted and jailed so suddenly and unexpectedly that they feel as if they've been hit by an avalanche and simply can't believe it. These "red pashas" meet up in prison for group readings of Hoxha's works, and during their discussions they confirm their faith in his infallibility, as if they weren't behind bars at all. Many of them think their entire detention is a big test they've been set by their wise leader and that, any moment now, they'll be released.

Whenever their beloved Supreme Comrade appears on the television screen, a number of the pashas start to sniffle.

"How I miss that great man!" Dashnor Mamaqi exclaims—until recently, editor-in-chief of *Zëri i Popullit* (*Voice of the People*), the official organ of the ruling party.

And in order to prove his ideological acuity, he sends the dear leader an official letter that gently prompts him to wage class war inside the prisons, too.

"We are not equal, after all," he writes. "Here in Ballsh we are surrounded by enemies of the people, whom we should crack down on as fast as possible. Class war must be waged in prison, just as it is in the outside world. Please provide some suggestions and a plan of action."

Unfortunately, no suggestions ever come, and without orders from the dictator, nothing can be done.

———

"Yes, take the soap handed to you by a traitor to the fatherland, but know that no soap will wash away your shame or the blood on your hands."

All the prisoners fall silent, and the man to whom these words are addressed stands mute, as if carved out of stone, his head bowed. The greater the successes announced by the authorities, the more enemies of the people have to be reeducated, and the more often former prosecutors, judges, and policemen come face-to-face with the people they sent to hell in the past. During morning ablutions, the victim watches in the mirror, following the reflection of his fallen torturer. Enemies of the people keep arriving, and living conditions in Ballsh look increasingly like a waiting room in hell: Prisoners sleep on the floor, side by side, and when there seems to be no room left in the cell for anyone else, yet another man appears in the doorway.

In the end, as a result of prison overcrowding—that is to say, thanks to the infinite mercy of the Supreme Comrade—in 1982 an amnesty is declared for all those with sentences under ten years. And that includes Gjeto Vocaj.

———

News spreads around the village of Koman that among these honest people, an extremely dangerous traitor has appeared. The enemy of the
people, his enemy wife, and their two enemy sons spend three days and
three nights under the open sky, waiting for the arrival of the village
chairman, who is sitting at home waiting for the rain to stop. On the first
night Gjeto sees some figures hurrying toward them in the darkness. The
villagers have brought them some bread.

It turns out that the only shelter the authorities can offer a traitor who
is to be interned for five years is a goat shed, with no windows, doors, or
electricity, because what do goats and traitors need electricity for? But just
behind the shed there is a beautiful lake full of fish, and next to the lake
there are trees with branches that bow under the weight of their fruit.

It soon transpires that, although growing vegetables is forbidden, the
local authorities are hungry, too. Gjeto plants beans and onions and swaps
the fish he catches in the lake for bread and cheese. This sends the local
spy into a blind fury—again and again he duly reports it to the authorities,
but every time the police are due to turn up for an inspection, Gjeto is
tipped off by the locals and hides his fishing gear in a safe place.

"False information," declare the authorities.

The spy is as stupid as he is zealous, and as he is always hanging around,
eager to start a conversation, one day Gjeto stops him.

"Please don't give me away, my friend," he says, "but tonight I'm going
to Shkodër without permission. You're the only person I trust."

The spy nods like a drunken woodpecker. In the middle of the night,
Gjeto is woken by someone hammering at the door.

"False information," notes the policeman, spitting curses to left and
right.

———

Meanwhile, in the northern village of Pult, where the authorities have
placed Nika and Lili with their two sons, people sometimes whisper about
bread made with wheat, and how they long to eat just one warm slice of
it. The local shop has nothing but hard cornbread that might as well be
made of stone.

Today, sitting on a designer chair and drinking coffee, Nika shakes his head.

"At home we used to joke that, when the Yugoslavs came, we'd shelter in the bunkers and cover them in slices of bread, because they were so hard, they'd provide excellent protection against the bullets. As a pair of teachers, my wife and I earned more than others, but even so, we had nothing. As the citizens of a proud and wonderful country, we thought we were the center of the universe, but actually no one cared a jot about us. The propaganda promoted the idea that Albania was a fortress made of granite, but that granite was crumbling with every day that passed."

———

Not suspecting that spies also inform on spies, everyone who placed denunciations on the altar of the Sigurimi is invited to the promotional event for Gjeto Vocaj's autobiography, *A Fatal Encounter with the Dictator*. Gjeto also leaves a copy of the book in the favorite café of the investigator who interrogated him so professionally. He doesn't forget to add an inscription: "Check I didn't make any mistakes."

———

Nika was at the book launch, too. After the fall of the dictatorship, he completed a law degree, became a real estate agent and legal adviser, and now he works in accounting. He financed the restaurant where I met Gjeto for the first time, but he stresses that it's his son's business.

"Talking about yourself is terribly boring," he says, laughing, when I question him about the story of the child prodigy. "If journalists want to meet me, I only agree to do it because of Gjeto. And anyway, you can always watch us on YouTube. Honestly! Can you imagine how much the world has changed? I come from a village that didn't yet have a school or electricity in the 1950s. What I gained from communism is that now, any obstacles in my life seem like nothing compared with the past. If I'd been born in the present day, I'd have no idea how strong a person can be."

Once upon a time, Nika spent an hour and a half climbing a hill to see the lights of electrified Shkodër. Now it takes me a couple of seconds to type his name into the search box on YouTube. I watch the two aging men smiling into the camera: the good teacher and his brilliant pupil, who used to say they were like a single person, and now just say they're friends.

The Broken Tree

"YOU CAN KILL ME HERE and now, because I won't sign any papers."

That's what he told them.

But the police chief looked him straight in the eye and smiled.

"Listen. You're going to live and you're going to beg me to let you sign those papers."

The cop was looking down on him, because Anastas was sitting in front of him on a chair, but if Anastas had stood up, that short-ass police chief would have had to crane his neck. Because Anastas was a good six-and-a-half-feet tall and weighed about 240 pounds—the guy was as big as a 300-year-old oak tree, people like him are rare. And when you looked at him, he radiated the nobility and serenity of an oak tree. So no wonder he was the local leader of the Aromanians, a Romanian-speaking ethnicity who live in the south of Albania. Anyone could come to him if they had an issue, and everyone listened to him because there was truth and integrity in him. He was like the water from a mountain stream. You drink it, and you know it can't poison you.

The Sigurimi needed him to be clean like that. They wanted a good man in their pocket, someone who had natural authority. He didn't have to lock anyone in a cellar for them to obey him. He didn't have to write slogans in stones on every hillside to prove how great he was. He didn't have to terrorize or kill anyone for them to respect him.

They summoned him and said: "You're going to inform for us."

But he said he wouldn't sign, and they realized that the man sitting in front of them would sooner die than become a spy. Since his honor meant more to him than his life, whose honor did they have to trample for it to be worse than death?

They went and fetched his daughter. Twenty years old.

Beautiful, one of those girls who are born more beautiful than the hills. They put her in the next room, where the police chief tore off her dress. He punched her in the face, splitting her lip. Then he hit her on the head, on the temples. She was covered in blood. She was screaming. Her father heard her screaming but didn't know who it was. The police chief beat her up while two police officers held her down and a doctor looked on. After a while the doctor raised a hand and said: "That's enough."

They brought his daughter in to him in nothing but her underwear, in a short white vest covered in blood. She had so much blood on her face it was hard to recognize her.

"Daddy," she sobbed. "What have I done to them, what have I done? Help me . . ."

Shortly before, she'd been at home, in the kitchen, they'd dragged her away from her cooking. How can it be that one minute you're a twenty-year-old girl, young and beautiful, doing things around the house, and then suddenly you're standing in front of a man who glares at you, punches you in the face, and rips off your clothes without a word? How can you understand that? She was crying like mad because she had no idea what was going on.

The police chief hit her again, in front of her father. So the father was looking at his daughter, the doctor was looking at the blood, the policemen were looking at the girl's naked body, and the police chief was looking at the man for whom this whole show had been arranged.

"If you don't sign, then each of us will fuck her in turn, right here, right before your eyes."

For an Albanian woman, rape is worse than death. It's like dying every day for the rest of your life. And her father knew it. His daughter's life would be over. That sort of thing couldn't be kept hidden, and no one would ever forget about it. He knew that, so he burst out howling. It was like he'd lost his mind. He curled up and just howled.

They even ripped the vest off her. The two policemen simply couldn't wait—they were ready. They lunged toward her. That was when her father cried out: "Please, I beg you, give me the document, I'll sign anything."

————

That's what it was like back then. If you were wondering why so many people were spies, there's your answer. They could always find a way to break even the best character. Just destroying you was never enough for them. They wanted to destroy whatever you loved most. Drita, is there anything good to eat in the house? Bring her some honey! We've got such good honey, from the local meadows. Do you like it? You're not eating a thing. Have some, it's good honey, that's the way we make it around here, with crystals as big as pebbles in it.

But that story had a happy ending—I think I can put it that way. The girl was semiconscious, horribly beaten up, but when they let her go, she told her boyfriend what had happened. He was from a village near the border, and he insisted they must escape. The border was a barbed wire fence, sometimes double-strand, sometimes electrified, with one guard tower beside another. The guards had a perfect view. But the lad knew that land better than those guys in the towers, he knew every path, every hillock, and he'd been thinking about it for a long time. And a week later they escaped in the night. Don't ask me how, because I don't know. Maybe they succeeded because they had nothing else to lose and despair carried them over the border? They were running away from something much worse than death. I guess that makes it easier to escape.

They sent the father to Spaç as a punishment, because that was the worst place of all, and that's where he told me the story. He didn't have to lie anymore, he didn't have to spy, they couldn't do anything to him in there. He was in prison, and he was free. He could go on living there in that everyday suffering of ours, or he could die in peace, because he knew his daughter was far away, and not even the authorities had arms long enough to reach her.

Eat up your honey—don't you like it? You see, it all ended happily.

Everything and Nothing

FAR, FAR AWAY, IN NËNMAVRIQ, one of the villages scattered among the high mountains of the north, there was an old stone church, modest and austere, with just one piece of treasure inside it: a mediaeval crown set with jewels. A young teacher called Dhurata Mulleti would go to the church in the evenings and sit in a pew. One day the priest stopped her and asked: "Why do you come here? You're a Muslim, aren't you?"

At first Dhurata said nothing, until suddenly she blurted: "In the evenings, the light bounces off the jewels in the crown and makes a rainbow on the wall . . . It's the most beautiful thing I've ever seen. Sometimes I imagine I'm wearing the crown—"

"You're blaspheming, child," interrupted the priest. But he didn't scold her or throw her out of the church.

That was early in 1967. Soon after, purges began among the clergy and Sigurimi agents came to the church. At first the priest protested, but when he realized there was no hope left, he insisted they summon Dhurata.

The Sigurimi knocked on the girl's door.

"The priest is asking for you," they said.

"He's denounced me to them for wanting to be a queen!" she thought. She entered the church, trembling. The priest cast her a glance filled with utter exhaustion and said: "They're taking everything away. Please put the crown on for a moment. Without knowing it, you were the harbinger of our fate."

Dhurata had long, fair hair. When she put the crown on her head she looked so beautiful that even the Sigurimi agents smiled. But then their faces hardened again, and without looking at anyone, they loaded a truck with wooden crosses, pictures, and candlesticks, every last thing they could take. They also took the crown and dragged the priest to their car. The church was filled with emptiness.

———

"Perhaps I shouldn't be wearing this pinny while I'm talking to you," says Sister Roza with a smile, smoothing down her blue nylon dress.

I look at her calm, grandmotherly face and her eyes, with irises that are brown in the middle, fading to blue at the edges. Soon after, Sister Roza shows me a photograph dating from 1942, of a group of Franciscan novices: she is sitting in the front row, among the youngest girls, as eleven-year-old Gjina, because that was her name before she took her vows. In the second row, with her hands in her lap, is Maria Tuci, age fourteen, with an intense, almost somber look on her face. The gravity of her expression distinguishes her from the other girls. Of all of them, it's Maria who will suffer the most, and who will become the second woman in the history of Albania to be beatified, after Mother Teresa.

"I was only ten years old when I joined the Franciscan convent school," says Sister Roza with a smile. "They kept telling me I was too young, that I wasn't old enough to be so close to God, but I could feel that He was giving me strength. I sat at my desk, I listened to the teachers, I sang the songs, and I couldn't imagine being anywhere else, I felt that I was full of God. But then along came the communists—they immediately closed the Catholic schools and reduced everything to dust . . .

"I have no words to describe it. All the wonderful people I knew were ruined or killed. The cleverest, the brightest ones . . . I listened to them at Mass with an open heart, and then again and again came the news: In 1946 Fathers Daniel Dajani, Gjon Shllaku, and Giovanni Fausti were shot dead in Shkodër against the cemetery wall, Bishop Frano Gjini was tortured and shot, Father Deda was tortured to death . . . Every time, my heart broke, because they were taking our best clergymen, the ones they feared because they might have put up resistance.

"And they didn't kill them just like that. They tortured them horrifically before they died, as if they gained strength by inflicting that suffering, they'd half-drown them in the sewage well, they wouldn't let them go to the toilet, they starved them . . . Their bones would snap like dry twigs . . .

"I'll tell you about Maria Tuci as I saw her then . . . At school Maria always had a kind word for me. She was calm and intelligent, with a strong spirit. I lost touch with her in 1946 when the Franciscans sent her to a school in the Mirdita district to teach the children. When the local Party secretary Bardhok Biba was murdered, she, her brother, and three hundred other people were sent to prison. She was so young—she was only twenty-two . . . Apparently at her first interrogation the investigator Hilmi Seiti told her: "I'm going to make you unrecognizable."

"They'd push Maria into a large sack, throw feral cats in there with her, and then hit the sack with sticks as hard as they could, so the creatures went mad with pain and clawed her body to shreds. Eventually Maria was so badly weakened that she ended up in the hospital with pneumonia. I went to visit her, but when I entered the ward, I couldn't see her anywhere. It was only when I heard someone calling: 'Gjina, Gjina!' that I stopped in mid-step. That figure on the bed in the corner of the ward . . . Nothing but skin and bones, with a skeletal nose . . . 'Lord God Almighty,' I thought, 'what have they done to her to make her look like that?' Because in the past, she had been a normal, healthy, beautiful young woman . . . She was the prettiest of us all . . . And she was stronger than any of us, too, because at once she said: 'Gjina, I've got pneumonia, but all they're giving me is penicillin, please try to get me something stronger.' 'Of course,' I replied, 'I'll see to everything necessary,' because by then I was doing a nursing course, but I could see from her neck and forearms that it was very bad—they must have beaten and starved her extremely harshly. Only her eyes were still the same.

"'I've got to get out of here,' she whispered, and I nodded.

"She died a week later, before I'd had time to get her the medicine.

Apparently, just before she died, she told one of her relatives that now she'd be free.

"Compared to Maria, I never suffered at all. Before leaving the house, I'd stop for a moment by the door and repeat silently: 'Lord without sin, protect me from all evil.' And there was no shortage of evil—evil was everywhere."

———

In the mid-1960s, Enver Hoxha decided to deal with God once and for all. Faith was distracting the Albanians from the one legitimate ideology, so the regime declared war on all religions. The persecution of imams, Orthodox clerics, and Bektashi babas had started as soon as Hoxha took power, but now the cruelest fate befell the Catholic priests, who were murdered for "spying on behalf of the Vatican, anti-state activity, and betrayal of the fatherland." The authorities hated everything Western, and Catholicism in Albania had always been supported by Italy and former Austria-Hungary—in other words, by the imperialists. Clergymen were shot dead, drowned in cesspits, beaten to death, or strangled. Many lost their lives in labor camps.

But even that was still not enough suffering. In February 1967, the Supreme Comrade called on the country's young people to wage war against "religious superstitions." "No more obscurantism and mysticism!" thundered the leader. "Socialism is built on hard toil, not prayers."

Newspapers throughout Albania tried to convince the new socialist nation that religion was a major obstacle to the country's further development, a stronghold of conservatism, the enemy of women's emancipation, and "mendacity in the service of foreign forces." The regime wanted the young people to do its dirty work.

Soon the most ideologically conditioned eagerly set about pillaging churches and destroying chapels. First to seize their pickaxes were students from Durrës, then they were joined by the young people of Lezhë; the campaign took place within the atmosphere of a propaganda picnic. Those with a bad family background were particularly zealous, because they wanted to show they deserved a second chance. People in the countryside destroyed their local churches, while the authorities bent over backwards to convince society of the legitimacy of their new plan: "Who could believe in Adam and Eve when we know what Neanderthals looked like? Why on earth do we need faith when we have science? Does Albania really need those greedy scroungers who do nothing but sponge money off hardworking people? Enough of these superstitions! We need buildings that are more functional than churches!"

———

"I watched as my beloved cathedral in Shkodër was turned into a large sports hall and the crowds cheered," says Sister Roza. "Catholic and Orthodox churches and mosques were demolished before my eyes and replaced with warehouses, theaters, cinemas, and cultural centers. Earlier, we'd been able to meet in church at least once a week, read the Gospel, and sing together. In 1967, all that was taken away from us. But despite the fear, before every meal we'd make the sign of the cross, even though I was aware that one of the priests I knew had gone to prison because his nephews had informed on him for praying. We still celebrated Christmas, but on that day we weren't even allowed to cook meat, because the spies would instantly have denounced us to the authorities. The shops were closed just before the holiday in case someone had a coupon for meat or eggs that they wanted to use. That's why on December 25 we'd gather in a circle, a very tight one, just my parents and us five children, and we'd sing carols almost silently. My brother, who used to play the recorder in church, now blew so gently that you could barely hear him. We were very fortunate that we could trust each other."

———

Since God no longer existed, former priests finally had to make themselves useful, the authorities declared and sent them to do hard labor on the cooperative farms. The most defiant and best educated ended up in prison—mostly in Spaç and Burrel. The regime continued to spill blood: In 1971 Father Shtjefën Kurti, earlier jailed for seventeen years, was shot for secretly baptizing a child; four other priests were killed by firing squad for being anti-communist and enemies of the people.

On religious holidays, the authorities invented special tasks for the citizens to perform, such as working to construct a canal or pave a new street, so that people came home completely exhausted. In the Christmas season, the residents of Shkodër were sent to clean cesspits. Atheism was triumphant—the authorities were so pleased with its progress that in 1973, in a former Franciscan college in Shkodër, they opened a Museum of Atheism, inspired by similar institutions in the Soviet Union.

Believers who dared to practice their religion at home continued to be tracked down. Disguised Sigurimi agents would call on their neighbors to scent out evidence of religious activity and submit the appropriate reports. In 1983, in Mirdita, someone denounced an old woman to the authorities for teaching prayers to her grandchildren; she died under torture. Many people helped the regime on their own initiative—teachers proved particularly useful in this regard.

"Pay attention!" says the teacher. "I'm going to ask you a tricky question, and whoever answers correctly will get a reward. What is this?"

And she draws two intersecting lines on the board. The children sit in startled silence—nobody knows the answer. Finally, one little boy can't stop himself from crying out triumphantly: "A cross!"

The teacher nods.

"Very good," she says. "Ask your mom and dad to come to school tomorrow. There's something I'd like to say to them."

"I knew that people still concealed Bibles, icons, and copies of the Quran in the attic and under the floorboards; that they gathered at cemeteries, in private homes, and in highland valleys to celebrate Mass; that they took food to imprisoned clergymen and kept liturgical vessels and vestments safe in hiding. I myself used to bury rosaries and prayer books in the woods.

"I managed to graduate from nursing school, and from then on I traveled from village to village, looking after and treating children. Since I couldn't live for God, I lived for others, and every day I gave them as much as I could. That was my act of resistance against the authorities. Once I gave a little boy a piggyback and carried him to the nearest hospital, because I could see that his fever was making him short of breath, and that way I saved his life. In spite of all, I've had a good life, I have felt needed, and people have responded to me with kindness. As a nun, in the eyes of the authorities I'd have been evil, but as a nurse, I was noble and useful, and every year I was awarded certificates of merit.

"I have never married—how could I? I've felt like a nun my entire life—but in lay clothing. Communism was a system of verbs, not ideas—we ate, we worked, we died, and that was all. The philosophy of Marxism-Leninism was imposed on us, but it was empty—as people of communism we were all empty. And now? Now life is beautiful, faith is beautiful. In 1991 I returned to the convent, and finally I'm among the sisters whom I first met in the 1940s. We have all felt like nuns our entire lives. Today the Albanians may not be churchgoers, but at least they're free. There's nothing finer than freedom."

———

Maria Tuci looks down at us from her portrait: a calm face with regular features and an intense look in her eyes. As I'm saying goodbye to Sister Roza, Sister Teresa, who until now has only been listening to us, offers to show me the grave of the Blessed Maria.

"So much suffering," she says, once we're standing beside the small, white tomb. "Nowadays we take life for granted. It's hard to believe that only a few decades ago the regime could torture a young woman—cripple, starve, and disfigure her beyond recognition—simply because she believed in God, simply because she'd been labeled an enemy. Nowadays the young are free, and also weak. In the past they had to be strong in order to die with dignity."

Circles

WHAT IS DESTINY? THE RIVER of events that flows through our lives?

Imagine this: Life is a river formed of two streams that join together. The first is fate: everything that happens because of God's will—major forces that are stronger than us. We're defenseless against them. You were born in Poland, I was born in Albania, at one point in time and not another, and none of it depended on us.

But there's also the second stream, which I'll call determination: all the events on which we have an influence, that we shape by means of our own will. What we want to do, who we want to be. Anyone would want these two streams to form a single current, for blind fate to match our inclinations and desires. I was born in wretched Albania—my God, why not in France? You were born in Poland, why not in Germany? That's our fate—we can't escape it, but we can put up resistance. We can refuse to let it rule our lives.

My name is Fatos Lubonja and I've always known I wanted to be a writer. I used my years of incarceration to think and to read; I can't say that time was lost. Even shoveling tons of rocks down a mine is an experience that shapes you. That was my fate: seventeen years in prison. I had to accept them and give them meaning. It's the same for everyone, regardless of what happens to us, whether it's illness or prison, loss or disaster. In every situation we should try to make sense of our fate, face up to it, confront it. Not crack under the weight of life.

The First Circle: Rubble

In prison, I worked three shifts, pushing huge, heavy carts right past the guards who could have destroyed me at any moment. Every day, life was a fight for survival, because my job in the mine was to deepen the tunnels. I drilled holes in the walls—not too big, not too small. Then we filled them with dynamite and lit the fuse. The explosion blew up the world around it. We felt the shocks running through our bodies. Then I had to clear the tunnel, remove the rocks, and make new holes. Shift after shift, day after day.

Every day takes something away from you. You live in a state of heightened alert, constantly aware of danger. I almost lost my life on two occasions. Once, without really knowing why, I simply walked out of the tunnel, and thirty seconds later there was a tremor, then a huge bang . . . There I was, alive, gazing at the rubble in front of me that could have been my grave. The second time, I made a mistake and a massive chunk of rock fell on my head. If not for my helmet, I'd have been killed on the spot.

The Second Circle: Isolation

And there was torture, too. The most terrible moments were when they locked you in the isolation cell. I spent four months in there after my second sentence because I refused to work. I simply knew that work would mean the end of me, the physical end. My body would wear out. I'd been able to bear the first seven years. But after the second sentence, when I got another sixteen, I knew the work would kill me. I knew I had to resist. It had nothing to do with anti-communist ideology, it wasn't a revolt against the system. It was the pure pragmatics of survival—I simply wanted to save myself. I wanted them to move me to another prison where I could read and write.

Sometimes life is like that: You have to take a decision and run a risk. But my resistance could have set an example for others, so I had to be punished. I spent my first month in solitary confinement. Then they let me out, but a few days later my name was back on the list of foremen, which meant I'd have to get up the next morning and go to work. I didn't go. They came for me and said: "Go upstairs to the officer."

I refused. So back I went into solitary confinement. I demanded to see the Mirdita district prosecutor. After all, there was nothing in the penal code to say that political prisoners had to work.

The Third Circle: Hunger

"I'm going on hunger strike until the prosecutor shows up," I said.

I simply wanted them to transfer me. I remember the hunger as pain, acute pain. Day after day, a time of hunger. After thirteen days I was still conscious. I didn't feel well, but I still had some strength left. On the fourteenth day, the prosecutor arrived.

"If you don't go to work, you'll die here," he said.

"But I wasn't given the death penalty," I said. "Why are you condemning me to death? Transfer me to another prison."

They refused.

The Fourth Circle: Cold

And so I spent another month in solitary confinement, on a starvation diet, and in extreme cold. Because you must know that it was winter, and in the isolation cell you only had the right to a cotton vest, a thin cotton jacket, a pair of long johns, and trousers. That was all, in the middle of winter. Very little. And two blankets from nine at night until five in the morning. What didn't we do to try to hide those blankets from the guards, to conceal them somewhere in the cell! Unbelievable. The things a man will do to survive . . . We slept on wooden platforms, and whenever the guards came into the cell, we had to lift the lids of these platforms to show there was nothing inside. Some guards checked carefully, others just took a quick look, and then you could conceal a blanket from them. Some of the prisoners had a clever tactic: They hid the blanket in the corner just behind the door, and since the cells were tiny, when the guard opened the door, he had no idea the blanket was behind it, not in the box. Imagine pulling that sort of trick, just to have a blanket during the day.

During the third month of solitary confinement, they ordered me to undress. I refused.

"There's no law that requires prisoners to undress," I said.

"Upstairs."

With every fiber of my being I could sense that now I had to resist. There are times in life, the most extreme, the most heroic moments when you know you have to stay strong at all costs. And then . . . there are times when you're terrified.

For an hour and a half the guard hurled abuse and threatened me. I took a close look at his face, at his rage. But I'd made a decision: I had to resist. I continued to refuse. And then the guard turned to another guard, who had just come in, and asked: "Have you brought a towel?"

In moments of extreme stress, the brain works differently—it's like a ticking bomb, a camera that's recording everything, a machine that's going at full steam. The question went whirling around in my head: "'Have you brought a towel?' What towel? What does he mean by 'towel'?"

Three guards stood in front of me.

"Now get undressed," said one of them.

After all those weeks in solitary confinement, my body was like a matchstick that anyone could snap. I was in no state to fight them.

"No, I won't," I said.

At once they leaped on me and twisted my arms. They ripped off my jacket and vest. Then they realized I had another layer of material underneath—a special warm vest with a cotton lining that a friend had made for me.

"Look at him, the crafty swine! What's he got here?"

I lunged forward to take it back, but they knocked me to the ground.

"Criminals!" I shouted.

And then I understood what the towel was for. They stuffed it into my mouth so I couldn't scream.

The Fifth Circle: Pain

They handcuffed me and left me on my own. Then another guard came
and took me outside, beyond the prison. We were walking up the path
toward the mine, when, at some point, he told me to stop, took out a
black baton, and started beating me and screaming. He'd scream and hit
me. My God. A scream for each blow. Scream—hit, scream—hit. There
I stood, handcuffed and half naked, taking the blows.

Then he led me farther on. I was thinking: "I'm not going there. I'm
not going to work." We entered the tunnel.

"Are you going to work?"

"No."

And then he went crazy, something snapped inside him and he started
beating me furiously, until my whole body was black and blue. Finally
he started hitting me over the head, again and again, with all his might.

"I'm dying," I thought. My brain was sounding an alarm. "He's going
to kill me."

But I couldn't let him break me. Something inside me dug in its heels.

Throughout, my mind kept on working, trying to find a solution. Perhaps it was instinct, experience, the will to survive, or perhaps after all
those years in prison there were things that I knew without realizing.
Somehow I brought out a strange, low voice.

"It's you who's going to die," I said, as though something were speaking
from deep inside me.

I remembered that the guard was called Pjeter, so he was probably from
a Catholic family.

"Pjeter, what on earth are you doing?"

At these words he was stunned. The hand holding the baton froze in
midair. Something had happened that he'd never expected. As long as he
was the torturer and I was the victim, everything was clear. But suddenly,
in a strange way, I'd broken out of that scenario.

"Why won't you work?" he yelled.

"Because you've ended up in this organization, Pjeter," I continued to
play my part, booming away in that deep voice.

The guard decided I'd lost my mind, but he had no idea what to do about it. Finally, he said: "We're going back," and I was rejoicing at the simple fact that he'd stopped hitting me over the head. Because of course the whole time I was in handcuffs, so I couldn't even shield myself. Once we were getting near the prison, he asked me what the guards at the gate were called.

"He's got shoes," I said, playing the goat, to leave him in no doubt that he'd loosened a screw.

I went back into solitary confinement, and seven days later they suggested I write a letter to my family. "This is my last chance," I thought. I scribbled a mathematical equation, in which the unknown quantities were the names of my daughters. And the answer was two. A Ministry of the Interior official, who was in charge of prison statistics, arrived.

"If you don't go to work, you'll die in your cell," he said. "We're not going to make an exception for you. It's bad enough that I had to come here because of you."

I was finally disillusioned.

"In that case, I'm going to the wire."

"Going to the wire" meant committing suicide. If you approached the barbed-wire fence surrounding the prison, the guard was allowed to shoot you, because you were trying to escape. Two or three people in Spaç had committed suicide that way. The official left.

The Sixth Circle: Despair

Only recently, I read in my file that the prison governor had wanted to transfer me to another camp after just two months in isolation, but the ministry had withheld its consent. I don't know why, after four months, they finally gave permission for my transfer to Ballsh. When I arrived, I ran into a friend in the hall.

"My God, how great that you've ended up with us!" he said. "It's like heaven here!"

I was twenty-seven years old. I'd spent four years in Spaç. And it was only because I was young that I'd had the strength to withstand it all.

I had always wanted to be an author. I wanted to write at all costs, but I knew that in Spaç I would become a wreck, that the work would destroy my body and eventually kill me.

The fact that in Ballsh I could read and think completely changed my life. I knew that one day I'd write about everything that had happened in prison. I could distance myself from the suffering. I could try to understand why I was there and what the people around me were feeling. I could try to understand the guards enough to stop hating them, to think about why they were so simpleminded and brutal. I gradually stopped being nothing but my own terror. I could try to find inner calm. But that doesn't mean I didn't feel hatred. I hated the system so much I can understand to this day why militants go into the street and blow themselves up in a crowd—I can understand that hatred. Sometimes I dreamed I was a bomb that reduced the prison to a heap of rubble. Sometimes I thought: "We should all commit collective suicide, it's the only way to make ourselves heard." These were fantasies of despair, because in reality we all wanted to survive, we all wanted to be saved.

The Seventh Circle: Death

Throughout the four months I was kept in isolation, I never thought about death. When a soldier goes to war, he doesn't think about being killed in battle; he assumes he'll survive. When you board an airplane, you know that sometimes planes crash and all the passengers die, but you don't think about it. You hold on to the idea that everything will be OK. In solitary confinement the fear of death never leaves you, but what you think about most is survival. When I decided to go on hunger strike, I lost all my fear—I stopped being afraid of death. At that point I felt I could do anything, that I was stronger than anyone. But that kind of thought doesn't last long. The fear returns.

There was a priest in my cell, the future archbishop Frano Ilia, who was accused of spying for the Vatican. He was given the death penalty, but they had offered to convert it to a life sentence if he confessed to the charges. He had agreed. One day I asked him: "Frano, I don't believe there's anything after death, but you're a religious person, you believe in eternal life, so why did you agree? You could have said: 'No, it's not true,' and you'd have gone straight to heaven."

And he replied: "Even Jesus Christ went to Gethsemane before his crucifixion and begged his Father to spare him from suffering."

He wasn't prepared to be a martyr, just as Jesus wasn't prepared to suffer. The body wants to escape suffering at all costs. The body wants to live.

The Eighth Circle: Shadows

These days the people who tortured me are like shadows in my head. I met one of them in the street once, during a demonstration.

"Fatos!" he cried. "Do you recognize me? It's me, Gjergj!"

Of course I recognized him—he was the guard who used to kick us extremely brutally, a ruthless man. Now he was supporting us in the protests against the government of Sali Berisha.

One day I'd like to sit down opposite the people who tortured me and ask them: "Who were you then? Were you human beings?" But I know they're not capable of reflection. Only a few of them really understand what they did to others. The rest see themselves simply as tools in the hands of the system, and that's why they don't feel any responsibility for their actions.

I also met one of the three judges who sentenced me the second time, and who in 1979 sentenced three of my friends to death: Fadil Kokomani, Vangjel Lezho, and Xhelal Koprencka. On my way into a café, I was trying to let an old man go ahead of me, but he also stopped to let me go first, at which point he looked me in the face and asked: "Do you recognize me, sir? Can we get a coffee?"

And then I realized who was there in front of me. We sat down at a table.

That man had determined my fate and that of my friends. Perhaps you're wondering why I didn't punch him in the face? I think I just wanted to understand him. But I couldn't look at him. I just sat there and listened to his voice.

"Yes," he said. "I signed those convictions . . . I signed them and I know that was wrong. But did I have a choice? I'd have ended up in prison, just like you. Do you remember when Fadil Kokomani asked for some spectacles to read out his defense, and I gave him my own?"

I looked him in the eye, just as I had all those years ago. When there are charges against you and you enter the courtroom, you immediately scrutinize the judges' faces, you look for any trace of kindness or empathy in them, a modicum of humanity, you look for hope for yourself. Now, in the café, it occurred to me that perhaps he wasn't as bad a man as I'd thought.

"Did you realize the charges were fabricated?" I asked. "Did you really believe it was all true?"

"No . . . I mean, it was obvious . . . We knew the charges were made up."

They knew. So they could have said: "No, I won't sign this death sentence." They could have said: "I love the Party, I love the laws it passes, but I won't agree to tell lies." But they didn't say that. They signed it all.

Now, when I think about it . . . How much freedom did they have? Is your conscious mind free? They were like children whose lives lay in the hands of the adults, in the hands of the Party. They couldn't grow up, they couldn't be free. In a way that excuses them . . . But then, in those days, everyone made decisions. Everyone had a margin of freedom; everyone had a choice. Those who determined the lives of others could also choose to act dishonorably or do the right thing.

While I was in prison, I sometimes wondered why my father didn't do anything to reform the system—he was an influential communist, after all. Why did no one in Hoxha's entourage object to the regular purges? Nobody ever stopped Hoxha. Nobody ever stood up to him.

The Ninth Circle: The End

In my book, *In the Seventeenth Year*, I describe the situation of a prisoner in solitary confinement. His arms are twisted back and there's a gag in his mouth, and he's longing for the evening, when he'll be unchained and he can cover himself with a blanket and sleep until five in the morning. That kind of suffering could last for several days, a week or two, during which time your only thought was: "God, when will this day be over, when will I finally be able to sleep without handcuffs?" Then, when the punishment was over, you stayed in solitary confinement for another thirty days, and you thought: "God, when will they finally move me to a normal cell . . . ?" Later, you were put in a normal cell and your only thought was: "God, when will they finally set me free?"

All of that was bearable. Hell has many circles.

The program to build a network of bunkers, shelters, and tunnels was launched in the early 1970s and lasted until 1984. According to various sources, between 173,000 and half a million bunkers were built.

PART FOUR

STONE ON THE BORDER

Survival Strategies

BIBIKA KOKALARI, CHEMIST, COUSIN of the writer Musine Kokalari:

"Whenever I was walking down the street and saw a black car with an official inside it coming the other way, I'd lower my head and shake it gently to get rid of all my thoughts and empty my mind completely. 'They're so powerful,' I kept thinking, 'they're sure to have built a mind-reading machine by now. If they can bug all those houses, if they've taken control of everything, they must have got inside our heads, too. Now they're driving around the streets using a device to read our thoughts, and tomorrow someone will come knocking at my door. Think of nothing, think of nothing,' I kept telling myself, as I shook my head."

Janina Çina, translator:

"'Don't trust your own shirt,' we used to say. Meaning, don't trust yourself, don't trust your own skin, don't trust your husband or wife. I, for example, never talked to my husband about what he did at work. It was better not to know. I used to think: 'If and when they take me to be tortured I'd better have nothing in my head.'"

———

"It can't be worse"—if you say it aloud at home and the wall hears you, that's ten years signed and sealed. For turning the wall against the system.

It wasn't just that you couldn't make a critical remark, you couldn't even think a critical thought. Because if you thought it, sooner or later, you'd say it. If only to the wall. But the walls had ears, tongues, and good memories. Plenty of people found bugs under the table and cables outside the window that led to official ears. One word and you had manacles on your wrists, five or even fifteen years on your head, and the blows of a black baton on your back to straighten or break your spine. The spine that keeps you upright, and the spine that carries your soul.

That's what some used to say.

But others would say their lives were tolerable.

Because some went hungry and festered in prison, while others got married and brought children into the world.

As some were coming out of prison, others were entering adult life.

"What is freedom?" some would ask.

"Why do you need to know?" others would reply.

There's nothing unusual about the surrounding world, we simply live our daily lives—who'd trouble their conscience worrying about freedom? There were some who had washing machines, who never thought life was hard but were pleased by the advent of progress. They survived that time. You'd hardly notice them. They didn't gloat and they didn't feel fear. They didn't suffer. Each of them had a tiny patch of the state to cultivate. Each had a tiny share of power, and they clung to it tightly.

If there had to be suffering, people suffered. If it had to be seen, they watched the suffering. Some closed their eyes. Others narrowed them.

At a certain point, everyone became their own survival strategy. Some changed into ears and tongues. Others changed into walls and rocks. Under their thick skin they grew a layer of fear—and under that, a layer of shame or torpor.

A Stone on the Border

I DIDN'T KNOW WHAT the world outside Albania was like, and I couldn't imagine it. I lived in a country full of lies, where there was nothing to be had. What could you dream about? A piece of meat? A decent pair of shoes? Managing to get a bottle of milk for your child if you stood in line long enough? That was the extent of our dreams in a country whose borders were marked out with barbed wire. That's why I had only one dream: to escape.

Albania was like a reserve full of depressed animals. Does a creature that lives in a cage dream of getting out? The desire to save yourself and regain your freedom isn't a dream, it's an instinct. An animal struggles and keeps watch, never dropping its guard, because instinct is telling it to break free. When you set out on the road, you don't know if you're heading toward freedom or death, toward relief or perdition. You don't think about getting killed, you think: "Only this can save me." If you knew what lay in store for you, you might never leave the house.

———

I was born in the ethnically Greek village of Derviçan, under seven and a half miles from the border as the crow flies—and I'd always had that border under my skin. I used to see the hills on the horizon glowing pink at dusk, and I'd think: "On that side there are other villages, other rivers, other homes."

But our Albanian life was as plain and austere as a wax candle. Nothing belonged to us; everything depended on the state. When I was in my teens, my parents sent me to Gjirokastër to train to be a carpenter. And there in the workshop, I met three guys who were just as inquisitive and hungry for life as I was. We talked about everything, including other worlds.

"Apparently, in other countries everyone has a television."

"And a car!"

"No way!"

We couldn't imagine it. We snatched at scraps of news whirling on the wind: Someone had been to Yugoslavia and seen something there, someone had listened to the ads on Greek radio and had no idea what they were about. The propaganda shouted: "Defense of the border is our highest duty of all!" and the whole of Albania was encircled in barbed wire— higher here, lower there, single-strand here, double-strand there. None of us had a passport; a passport was an honor bestowed upon very few: Party hacks, athletes, and members of folk ensembles. And only when it was absolutely certain they wouldn't immediately use it to run away.

And anyone who did escape had to live with the knowledge that they'd left suffering in their wake. The families of traitors were punished in the same way as traitors. Usually they were interned in the most isolated and backward regions, where every day was a fight for survival, so that their suffering should serve as a lesson for others.

Sometimes, the border meant death, because the guards were allowed to shoot anyone in their line of sight, but sometimes not even death was the final punishment. In the 1980s, the guards tied the body of a fifteen-year-old boy they'd shot to the tow hook on the back of a truck and dragged him along a gravel road to his family's village. What they dumped beneath the biggest oak tree in the village was just a ragged mess. The authorities reduced a cheerful teenager to a bloody heap of rags, but what the hell for? To make us all feel afraid? To be sure we'd never forget?

And yet people still gambled with their lives. We talked about a family of nomads who in 1956 simply walked across the border while herding a large flock of sheep and found refuge in Greece, because it never occurred to the guards that even some dumb shepherds might have the sense to get away.

"Perhaps it's not all that hard . . ." we said to each other.

Is an animal that yearns to break free a brave creature or a stupid one? When an animal that lives in a cage is put into an even smaller one, does it stop to think: "They've stolen my life"?

There were four of us, a great bunch of guys, or so I thought, but in fact there were three of us and a spy. The fellow who informed on us had lost his job as a teacher, so now he needed to suck up to the authorities to get a foothold. We didn't know him well, but we soon counted him as a friend because we were stupid and trusting, and he was always a good laugh. If I could get my hands on him now . . . He ruined our lives, and now he's dead . . . My friends are dead, and so is Anastas, the Judas. He took his guilt with him to the grave.

The system came banging on my door when I was sixteen. I was just a silly, naive child who'd dared to have a dream and say it aloud. I should have been going to school but I went to prison instead—the worst school of life. They called me an enemy of the people, but I simply didn't understand that in Albania communism was in control, that the propaganda was etched on people's minds, and we lived in a trap. It was only in prison, in a concrete cell, that I saw Albania as a great big cage. I was stuck inside it all alone.

In their darkest hours people were kept alive by the thought of their family, but I never got a single letter or parcel, not a word for the whole five years I was in prison.

I was twenty-one when I was released. They fired me from my first job after a week, yelling "You traitor!" in my face. After that, no one wanted to hire me, although I went from one factory to the next and asked for help wherever I could. I was like a dog that anyone could kick.

When you're young, you don't know when to give in, you think you'll be able to shoulder any burden. I fell in love and got married, but when my wife fell pregnant, I realized what a dreadful life lay ahead of us. Every day I had to fight the system just to bring home food. Even at liberty I was like an animal in a cage.

My thoughts of escape kept recurring, last thing at night and first thing in the morning . . . Death on the border didn't frighten me—how could it be any different from the living death we were enduring every day? I was a young man, yet I felt old and lifeless. I didn't want to escape to make a great dream come true, I wasn't chasing a fantasy or some incredible plan. I wanted to escape the misery of our life, the lack of hope, the degradation. I wanted to escape because I was driven by the desire for a better life awaiting us on the other side, where I wouldn't have to speak to my wife in whispers, I wouldn't have to lie to my child, and we wouldn't have to wonder where our next meal was coming from. Where people would treat me like a human being, not a louse.

When my wife was six months pregnant, I finally convinced her that we should make a run for it. It was a race against time, her belly was growing and so were our problems. "We've got nothing to lose," I told her, although our lives were at stake. But we'd be fleeing as a family, the two of us. I had no one left, but she was hesitant because she felt sorry for her parents. In the end she agreed—perhaps because she loved me, or perhaps because she hated Albania. Perhaps she had run out of hope.

We left the house as if everything were normal, with just a few of slices of bread in our pockets, and off we went. In a country where there were hardly any cars and you had to fight for a seat on the bus, a bicycle or your own two legs were the only reliable means of transport. I'd spent my whole life walking to some place or other. And now I was walking, too—straight ahead, to meet my own fate.

We didn't talk much on the way. Step by step, mile after mile, we got closer to the border, keeping as far as possible from the checkpoints. I was single-minded, but she was getting more and more tired, holding her belly in silence.

I knew the area—I knew where there were the fewest guards and where the fence was lowest. Once we were quite near, I ran on ahead. "Get across as fast as possible, as fast as possible," I kept thinking. And I left her behind. I climbed up the fence, scratching my legs until they bled, but I couldn't feel a thing. I jumped down, ran straight ahead, and threw myself into the grass. I was overcome with joy. Just a while and she'd get there, too, and we'd be free. We'd make a new start. I gazed up at the sky, and for the moment I let my mind go blank. For the first time in ages I let myself stop thinking. I was free . . . or so I thought.

The sun was gradually setting, but I went on waiting, hidden in the grass. I thought about her, the fact that she was carrying our child, and that she was the only person I loved. An hour or so went by, but she still hadn't appeared. What had happened? I looked ahead of me, at the hills tightly surrounding me, filling the view. What should I do? Go back for her, or walk straight on to freedom, to a better life?

And at that moment I made a decision. I put my life on one side of the scales and love on the other, and I chose love. I didn't know what that choice would mean. I didn't know that she would have to make a choice, too.

I went back.

She was sitting on a stone, with her head bowed, holding her belly. The moment she saw me, the moment I looked her in the face . . . I realized, but it was too late. At once the guards surrounded me.

They'd found her much earlier, but when they noticed she was pregnant, they guessed she hadn't been on her own. They didn't know if I'd come back for her, but they'd waited. They'd been waiting for me, just as she had.

I don't know what she was thinking as she sat there on that stone. Had she been mentally begging me to return, or had she figured I wouldn't look back? As I gazed at her and her belly, I felt so terribly sorry.

I went back because I knew I had to be faithful to her. If you love someone, you're faithful. And you mustn't betray the person who loves you.

Right there, sitting on that stone, was the last time I ever saw her.

For attempting to escape the country—in other words, for betraying the fatherland—I was sentenced to twenty years in prison. My wife only got ten because she was pregnant. I don't know what any of it was like from her point of view, I don't know what she thought. Only scraps of information got through to me: that she'd had the baby in prison, that she'd given our son up for adoption, and that she wanted a divorce.

I was completely alone. Somewhere out there, far away, my son was living in an orphanage—the child for whom I'd risked everything—and he was alone, too.

I signed the divorce papers. Too bad, if that was what she wanted. Then I found out that just after the divorce she'd ended up in a mental hospital in Vlorë. Our shattered Albanian family. Me in prison, our son in an orphanage, her in an asylum. Three destinies like three snapped twigs.

I never tried to get in touch with her again. All I heard was that when she left hospital, her family married her off again. Someone told me she didn't want to do it, but they forced her. I'll never know if that was true. It doesn't matter now, anyway.

In prison the hardest thing was thinking about my son, and I thought about him every day. What was he like, what was he doing, was he like me? Had he taken his first steps, said his first word, drawn his first house? Did he know who his parents were? Did he bear me a grudge? Was he suffering? Did he feel trapped at the orphanage? Did he ever think about me? Had it occurred to him that we'd taken all that risk for his sake? That I'd gone back out of love for them? That by recrossing the border, I'd signed my own sentence, too?

Years went by—years of hard, forced labor, bleak and hopeless. Ten years at an oil refinery in Ballsh, then at a copper mine in Rubik, then in Laç . . . Draining marshes in central Albania. Dreadful work, which made people drop with exhaustion, like overworked cart horses. Then we'd go back to our cells, to be locked up like caged animals. Alongside the suffering, I could feel hatred and evil brewing inside me.

I came out after twenty years. They didn't take a single day off my sentence. I was free in a country of three million free prisoners. I had to learn all over again how to walk like a human, how to think like a human, how to breathe like one—because I walked, thought, and breathed like a prisoner. For years, day after day, I'd been taught discipline and terror, so I was entirely made up of discipline and terror. I felt as if everyone around me was giving me orders. Whenever I spoke to someone, I stood as straight as a ramrod. I had to learn freedom again from scratch, insofar as a former convict in an enslaved country can be free.

I immediately thought of my son. He was twenty; he'd lived his entire life at the orphanage. What kind of a man had he become in the care of the state that put me behind bars? What had he been told about me? Had his guardians instilled him in him hatred for his father, an enemy of the people? I badly wanted to see him—I longed to tell him everything. I wanted him to understand me and forgive me.

I found out that he was studying in Elbasan, and I managed to get in touch with some of his fellow students. In the end we agreed to meet; on the appointed day, I was to wait for him at the bus station in Gjirokastër. And I did. I scrutinized the faces of all the young men, looking for a sign, waiting for my heart to skip a beat. But none of the faces meant anything to me. I didn't recognize my son.

And yet he was there that day at the bus station in Gjirokastër. He came. He even walked past me. But it was 1982, and we were all stifled by terror. Neither of us dared to simply come up and ask: "Is it you?"

Only a week later we finally managed to meet, at a different place. We threw ourselves into each other's arms, without hesitation. Back then, even an ordinary, human gesture of that kind was an act of bravery. My son took a risk by hugging me, an enemy of the people, a former prisoner. But he badly wanted to have a father. And at forty-four years old, all I had to my name was twenty-five years in prison and a son, nothing else. People kept telling him: "Leave it—what good is a father like that to you? He'll only bring you trouble." But my son refused to listen to them. He'd grown up to be a good person. He'd grown up to be the son I'd always dreamed he'd be.

Meanwhile, the country was crumbling and grinding to a halt—there were no raw materials, the factories were at a standstill, there was no petrol for the machinery—but my life moved forwards as if it were finally on the right track. I got married again, and my second son was born; we lived in poverty, but I no longer had any dreams or expectations. "Just as long as there's no more suffering," I thought.

And then my wife ended up in prison. Seven years for stealing a radio. A sentence for her, me, and our son. We were left on our own, he and I. To get milk for him, I used to stand in line from four in the morning. I'd stand and stare into the darkness, waiting for the sun to rise at last. And when I saw it, I never thought it had come up that day to shine for me. I thought it had come up to scorch my face.

As soon as the system collapsed in 1991, I went to Greece with my sons. I wasn't expecting much of that country, because I was worn out by then—I could feel the years of labor in every bone—but once again I took a risk, this time for my sons. As simple as that. For them, life in Greece turned out to be a salvation—the older one found work, and the younger one went to college. Today, one of them lives in Sparta and the other in Canada, they're in no danger. They have a good life, they're safe.

And I'm here in Albania, on my native soil. Nothing bad can happen to me now—and nothing good, either. I have no illusions. I can say whatever I like about the fact that there's no work, there's no money and no future, and no one's going to punish me, so I'm a free man. When I was sixteen, I thought I was always going to fly high, but then someone clipped my wings. I fell and crashed to the ground. I could never rise again. Now there's nothing else ahead of me.

I often meet up with friends at this bar. We talk about the past, we go back to the same events hundreds of times, but there are things I simply don't want to remember because the pain is blinding.

I don't know if I've ever been happy. Perhaps when looking at my sons. But my life has consisted of short periods of calm punctuated by a series of unlucky blows. I don't know why fate spares some people and sends so much suffering to others. I don't know who writes our lives, I don't know whose hand was shaking so badly as they wrote mine. I did what I could to determine my own life, but I still spent twenty-five years in prison. I tried to live and think like a free man, but I still ended up living like an animal. If only I'd kept walking that time . . . If only I hadn't gone back for her . . .

Life takes you where it wants. If only I'd managed to escape . . . but I didn't. I failed to elude my own fate.

There's a poem by Martin Camaj:

> When I die, may I turn to stone
> On the confines of my land
> May I be a landmark
> I turned to stone while still alive, on that day when I crossed the
>   border and went back.

Freedom in the Village of Zogaj

"MY NAME IS XHEMAL TURISHTA, and I've been a fisherman all my life."

"And I am Ardiana, his wife. I've spent half my life at a factory."

"Here in Zogaj we never wanted for anything. Compared to the rest of Albania, we lived quite well. I'm sure no one ever went hungry."

"Another packet of coffee? Here you are. An extra pound of meat? No problem. More cheese than anywhere else, and more than enough fruit of various kinds."

"I could catch as many fish as I liked. In all the villages on the border, people had it better than in the towns. They ate fish day in, day out, they put up their own homes. They had a life."

"Whether they wanted to or not, the authorities used to spoil us. Because if they'd failed to take care of us, we'd have all escaped. But someone had to sit on the border and keep an eye on everyone else, didn't they?"

"We didn't really have a choice. And if you thought you had a choice, you were wrong. We were grateful to the authorities for letting us live the way they told us to. If they let you study, you were so happy you'd have gone to study how to count snowflakes, just as long as they didn't change their minds."

"Being born on the border was a gift from fate. But it was also agony, because the border tempted you, it called to you. And we saw our fair share of suffering, too. Our Lake Shkodër was a great source of hope, but it was a great big graveyard, too. But folks went into the water anyway. They'd get in, they'd see the lake ahead of them all the way to the horizon, but they'd carry on regardless. Would they get to the other side, or would the water swallow them up? What would it be, freedom or death?"

"The ones they caught were tortured horribly. The guards could beat them as much as they liked, so they tormented them for show, they bullied people to death so others would see. Three of the local boys tried to escape, just silly sixteen-year-olds who fancied a bit of freedom. When they caught them, they beat them up so badly . . . They laid them on the floor and put huge stone slabs on their backs, really heavy ones. That's a terrible torture—it doesn't just hurt, you feel like you're suffocating, too."

"The only thought in your head is that you're dying."

"If they saw someone trying to escape, they hunted him like a deer. Something was triggered inside them, some kind of inhuman cruelty. I remember the time they tracked down this one kid. First they circled him, shouting and gloating, and then they rammed him with their boat so his body got caught in the propeller. They reduced him to a pulp, ripped him to pieces. And they enjoyed it: 'Death to enemies of the fatherland!' If a guard shot someone on the border, he got a day off to have a rest."

"But they were people, too, weren't they? Sometimes they had human reactions—one time they'd shoot, another time they wouldn't. Once this woman came along, carrying her baby daughter, not more than a few months old. I can't think how she did it. After this, if you go over to the maple tree—that's to say through the border zone—you'll see it was impossible to get across. But she managed it. Just an ordinary little woman like me. And she was already on the other side when her baby started to cry and they caught her. Her husband had died a few days earlier, and the poor thing thought she had nothing else to lose. You got at least ten years for trying to escape, but they let her out after a year because she had a baby."

"How did she do it?"

"How should I know? We talked about running away lots of times, but I was afraid. And I couldn't leave my sickly mother behind."

"They'd have exiled our entire family if we'd escaped. Anyone who escaped had to remember that, even if they managed it, they were leaving their family to suffer."

"Now I'm sorry we didn't escape. Honestly. But we were always being told the Serbs were monsters who'd rape you as soon as you crossed the border. That fear held us back, but now I feel daily regret for the years wasted in Albania."

"Five people escaped from our village!"

"Yeah, they managed it!"

"And they've spread about the world. One's in America, one's in Australia. They've got a good life."

"And we had spies, too! Times have changed, but they're still here. And they put plenty of effort into it, they sure did! Always on the lookout, always lying in wait. They'd come up to the window to eavesdrop, but however cautious they were, sooner or later one or another of them would come a cropper. There were three spies in Zogaj. We knew who they were, so we kept an eye on them."

"We weren't allowed to circumcise our sons because it was a religious ritual, so we covered the windows with blankets and kept an ear cocked in case we heard someone coming. 'Let's hope the baby doesn't cry!' we thought."

"I once said at work that I liked Yugoslav songs. How stupid could I be?! But I got off lightly. I only had to submit a self-critical statement, saying I didn't know what had got into my head, because I'd never actually heard a Yugoslav song, and the most beautiful songs were our Albanian ones anyway . . ."

"One guy said Yugoslav bikes were better than Albanian ones. Seven years! And he left behind his wife, his child . . ."

"And what about Zef Tushi, who got five years because he complained about the bread?"

"And there was the time my aunt came for lunch and the police burst into the house, because she'd come from Shkodër without permission. Remember how they dragged her away from the table? She was quietly having her lunch, and they just grabbed her and took her away."

"Because as borderland residents, everyone in Shkodër had internal passports. To cross the bridge over the Buna they had to go to a special checkpoint to get their passport stamped. If there was a wedding here in the village, the guests from the neighboring villages had to get permission, too."

"And do you remember when my uncle ran away with his lover? I had an uncle who was an accountant, and he fell in love with a woman from Vermosh, who had a husband . . . 'All right then,' they thought, 'we'll run away!' They took some food with them and off they went. They just walked straight ahead, climbed up the fence, jumped down on the other side, and legged it. They kept running until they were gasping for breath, then they threw themselves into each other's arms because they'd crossed the border, and happily sat down for a bite to eat. And just then a guard appeared. 'What are you doing here?' he yells. Luckily, my uncle kept a cool head. 'What do you mean?' he says. 'Can't you see we're having a picnic?' And they were extremely lucky, because they only got a few months for having a picnic in the border zone."

"Tell her about the boys."

"The boys . . . There were three of them—the guards shot them dead trying to escape. And I helped carry the corpses back. Small, skinny guys. As we were carrying them, one of them slipped and his head kept hitting the stones. I felt bad about it, I wanted to pull him up, but the guard screamed: 'Stop! What are you doing?' I kept my mouth shut. 'It's none of your business, leave him!' he shouted. We walked on. But that boy's head kept bashing against the stones . . . It left traces of blood on them."

"But you mustn't get the wrong idea . . . The system had good sides, too. Everyone had a job, there were schools everywhere, nurses, midwives, health care for factory workers. If I'd had an urge to wander down the street stark naked, nothing would have happened to me, because it was so safe. But now? You spend years on end being afraid to leave the house. Zogaj is so beautiful, but nothing's being built here. We don't even have a right to this house, because no one will issue us with the papers for it. You could set up a business, but that's impossible without paying bribes, and without the right documents, no way! There are no playgrounds for the kids, no soccer pitches for the boys. Our folks hang about in the streets, because they have work for three months a year and then nothing."

"You might not believe it, but life was better for us then than it is now. With all that terror, all that poverty, it was better. I was arrested on the lake recently while trying to smuggle in some lamps from Montenegro. I got eight months, my son got five, and my nephew got six, even though they're both minors, and that's how they're starting out in life. My son still had fresh scars on his leg from an open fracture, and they kicked him on those bright red scars. How is that any different from communism?"

"And we have to do something, don't we? Make a living somehow. There's no other work, so you come up with whatever you can. How are we supposed to live off state benefits, off five thousand leks a month? Back then, we didn't have a TV, a washing machine, or a fridge; now we have all that, but every day's a battle."

"What do we need freedom for? We can complain as much as we like, but no one listens to us anyway. Freedom's worth nothing if there's no dignity."

The Zone

FOR AS LONG AS THEY CAN REMEMBER, nothing has ever changed here—the earth is still a rusty gold color, lizards flash past underfoot, and there's a gentle breeze blowing off the lake. The posts and the wire have gone, but otherwise everything is just as it was before. The earth remembers, the trees and rocks remember, only the people do everything they can to forget.

"Look how sharp these bits of crushed stone are," Senad says. "When the guards were dragging those bodies, that boy's head kept hitting these stones. That's why my father couldn't bear it."

"And this is where the fence ran, with barbed-wire entanglements on top of concrete posts." Bekim extends a hand. "Look how high it went up the hillside. It's one of several, and it was ten feet high. We're only halfway."

"Yes, there's still a long distance to go. How did that woman escape? It was impossible, and yet she got across all this bit, carrying a small child. It was the middle of winter—maybe the cold weather made the guards less vigilant?"

"Storms did that, too, so people used to escape when it was raining very hard and the wind was blowing like mad. The weather could kill them, but it could help them, too, just like the darkness. You had to be swallowed by the darkness, so nobody ever escaped when the moon was waxing."

"They used to cover themselves in pitch and then jump into the water, so the glow of their bodies wouldn't be visible. Sometimes they put a carved-out watermelon on their heads because it was dark and it blended with the blackness of the water."

"No one dared escape by land—everyone went across the lake. Our neighbor put his whole family onto a boat during a storm, when it was bucketing down so hard they could barely see each other. They set sail— he, his wife, and kids, with the wind roaring like mad, but they managed to get across the border. They were very close to Montenegro when the boat capsized. They all drowned except for the man, who managed to get to shore. The communists couldn't have dreamed up a better punishment."

"Sometimes, when someone was killed on the border, the policemen wrapped the body in barbed wire and drove it around the streets of Shkodër, so everyone could see that the world doesn't belong to the bold."

"In April 1990, Ramiz Alia promised to put a stop to murdering people on the border. A week later the guards killed a young man—they clearly found it hard to change their ways. In June they shot another guy in the back . . . Old habits!"

"There was also a young couple, a boy and a girl, whose parents wouldn't let them marry, so they decided to run away. As they were crossing the bridge over the Buna, a guard shot them, one after the other. A young man in uniform killed two young people who just wanted to be together. And that was in 1991, the final days of the system . . . To cover their tracks, the soldiers immediately buried them next to the bridge. They were dug up a year later, wrapped in a blanket, lying side by side . . ."

"And this is the army building, where the guards were stationed. Watch out, there are always lots of snakes in there. And over there, beyond those trees, it's already Montenegro."

"And did you know there was no one guarding the border on the other side? Who'd have wanted to escape into Albania? It would be like voluntarily swapping house arrest for a concentration camp."

Everyone Is Born Free

THE WATER WAS SO PIERCINGLY COLD that for the first few seconds he couldn't catch his breath. As a stream of needles coursed through his veins toward his heart, for a while the man felt as if his body were changing into a block of ice that would soon sink to the bottom.

"I'll never make it," he thought.

But there was no other way. The blackness of the water blending with the blackness of the night. Two bodies surrendering their heat to the icy river.

They'd tried to escape overland, along the river, but some local villagers had seen them in the darkness and raised the alert. The Sigurimi had taught people vigilance—they were to guard the border themselves, like hunting dogs. With a host of volunteers in every village, there was no shortage of eager stalkers.

It was early April, and the snow had only recently melted away. The people who had just sounded the alarm now crowded at the edge of the river to stare at them, deep underwater, as though they were looking at dead bodies. No one had expected them to leap into the water to certain death.

They were seized by the current of the Buna, which flows through Shkodër and straight on to the Adriatic, and it carried them away, into the darkness. Their winter clothes and heavy boots were dragging them to the bottom. Two young, strong bodies pitted against the great force of the river. Two men possessed by the idea of escape and ready to die for it.

"If I'd known what would happen . . . If I could have foretold how excruciating the pain would be, I'd never have done it," says seventy-year-old Zenel Drangu today.

The water carried him for four hours. A nonstop battle against overwhelming agony, against needles of ice that stabbed into his body, against fatigue and terror. He spent three days in Yugoslavia, the promised land for which he'd risked his life. And sixteen years in the prisons of communist Albania.

———

"Poverty made everyone equal in the countryside—we had to fight to put bread in our mouths like all the rest. Two pounds of cheese a week, two pounds of meat a month. I remember my nine brothers' and sisters' faces in the candlelight, I remember the taste of oranges and apples that we ate only at New Year. When the Bajram holiday came, our parents bought each of us new clothes—shoes, trousers, a shirt, all soft and brand-new. Nowadays children have everything, but, back then, getting those fragrant new clothes once a year was a wonderful thing for me.

"Our parents taught us that we were all the same, Catholics and Muslims, and that whatever happened, we mustn't cheat or steal. Throughout my childhood, I remember struggling with hunger, stifling it, deceiving it; there was never enough food, hunger always had us in its sights.

"I finished a one-year training course for drivers, and from the 1970s onward I worked in Shkodër for a timber-transport company. As I drove around Albania, the thought of escape traveled with me in the passenger seat. Up in the driver's cab, I saw the everyday poverty, the streets that were so narrow I sometimes had to reverse several hundred feet to let an oncoming car pass, and I thought about how according to the propaganda we were striding forward, and yet it was plain to see that we were going backward by the day. The more inflated the propaganda, the more the country collapsed.

"'You live better than any other nation in the world! People in the West have to sleep under bridges!'—and they'd show us photos from Africa. Once an Albanian opera singer went on tour to Yugoslavia. His Yugoslav colleague drove him around the country in his own car. 'How is it possible for an ordinary man to have his own car?' asked the Albanian on his return. His amazement earned him ten years in prison, so he had plenty of time to wonder about it without confusing others.

"At workplaces, there were special committees to check whether the citizens were dressed appropriately, according to the system's taste. If not, they were capable of tearing the clothes off a person's back in front of everyone. Or they paraded around with scissors to trim people's hair if it was too long. All Albanians were supposed to be cut from the same cloth, with Enver Hoxha's stamp on their chests.

"I had very modest dreams: a shiny nylon shirt from Yugoslavia, which cost a whole month's salary, and a pair of glossy shoes imported from Czechoslovakia. I couldn't imagine anything finer."

———

Their shoes turned to stone, and their bodies were like blocks of wood. Finally, the river tossed them to shore on the other side, on the outskirts of the town of Ulcinj.

Their first steps in a free country. Pain gripping their bodies in its pincers, and euphoria bursting inside them. The two men hugged each other, bewildered. They couldn't believe they were alive, that they had managed to survive.

They walked through streams of ice-cold rain that lashed at their frozen bodies but was on their side, because it washed away their footprints. They crossed some marshland and came upon a fisherman—an Albanian, as it turned out—an ordinary, shriveled man who smiled when they told him they'd escaped.

"You'd better warm up," he advised them and took them to his house.

He gave them some clothes and blankets to wrap themselves in. He nodded as they told him they wanted to get to Italy as quickly as possible, anything to avoid catching the eye of the Yugoslav police, who would immediately hand them over to the Albanians.

"Yes, yes," he eagerly agreed. "You must be off as soon as you can, you'll blend into the crowd in Ulcinj, and once you leave town it'll be easier."

And that was when a constable appeared in the doorway. For notifying the police and having no scruples, the communist authorities paid the fisherman in dinars.

———

"'Why did you run away?' the police chief asked through an interpreter. 'Because death is better than life in Albania,' I said. They thought the government had sent us—that we were spies—so they asked us about everything, the border, the garrisons, the state of the army, but what could we have known about that?

"The interpreter was a small, fidgety upstart, who glared hatefully at me every time I opened my mouth. 'What would you do if Yugoslavia attacked Albania?' asked a stern, burly man—the head of the UDBA, the Yugoslav equivalent of the Sigurimi. 'I'd have nothing against Yugoslavia taking us over. Life in Albania is so miserable that any invader would be a savior.'

"The interpreter was horrified. Instead of translating, he looked at me and snarled: 'You motherfucker!' And I said, 'I thought I was being interrogated by the UDBA, not the Sigurimi, you son of a bitch.' We were spoiling for a fight. 'I'll see you in Shkodër in three days, you scum,' the interpreter said.

"We were still under the illusion that the worst wouldn't happen, and that they wouldn't send us back to Albania. Three days later, they put us in a car, with two soldiers sitting between us. I was still kidding myself. After about half an hour, the car stopped beside another car, out of which stepped two high-ranking officials in civilian clothes. I realized we were on the border, so when they came near me I spat in their faces. 'Bastards!'

I cried in despair. 'You're condemning us to death! We're not even thirty years old, and we're going to suffer for the rest of our lives!'

"It was cloudy, and there was light rain falling on my face. The Albanians and the Yugoslavs looked on calmly as I struggled. They didn't say a word. And then, right in front of us, they swapped cigarettes. The Albanians gave the Yugoslavs Taraboshes, and the Yugoslavs gave the Albanians Moravas. The best cigarettes in the country in exchange for our lives."

The trial was a simple formality, a showpiece for the people gathered in the room. There were more than a thousand packed inside, eager to get a glimpse of the traitors, and outside in front of the court building stood three times as many again, listening to every word through a loudspeaker.

"These degenerate youths want to go to the US, then come back and infect others with their decadent ideology!"

"Traitors to the fatherland!"

Zenel Drangu's trial was recorded and shown in cinemas as a warning. At one point, the representative of a youth group who was present in the courtroom stood up and cried: "We, the young people of Shkodër, demand the highest penalty for these degenerates: the hangman's noose!"

Zenel had realized what fate was in store for him during the interrogations. As soon as the guards had taken them to the army buildings on the border, one of the men had told them they were heading for the firing squad. But Zenel had been so devastated and furious at the time that nothing had sunk in.

"Better a tragic death than endless suffering," he thought and waited for the beating to start, but the guards didn't hit them; they just smiled.

"We'd have caught you wherever you went."

As they drove into the city, Zenel took a good look at every person, every building, every tree.

"You know you're seeing Shkodër for the last time?" the commanding officer said.

In the interrogation room, they didn't even ask why they'd run away, as if it were obvious; they were only interested in who had known about their plans.

"I didn't admit it, but I had talked to two of my friends about it in advance," recalls Zenel. "And I can imagine how scared they must have been right then. They were well aware that the Sigurimi used awful methods to extract information. Some people can withstand torture, but some will say anything because they're afraid of pain. When I'd had to fight against the current of the Buna I'd realized just how strong my spirit was, and what a powerful body I had. I knew I'd be able to endure all the suffering that lay ahead of me."

The court announced its sentence: twenty years in prison for betraying the country.

"We spared you, you should be grateful," hissed the guard who led Zenel to his cell.

"I'd rather you killed me."

"You son of a bitch!" shouted the guard. "We'll break your back. You're going to be digging down a mine until you drop dead."

"The rays of the sun tanned our wrinkles, scars, and furrows. Six hundred identical prison uniforms. The prisoners would say in greeting: 'Don't ask how many years they gave me, ask how long I've been here already.' Standing before me were weary, hunched fifty-year-olds who'd been sent there as young men. Just like me. Wasted lives.

"I didn't break down because I realized I'd survive the suffering, too, just as they had. I hadn't known I was capable of surviving several hours in icy water and several weeks of torture. Down the mine we suffered on a daily basis, and yet every day we lined up to go to work.

"It was in Spaç that I first realized how strong a man can be—and how cruel. Nobody ordered them to do it, but sometimes the guards tortured us against the rules, just for fun, as if they enjoyed our pain. Sometimes they kept me tied up outside for eight hours in the winter, when the temperature dropped to 5°F. Once in a while they'd come and tighten the frozen handcuffs, which carved gashes into my wrists, so that I'd suffer even more. Or they tied your body to a post and hung stones weighing fifty or sixty pounds to your dangling arms. They didn't have to do that. But they did. Those men had been selected to inflict pain. Nobody was giving them orders, they just thought up their own ways to do it.

"One time a guard was whacking me with a baton, and when he stopped to catch his breath, I raised my head and said: 'I'll be here until I die, so I've nothing to lose. Hit me again and I'll find a way to kill you.' And I watched as he put down the baton."

———

Eighteen triple bunk beds in a small space. Fifty-four prisoners get up at five-thirty. Some wash, others haven't the strength to put a slice of bread in their mouths. Some fight every day for cleanliness and dignity, others have given in to lice and exhaustion.

Straw mattresses that haven't been changed in ten years. Every two or three weeks, the guards turn them upside down just to torment the prisoners—looking for God knows what. A heavy stench of despair and straw dust fill the air. Sometimes high-ranking officials come for inspections, and they tell the prisoners how lucky they are to live in such a wonderful, democratic country as Albania. Even the cells of enemies of the people have mattresses and blankets; the authorities treat everyone with respect. Are there any questions?

Someone stands up.

"Before I ask a question, I'd like to know if I'll get an answer, and if I'll face any consequences."

"Go ahead," says the prison governor, graciously giving permission.

"Must everything that is born also die?"

"Yes," nods the official. "That is the law of nature."

"In that case, when will communism die?"

He hadn't closed his mouth before they'd seized him under the arms. No one ever heard of him again.

———

"'Either I'll get out of here or they'll shoot me,' my friend kept saying. He was obsessed with the idea of escape. I understood him better than anyone else.

"One day, I was working with a fellow prisoner to reinforce some new corridors in a part of the mine that hadn't been exploited yet. There were no guards with us. My workmate set off down the tunnel and I was left alone, when suddenly I discovered a nearby recess in the wall. I went into it, walked on about fifty feet, and realized it was a tunnel leading to the soldiers' bunker that adjoined the mine. That is—to the outside world. My knees went weak.

"But I immediately went back, and I didn't tell anyone about it, not even the man who was working with me. And yet from then on, the thought of that tunnel haunted me every day of the week.

"And when my friend said yet again that he couldn't stand it any longer, I took him to one side.

"'Listen,' I said. 'When you go to gallery twenty-two, look at the ceiling and start counting. You'll pass fifty wooden beams and there'll be a stone on the right. Push it to one side—it's the entrance to a tunnel that leads outside.'

"My friend stared at me as if he'd heard a fairy tale. 'Let's escape together!' he cried. 'I've tried that before,' I said, 'and the Yugoslavs packed me up and sent me back. The only escape from prison is into oblivion.'"

———

Chess, dominoes, dice, and books. Sometimes prisoners from Shkodër or Korçë played guitars, but the merrier it was in the cells, the sooner the guards appeared. They could take the guitars away whenever they wanted.

And when the prisoners went to the governor to complain, he'd shout: "Give them back their guitars immediately!"

But moments later the guards would smile and say: "In your wildest dreams . . ."

The prison staff put on these little performances to show the convicts that nothing was in their control.

It was worst for the older prisoners. They couldn't work, so they received minimal rations: two teaspoons of sugar, a tablespoon of of oil, a piece of bread. That's what it said in the regulations, but the prison management regularly stole from them.

In fact, everybody stole: the management, the cooks, the guards; the food that ended up on the prisoners' plates always had a piece missing, sliced off by a thief.

Flies buzzed around the ladle, and the rice and the pasta were teeming with maggots. In theory, the prisoners were entitled to about a pound of meat a day, but meat was the first thing to get stolen. They only saw sweets and fruit at New Year. That's why parcels from their families were worth their weight in gold, and so were the blessed jams and equally blessed cigarettes they contained: deliveries from another world, where some people took the food out of their own mouths to try to give others a small touch of relief.

———

"My friend started looking for a partner. He told one prisoner, then another, until finally the news reached the governor. Soon after, a young guy started hanging around me, a former soccer player from Tirana. He kept trying to persuade me to join a group of several others who were planning to escape. I told him the same thing I'd said to my friend: that I'd tried it once, and my family had already suffered enough because of me. But he kept insisting, tempting me like the serpent.

"'Don't you get it?' I told him. 'You can't escape from here. And even if you do get out, everyone in the vicinity will be after you. The most innocent child will give you away for a sweet, if you don't starve to death first.'

"The next day he came along with the same old story. 'Listen,' I said. 'If you don't stop, I'll report you.'

"At that point, I didn't yet know that the lad, our footballer, had been sent to me by the governor."

———

If you looked up in Spaç, all you saw above you was a dark turquoise scrap of sky and nothing else. The prisoners were surrounded on all sides by steep walls of rock. Mehmet Shehu had picked this place on purpose. He knew that the mountains would lock the prisoners inside an even smaller cage.

"Perfect for political prisoners," he said, observing the terrain from onboard a helicopter.

Anyone who escaped in winter had to force their way through snow-drifts over six feet high and try to hide from view like a surrounded animal. The brown prison uniforms would stand out against the white snow, and the shaven heads would catch the eye of any upright citizen.

And yet there were prisoners who did try to escape. Among them was Dalip Gaba from Vlorë, a senior Sigurimi official who ended up in Spaç after another wave of purges. One night in the middle of winter, he wrapped himself in a sheet and walked up to the fence. The entire area was bathed in the glare of the floodlights, but Dalip, wrapped in white, blended into the snow. Even though there was a sentry box very nearby, the guard didn't notice him. Calmly, methodically, Dalip cut through the double row of wire in the fence.

Snow was the enemy, but it could also be an ally. When on the ground, it mercilessly showed your footprints; when falling, it quietly erased all trace of them. After a week's pursuit, they caught Dalip, a heroic, worn-out creature wrapped in the bedsheet, half dead from starvation and exhaustion.

Another man who spent twenty years in prison was Ahmet Hoxha from Kolonjë near Gjirokastër; he'd ended up in Spaç at the age of eighteen. The narcs never let him out of their sight, because he'd already tried to escape twice, and yet one day he and Salim, a policeman from Dibra, managed to go through one of the army tunnels and get outside.

According to legend, they caught Ahmet Hoxha a few hundred yards from the Yugoslav border, when he'd already managed to get across the Black Drin and was only a step away from freedom. But Ahmet's brother says the police already had a fix on him beyond Gjirokastër, just a mile or two from his family home where he'd tried to hide.

Thirty-eight years of life, twenty years in prison, five days of freedom. For trying to escape again, Ahmet was shot. Although he had the right to ask the authorities to spare his life, he didn't.

––––––

The regime never stinted on suffering, but it wasn't so lavish with the death sentences because it needed slaves to fill nine hundred mine carts with ore every twenty-four hours. As citizens, the prisoners were nobodies, but as a cheap labor force, they were everything to the authorities. Every time a prisoner exceeded the work norm, the system took five days off his sentence, but such a major effort wore out the body in no time, which was why everyone tried to avoid work.

During the Second World War, Italian geologists had already done some work at the site of the Spaç mine. They had mainly extracted copper but also pyrite and gold, because the small mine was rich in deposits of various metals. There were no roads or vehicles, so the entire output was transported by mules.

With the arrival of communism, the role of the mules was taken over by prisoners. A two-ton mine cart would be pulled by two people, sometimes just one. The work norms had to be met at all costs, but following orders from above, no one actually checked them. The prison governor received instructions from his superiors in Kukës, who were obeying directives from the Ministry of the Interior, and the minister did as Enver Hoxha said without question. Each link in this chain wanted to come out of it as best they could, and each one falsified the data to please his boss. They all assured each other that the work norm had been completed on time, significantly exceeding the plans.

Sometimes the governor, wearing worker's garb, would cry: "Fill the carts with this!"

And when the prisoners replied that it was just mud, without any copper, he'd yell: "Don't ask questions! Get to work!"

Sometimes the mine took lives. On one occasion, a landslide of pyrite fell on a prisoner, suffocating him. His family couldn't get his body back, because the guards quietly buried him on a hillside near the prison. Even in death, he remained a prisoner. The hill conceals unidentified bodies to this day.

————

"I had a best friend, Ahmet Izbiu, who was crumbling before my eyes and who completely broke down when he heard that his mother had died. I always tried to keep an eye on him, because I knew he was in a bad way. One day, Ahmet took advantage of a moment when we were resting in the courtyard after an especially tough shift. He just stood up and began walking toward the fence. I leaped to my feet and ran straight to the guard. I begged him to let me catch Ahmet, I shouted into his face, even though we were forbidden to talk to the guards, but he just stared at me as if I were thin air. He looked through me into the distance, and then he simply turned around, raised his gun to his eye, and pulled the trigger.

"Ahmet fell below the fence at a single shot.

"The only escape from Spaç was into oblivion.

"None of us knows if heaven, purgatory, or hell is waiting for us when we die, we don't know if we'll be punished for evil and rewarded for good, but we prisoners can be sure of one thing: Man is capable of creating hell on earth for his fellow man. Many years after I left prison, I went to Auschwitz, and I heard about the Poles whom the Germans murdered for helping Jews to escape from the camp. I stood by one of the barracks and I burst into tears.

"It took me two years after coming out of prison to learn to tell faces apart, because everyone looked the same to me. One day, I went to Tirana with my brother. It was 1988. I was crossing Skanderbeg Square, gazing at the golden statue of Hoxha towering above us, and suddenly I stopped. 'Can it be possible? Am I really free?' I asked my brother, feeling as helpless as a child. 'Is no one going to come up behind me and shout: Stop! Where do you think you're going?'

"Even a canary born in a cage dreams of freedom. People think it's singing, but it's crying. Every creature is born free and should remain free.

"Apparently in democratic Albania we're all free, but the people who did us harm have escaped punishment. Democracy hasn't brought justice, and Sali Berisha did nothing to punish the guilty. But as a nation, we should be judging Enver Hoxha, we should be facing up to what he did to us. Can a man who is a murderer for some be a hero for others?"

The Many Deaths of Enver Hoxha

AND SO THE RED PHARAOH passed away—the man who was never going to die. The man to whom everyone said: "Take the years I have left and add them to your own." Immortal in life and immortal after death.

In his final months, he looked like a waxwork: exhausted by diabetes, puffy, his face coated in a thick layer of powder, with unseeing eyes, growing ever weaker, ever more paranoid, ever more acutely cut off from reality. Anyone who had the opportunity to take a close look at him in early 1985 could tell his days were numbered, but no one dared say it aloud.

At dawn on April 11, 1985, an announcement was issued to all activists: "Despite the enormous, tireless efforts of the Party and the Central Committee, Comrade Enver Hoxha has died."

The children thought their dearest uncle had passed away—the person who always cared about them. The young people thought their psychopathic father had died—the man who was always supervising and punishing them. The elderly, who remembered how the propaganda had been cranked up, thought the biggest fraud in the history of Albania was no more.

What do you do when the god who was never going to die suddenly disappears?

———

On April 11, little Alban Hajdinaj spent the morning at school in Mallakastër. Today, Alban is an artist, and he's sitting with me in the Bar Iliria, smiling at his memories.

"I remember it all very well," he says, "because that was a day when something terrible and something astonishing happened. He died.

"For a long time the dictator's health had been a strictly guarded secret, so he hadn't appeared in public for months. Many people didn't realize quite how sick he was. When he died, they exclaimed: 'How on earth? It's impossible!' It was inconceivable, especially for us children.

"I thought it was going to be a day like any other. Our first lesson was over, and we were waiting for the next teacher to arrive. Someone was throwing little bits of paper around, someone was shrieking, someone was yanking someone else. Half an hour passed. The break was long over when finally the teacher came in, but her face was chalky white, and we immediately realized that something had happened.

"She stood in the middle of the classroom, took a deep breath like an actress on stage, and whispered: 'A terrible thing has happened. Comrade Hoxha has died'—and she burst into tears.

"And then, like tumbling dominoes, one after another the children started crying, and so did I. We weren't crying because we loved our leader so much, we were crying because something completely unexpected had happened and the shock made us all feel very tense.

"In those days, everyone had to complete junior school, no matter what. In our class there was a poor guy who'd repeated the fifth year several times, older than us and as big as a bear. The police had to bring him to school by force.

"And that day, he burst into tears, too: He roared dismally in that deep, manly voice of his, drowning out our shrill, childish sobs; he roared like a wounded animal gasping out its last breath. We all turned around to look at him. The fact that this large, swarthy man could cry like that was just as surprising as the fact that Hoxha was dead. We stared at him dumbfounded.

"And then someone snorted, and suddenly the whole class was shaking with laughter. The dismayed teacher ran away but came back after awhile and said: 'Go home—on a day like this you should be with your parents.'

"When I went outside, everyone around me seemed bewildered and horrified. As I walked home, like every child, I wondered: 'What will happen now?' After all, Enver Hoxha was the invincible champion who protected us against all the evil in the world. As long as Enver was guarding Albania, no enemy could touch us. We were taught that during the Second World War it was he who had fought all Albania's enemies, and later, he'd stood up to Yugoslavia and the Soviet Union. So I thought: 'What are we going to do when the invasion starts? How are we going to defend ourselves?'

"I got home and saw to my surprise that my grandparents were sitting in their armchairs and didn't seem at all distressed. Just two old people, drinking coffee like every other day. 'Granddad, grandma!' I cried. 'Comrade Enver has died!' 'Yes, yes,' they said, 'we know.'

"I looked at them in shock. 'Granddad,' I said. 'Enver's died!' 'We're all going to die one day. What's so odd about it?'

"I was speechless. It was a day of great surprises.

"In my eyes, Enver was a superman. In my grandparents' eyes, he was someone completely different. They had no illusions about him. Brainwashing didn't work on people who remembered the Second World War and how the communists came to power. They knew what had really happened, they just couldn't talk about it. Right before their eyes, the propaganda had wiped out the history they remembered and replaced it with a new, carefully designed past. All aimed at Albanian children, who when they grew up would believe the authorities unconditionally, just as I did.

"My father was far more indoctrinated than my grandfather. When he was nine, he went to live at a boarding school in Tirana and became a model pupil of Albanian communism. Today he's seventy, and he won't change now. He still votes for the Socialist Party, he's not capable of thinking critically. But my grandfather belonged to the old world.

"'What will happen now?' I asked him that day. 'Nothing,' he said and shrugged. 'Life will carry on.'"

In each Albanian home the scene was different.

Ilva Daci, who's now a notary, was six years old at the time and remembers the tears pouring down her schoolteacher's cheeks.

"Children!" cried the desperate woman. "Go home, Uncle Enver has died!"

Ilva shouted in the doorway: "Mama, Babi, Uncle Enver has died!" but her parents weren't there, and her grandma refused to believe her.

"Child!" she said. "Be quiet this instant, those words will get your father ten years!"

Terrified, Ilva hid in the garden, and it was only that evening when they were sitting in front of the television that she saw her father staring at the screen with a blissful smile on his face while her mother and grandma sobbed.

"Why are you crying, you idiots?" He slapped his knee. "It's a good thing he's gone!"

"Four of us met at a café in Gjirokastër," says Fredi Muci, an engineer who was in his thirties at the time. "The poverty was dreadful by then. They served coffee but nothing else, so we'd brought our own piece of cheese, which we put on the table, and we drank.

"'It's lucky there's cheese, there might not be any,' said one of my friends. Another sighed: 'Our dear Enver has died.' We nodded. The people sitting around us were downcast but alert. Everyone was watching everyone else, we were all a bit frightened, we all wanted to say something, but the authorities could put a price of several years in prison on a single remark. So we sat there like stones, in silence, with just the occasional sigh.

"'They've laid Enver in his coffin,' someone ventured again. 'Yeah . . .' mumbled another of my friends. 'Now that he's in it, they'd better nail it shut properly!'

"And then the other guy snorted so hard the cheese came out of his nose. The third one nearly choked, too, but without making a sound, because laughing on the day Enver died was sure to get you at least six years!

"We took the cheese and left, quickly, to avoid drawing attention to ourselves. We thought we'd go to the factory to see what was happening at work, but there was no one at the machines—they were all sitting in a circle, sobbing, wailing, gasping for breath. I stood there staring at them, with the salty taste of cheese on my tongue . . ."

———

The Red Pharaoh was dead—so his slaves had to weep. And so began the cycle of collective howling and sobbing, hand-wringing, whimpering and sniffling, monotonous wailing, modulated wailing, extended and sudden blubbering. Some did it louder and for longer, others let it all out, yet others were in a state of tearless stupefaction. Slices of onion hidden in pockets were secretly wiped over eyelids. Matches poked into the corners of eyes made blood vessels burst in an effective and useful way.

"He looks the picture of misery" meant that he was suffering appropriately. Muted, moderate, unconvincing grief could land you in prison. Just a small degree of suffering was like no suffering at all, it was tantamount to being pleased about the death—and so several years of forced isolation were prescribed, to give the reactionary individual the chance to reconsider his attitude in peace and quiet.

To show that after the captain's death no passenger would abandon the sinking ship, the regime started tracking down new enemies. People ended up behind bars on absurd charges: "He smiled on the day of Hoxha's death;" "He looked happy when the whole nation was crying." All the rats that had looked around for a lifeboat were imprisoned on the lower deck.

———

"There were six of us boys from Vlorë, we were watching Enver's funeral on television together," recalls Astrit Beqiri, a translator. "We felt neither sorrow nor relief. Basically, we weren't bothered about Enver. We were young, we stuck together, we trusted each other. In those days, if you told a friend what you were thinking, you'd immediately wonder: 'How many years in prison for the words that just slipped out?'

"And one of us . . . God, it seems unreal now . . . Our friend stared at the TV and giggled. Yes, he giggled!

"'Look at Lenka's handbag,' he said—Lenka Cuko was a high-up commie official. 'Look how ugly it is! She could have made more of an effort for Enver's funeral!'

"If in the privacy of your own home, instead of crying you could laugh among friends, it meant Enver really was dead!"

―――――

"There should be no date of death on this marble," Ramiz Alia said over Enver's grave. "It should just say: 'Born October 16, 1908.' Only that date defines Enver Hoxha—his date of birth—and so it shall be for ever, for this man knows no death. Enver Hoxha is immortal!"

Throughout the country, new slogans appeared overnight on inside and outside walls: ENVER LIVES. And THE WORKS OF ENVER HOXHA WILL NEVER BE FORGOTTEN.

―――――

"We used to dream of Hoxha's death, all of us prisoners," Fatos Lubonja says with a faint smile. "His death would have brought us closer to freedom. When Stalin died, something changed throughout the Soviet Union, and we were counting on the same thing happening in Albania.

"Our hopes were first raised in December 1973, when Hoxha had a heart attack, but we soon realized he'd come out of it just as strong as before.

"In 1981, a television set appeared at the prison. Of course, we only watched the news from Tirana, and once in a while, Enver. But just by looking at him you could see he was feeling worse and worse. In 1984, a rumor went around that Hoxha was too weak to appear at the celebrations on November 29, the fortieth anniversary of the communists' entry into Tirana. That day we were forced to sit in front of the television. We watched it, and there he was. He was there, after all . . . We were tremendously disappointed. But for the first time, he wasn't standing up straight—he was leaning on something like a chair. In Albanian we say: 'He's got sores from sitting on his ass.' And my friend cheered us up by saying: 'Oh well, perhaps he's got sores at least!'

"Apparently there's a Chinese saying: 'If you want to see your enemy's coffin, stand on the riverbank and one day it will float past.' And eventually, the dictator's coffin did come floating by. The news traveled from cell to cell: 'He's dead!'

"I felt great joy—and great fear of showing that joy. First thing in the morning, two or three of us were put in solitary, because the authorities had to show us they were still strong. They wanted to frighten us. But then—something unlikely happened. We were watching the funeral ceremony, we sat there quite calmly, with stony faces and joy in our hearts. And there was one prisoner among us who'd first tried to commit suicide, and then become mentally ill. Since then, he'd never stopped trying to prove how much he loved the Party. And as soon as they'd lowered the coffin in the grave, we heard: 'Stand up, because the greatest man in Albania has just been laid to rest.' We turned around. Fortunately, it was just our silly, deranged Alen. Even the guards had no alternative but to ignore him.

"But then some prisoners came up with the idea that we should all demonstrate our grief by sending Nexhmije Hoxha a telegram with our condolences. We were sitting in the canteen, feeling that the time had come when one of us was going to be sacrificed. We sensed it was a provocation, and that the authorities were looking for rebels. And I had two sentences to my name, so I would be first in line to be picked off. The prisoners who collaborated with the guards came along and read out the telegram. No one said a word. The next day, a friend of mine from barracks number one took me aside and whispered: 'Fatos, they brought us the telegram and insisted that we sign it.' 'Oh my God . . .' 'And we did. Ilir Malili was the only one who didn't sign it. And now they've moved on.'

"So that was it. Sign it—and you'll survive. Don't sign it—and you're done for. Sign it—and you'll have to face up to your own shame. Don't sign it—and you'll have to face up to your own death. I was terrified, because I knew I wouldn't sign it, but I also knew I didn't want to die. And everyone was signing it, even the bravest people.

"Except that sometimes the really brave people turn out to be the ones you'd least expect.

"The guards went into barracks number two. I was in number three. The telegram had to be signed in front of everyone. One prisoner gave the signal to say we're starting, but when the guards approached the first man in line, who was another slightly crazy guy, he looked at them and announced: 'Sorry, but I'm just off for a piss.' And off he went.

"That gave other people courage. They refused. The guards never even got to barracks number three, my one.

"Incidentally, I saw how quickly legends are born in prison. Only a month after these events, one of the others told me: 'You know, I was ready to sign, but when I heard you say, "Let them kill me! Let them kill my entire family but I won't sign!" I instantly changed my mind.'

"Of course, I never said anything of the sort! I knew I wouldn't sign the telegram, but I never made any kind of passionate appeal. It was just that the man honestly believed that was what had happened, because he was fighting an internal battle to preserve his own dignity.

"Yes. The guards did what they could to poison our great joy with extreme terror."

———

And then six years went by, and the memorialized figure of the dictator crashed to the ground with a thud. An enraged crowd pulled down his statue in the center of Tirana, and thus symbolically murdered the man who was meant to be immortal. This time it was the spirit of Hoxha that was killed. It had continued to hover over Albania through the years when communism was in its death throes.

"I was at home when I heard from my neighbors that Hoxha's statue was coming down," recalls Alban Hajdinaj. "It was broadcast live on television. Today, people say it was all orchestrated by the secret services, that the students wanted to bring down the old system, but they were being manipulated by Ramiz Alia, who knew the fall of communism was inevitable and wanted to take control of the opposition and have his own people in the Democratic Party. Perhaps that's why we're still partly stuck in communism.

"In hindsight, even that watershed moment seems faked. I don't know if people rushed into the streets entirely spontaneously. I don't know who was clean then. Sali Berisha went to negotiate with the students as the authorities' envoy, and then he switched to their side and led them into the streets, but today people say he was planted there by Alia. Even while the system was being brought down there were no heroes we might still believe in today."

———

A painting by Enkelejd Zonja, one of Albania's leading contemporary artists, depicts Enver Hoxha as a resurrected Jesus Christ allowing doubting Thomas to stick a finger into his heart.

"See?" he seems to be saying, with a gentle smile on his face. "I never died at all."

Hoxha's determined way of baring his chest makes us think of Clark Kent, tearing off his shirt to transform into Superman. His body emanates strength, his face is ageless, unmarked by earthly suffering. Hoxha looks like a figure from a propaganda poster—he's bigger than the other men in the painting, brighter, as pink as a bunch of peonies.

"To the extent that a man can become God, Enver became God for us," says Zonja. "But look at his red tie that goes flying across the painting like a ribbon or a hangman's noose. Enver rose from the dead, but his statue was hanged. We all remember how, in 1991, just before it shattered, the statue of Hoxha leaned over and hung in the air like Benito Mussolini's dead body. It was the symbolic hanging of the dictator to whom we could no longer do anything."

"And the man sticking his finger into his heart?"

"He looks like my father, a retired history professor. He still believes the system fought for equality and guaranteed our security. If the authorities had persecuted us, my father would probably have been more critical, but we lived carefully and fate was kind to us.

"I needed a model for the figure of the old man who's also staring at the dictator. I found a withered-looking guy picking up trash in the street. When he came into my studio, he dropped a black bag on the floor, and a Coca-Cola can rolled out of it. That's why the young man in the picture is holding a can and looking in a completely different direction. The resurrected Hoxha doesn't interest him at all. The youngest generation are cutting themselves off from the past and thinking only about the future, because the present has utterly failed to meet their expectations."

Zonja's painting portrays Hoxha's symbolic victory from beyond the grave—Enver cannot be forgotten or wiped from the pages of history. The myth of Skanderbeg, the great national hero who bravely stood up to the Turks in the Middle Ages, and the myth of Hoxha are the country's two most distinctive reference points. The specter of the leader still hangs over Albania and still has an effect on its society.

Nowadays the Albanian kukudh, the phantom that was said to feed on blood, feeds on people's memories.

––––––

Alban Hajdinaj puts a packet of cigarettes down on the café bill, then picks it up again.

"In 2016, I was taking a family photo out of its frame when I noticed there was a picture of Enver Hoxha underneath it. My grandmother had put our family into a frame that had once held an official portrait of the dictator. Hoxha was there for years, hidden like the skeleton in a cupboard. But of course the regime wasn't just him, it was also thousands of ordinary people who obediently carried out his orders and did harm to others of their own free will. People kept portraits of him in their houses out of opportunism or out of faith. We, the new generation, can't blame ourselves for the past, but nor can we pass over our history in silence forever, however repugnant we find it. We have to confront what happened and come to terms with the past.

"There's a picture frame in every home that conceals the pain and the shame of it. That's why I've made a film in which I recreate the moment when I discovered Hoxha's photograph. The dictator is there in the background of every family's history; every single family, whether consciously or not, certified the authorities' methods and submitted to them. This is me, here's my family, and here's Hoxha's photo in a frame on the side table, in a completely new context—one shows free Albania; the other, enslaved Albania."

Are They People Like Us?

HERE WE HAVE IT: an object broadcasting words and pictures that transformed the lives of everyone in the vicinity. Amid the boredom of identical days, it radiated a light that drew people to it like moths from the entire neighborhood. What an extraordinary invention! Science had worked magic!

Those who could install this border-crossing device in their living rooms were fortunate indeed. But the marvelous box only reached a select few. There were no homegrown pictures or Western wonders for enemies of the people! The worthiest members of the nomenklatura were another matter—of course they could and should stare at the TV screen, they could even get away with watching capitalist propaganda, because someone had to know what the enemy was up to, didn't they?

But to have a television set, you had to tighten your belt, swallow hard, and get your hands on eight months' wages. People said goodbye to sewing machines, clothes, mirrors, and books, just to fit their home with a new window onto the world.

And then they'd watch *La Dolce Vita* and wait impatiently for the commercial break.

———

When the television frenzy began in the early 1970s, the authorities hadn't yet sensed that the sight of foreign luxuries might confuse the Albanian citizens. The city of Durrës had an eye on Italy, Pogradec had one on Yugoslavia, and Shkodër had both. The residents of Gjirokastër could sometimes catch glimpses of Greek channels. Soon homemade tin-can transistors appeared, which amplified the signals coming from these other worlds. The men would hide the aerial in a cupboard during the daytime, and at night they'd climb onto the roof to set it up in an inappropriate direction.

"Apparently, it's all just stage sets," people whispered. "There's one world on television and another in real life. They string us along here, too, don't they?"

In his book *Everyone Goes Mad in His Own Way*, Stefan Çapaliku describes the arrival of a Soviet Rubin television in his house, brought back from a foreign delegation by his father, a distinguished agronomist. It was the memorable year 1968.

"From then on," writes Çapaliku, "the TV room looked like a furniture shop, and every neighbor for whom there wasn't a seat had to come with his own stool or chair." From one day to the next, twenty people in the neighborhood started learning Italian just to be able to keep up with the beautiful world on the television. "We listened to our Italian teacher as if he were reading us the Old Testament. He was the priest, and we were the students of the catechism."

As the spring timidly began, the Western world came seeping in through the sealed borders. The authorities kept talking of the need for modernization and shaking their fist at the wicked conservative forces that were stifling young people's freedom, but apart from ideology, perpetual tedium, and terror, they had nothing to offer anyone. So voices started coming from inside the Party again: "The West is bringing our ruin, stirring up futile yearning, and tormenting people with indecent desires!" The three-year thaw was over, and the long winter was back. In 1974, the authorities installed jamming devices in the biggest cities to put a stop to peeping at foreigners.

Down with Western degeneracy!

No more bewitching songs, quirky music videos, or humming under your breath.

No more cars, handbags, or swimming pools.

No more daydreams, longings, or fantasies.

Instead, the mandatory schedule: four hours of Albanian television each day—a twenty-minute children's program called *School and Life*; a half-hour program called *Advice and Practical Knowledge*; a feature film that was only an hour long, because the capitalist filth had to be cut out of it; then *The Voice of Youth* and the documentary *Around Our Country*. For fans of culture there was *Culture and Life*; for fans of farmwork there was the *Program for Agricultural Workers*; and for two million patriots, that is to say everyone, there was *Glorious Moments from the History of Our Nation*. That was the extent of Albanian television in 1976.

"The news about the jamming was as shocking and tragic as if we'd found out a kid we'd been playing football with five minutes ago had just died of a heart attack," writes Stefan Çapaliku.

Fortunately, in the late 1980s, the whole of Albania stopped functioning, including the jamming devices. So, thanks to Yugoslav television, some Albanians could get to know the gold, rhinestones, and bathrobes of *Dynasty*, while who should appear on national television but Isaura the slave girl—the heroine of an eponymous Brazilian soap that enjoys great popularity in Eastern Europe.

The foreign characters on television had eyes, hands, and everything else, but they seemed to be made of a different material. "Are they people like us?" wondered the Albanians. The cheerful Italians, for instance, cheekily carefree, they go through life with their heads held high, they have no reason to feel fear. They get into their cars and speed ahead, the wind streams in through the open windows and ruffles their hair. In Greek serials, the criminals leap onto ships and sail across the sea, as an intrepid policeman tears after them in a motorboat.

Everyone knows who's good and who's bad.

Everyone knows where the border lies.

Everyone knows that anyone who tries to escape will be caught.

And right there, on the other side of the screen, is another world. You just have to smash the glass.

In 1960, there were 1,900 passenger cars on Albanian roads. By the 1980s, this number had risen to 6,000 to 7,000.

PART FIVE

THE
FORTRESS
CRUMBLES

Pretty Papers

THE CHILDREN'S ANSWER TO THE COLORFUL PROPAGANDA albums were scrapbooks into which they glued bits of foreign packaging— iridescent pieces of a faraway world, known as *letra të bukura*, "pretty papers." An alternative reality manifested itself in the form of shreds of paper, confirming the painful suspicion that somewhere out there were different lands filled with wonderful, wild abundance, beyond the reach of the Albanians.

Sometimes, in a surge of generosity, someone who'd received a parcel would give away a piece of trash. A resident of Durrës or Vlorë would fish an Italian candy wrapper out of the sea and present it to a loved one. Sometimes the children played a game, trying to guess what it had contained. A lollipop, perhaps? Maybe a chocolate bar? Or maybe . . . chocolate wafers! After the beloved leader's death, Albania contracted economically—there was no glass, steel, or fertilizer, and people went to the shops with their own jars or paper cones.

Meanwhile, scraps of the outside world came floating in on the water, down the rivers, or across the deep blue sea; they caught in the bulrushes or swept past on a rapid current, so fast you couldn't catch them. The trees looked down on the little figures bent over the water. The hills watched their outstretched fingers trying to grab an object as it floated away. Oh, to find a pair of shoes! A foreign shoe was a bit of luck, because it had a foreign sole. With a foreign sole, you could make a good Albanian shoe. You could go far in a shoe like that—all the way to the border and back again.

Stories did the rounds about people who worshipped capitalism in their communist apartments, hiding empty Coca-Cola cans—a vulgar and dangerous drink—at the back of the cupboard. There was some debate about what it tasted like, but it was hard to reach a common position on that point. One day, by knowing the right people, a loving father managed to procure a can of this miraculous stuff, so he pulled the curtains shut and called his kids into the room. He gave the can a really good shake, in the usual way—every drink needs a shake before serving, from kefir to compote, doesn't it? Up and down he shook the can, while the kids whined and shouted, gradually the tension increased, until finally he opened it . . . There was a terrific bang, and everyone fell to the floor. Streams of brown liquid trickled into the carpet.

Another man managed to get hold of some bananas, but the skin was hard and tasted horrible. To hell with bananas, all that fuss over nothing!

And when a boy from Gjirokastër wrote "Pepsi" on the back page of his notebook, his parents had to spend hours explaining to the headmaster how on earth their child knew such a filthy, ugly word.

Parcels from other worlds brought the weirdest objects, such as a scented substance in a stick, which one family thought must be antiperspirant. And you could just about spread it on—it even had a scent, quite a nice one, too, if you weren't fussy—it was just that it made your armpits terribly sticky. Oh well, you shouldn't expect too much! Finally, the new era brought a revelation: the green tube was a stick of glue.

The customs inspectors rated some items in the parcels as just a moderate threat—lacy underwear, for example—but other things proved unacceptable, such as a baseball cap with a clover-shaped patch sewn onto it. Just think, comrades, they say four-leaf clovers bring good luck, but look at this cap: only three leaves! Someone's making sly fun of our system, someone's implying there's no good fortune to be had here in

Albania! What an idea! Pass the razor, please, we'll soon deal with this treacherous three-leafed clover.

Later on, the recipients opened their parcel, took out the baseball cap with a hole in the front, put a finger through it, and sighed. What's to be done? We'll put a smart patch on it to look Western, but in Albanian style. We'll just have to write to Uncle and ask what on earth was on the cap that made the inspectors cut it out . . .

No One Feels Guilty

Exit Father

My father was one of those ordinary citizens who went out for cigarettes and never came back. That night we waited for him, our hearts
pounding with fear, casting glances at his books, his favorite armchair,
his glasses case, and his reading lamp. It was only the next day that some
men in identical beige overcoats hammered on our door. Their faces
were stern and their movements guarded. They said our father had been
arrested on a charge of terrorism.

My mother lowered her head and her long, dark hair fell over her face,
cutting her off from us like a curtain.

Three days later, they came back and went through the house as if
it were their own. They ordered us to pack our lives into suitcases and
move immediately to the countryside, to Bubq near Fushë-Krui. It was
1984.

I packed my father's books into boxes: Balzac, Stendhal, Hugo,
Tolstoy, and I couldn't stop thinking about how, when I was little, my
father would get me to read, because he personally had found refuge in

literature. "Albanian indoctrination is a waste of time," he often said, and handed me foreign classics. Where would he find refuge now?

They said my father had tried to kill Hoxha and overthrow the people's power, and death awaited him . . . An unassuming teacher, the mild-mannered author of several books. My childhood hero, who taught me to read. People like him, educated and sensitive, were the greatest threat to the regime. It was becoming more monstrous right before our eyes, sinking into madness, losing what remained of its reason, and devouring us all, one by one, the guilty and the innocent alike.

Many years after, I thought about what my father had been through. When a man learns he has been condemned to death, he has to come to terms with his fate and cut all his ties with the world. Imagine it like this: Life is a complicated machine with lots of ropes tied to it. The condemned man has to cut them to make the machine stop. He cuts the first rope: love for his children. But the machine goes on working. He cuts the second one: love for his wife. But that doesn't stop it either. Finally, he cuts the last one: his own love of life. Now, he can cross to the other side and go to his death. Just then, the door opens and a messenger arrives.

"You're an enemy of the people, you're a miserable waste of space, you're worthless scum, but we're going to spare your life!"

And he leans over the convict, unaware that he's looking at a shell—a deaf, blind wreck of a man who can't make out what he's saying, in whom life is closing down. But finally the victim starts to understand, and he's faced with a seemingly impossible task: He's got to start up that machine again. Tie those ropes back onto it. I know how long it took my father to come back. I used to sleep in the same room as him, because he'd wake up in the middle of the night shouting, and I'd try to calm him down. I did what I could to help him get used to the life he'd recovered.

My name is Shpëtim Kelmendi. I'm a writer and poet, and this is the first time I have ever talked about what happened to my family. I've never wanted my personal life to influence the way my writing is perceived.

Exit Mother

My mother had black hair, a white face, and eyebrows as dark as a raven's wings. I've only inherited her eyes; throughout my childhood she seemed impossibly, stunningly beautiful. When they took my father and interned us in Bubq, she had to take on the entire burden of looking after the eight of us. In times of direst need, she sold her own clothes to feed us. Finally she cut off her long, shiny hair that flowed down her back in a black wave; it earned her enough to buy some bread and potatoes.

Sometimes we had nothing to eat for two whole days. The longest I went without food was nine days. I'll never forget the time my mother took a few boiled potatoes from a bowl on the table and said: "Children, you've had enough now. Let's give some to the neighbors, let them eat their fill for once."

I was shocked: Firstly, because she was taking food away from us, and then, because she was giving it to others. One could hardly afford to make that kind of gesture in those days. It occurred to me that my mother was a really good person, too good for those times.

Every day she had to cope with our hunger, with the pleas written on our faces, with our fragility and our weakness, and that helplessness killed her. She died of cancer, but I'm sure her illness was born out of suffering, out of the pain of being unable to change anything, of being unable to help us properly. She was only forty-nine when we buried her.

Just before she died, we went to visit our father. Looking at her, I could already see the effects of the illness. But my mother said: "Not a word. We're not going to add to your father's worries."

I watched her as she talked to him; she was cheerful and loving, with a gentle smile on her face. I trembled inside as I saw how strong she was—a rock. That was the last time they ever saw each other.

She received no medical care, and we had no way to relieve her pain. She died in my arms. "How could death take someone so beautiful away from me?" I thought.

I've never known Albanian men to be half as strong as Albanian women. Because the women suffered in many ways: as workers at the

factory conveyor belt and as servants at home, as mothers, wives, daughters, and sisters, and as model workers, toiling away at cooperative farms,
unappreciated, misunderstood, entrenched in sacrifice. How did they
cope in that inhumane system, working beyond their strength every
day of the week? I know one thing: Albanian mothers never think of
themselves—they only ever think of their children. When my mother
was very ill, I would sleep in the same room to check up on her at night,
and, as it was very cold, I would cover her with a warm blanket and sleep
under a thin one myself. But I'd wake up in the morning to find myself
under the warm one, because during the night my dying mother still
had enough strength to swap our blankets. That's what she was like, to
the very end.

On My Own

For the system to last, we all had to be afraid, because people who are
afraid keep quiet. If the terror had eased, we'd have started saying that
life was unbearable, and we'd have tried to bring down the system, and
that's exactly what Hoxha wanted to avoid at any cost.

The propaganda stuck to us like shit to the sole of your shoe. I had a
classmate who was very cunning, but all his intelligence was spent on
thinking up ways of talking bullshit. Whatever the teacher asked him—
about the growth cycle of the potato, for instance—my friend would start
prattling: "The Party places special emphasis on the promotion of potato
cultivation, so that the Albanian people will never experience hunger,
because the potato is their bread and meat."

What could the teacher do to someone like that?

"All right," he'd mutter. "Sit down."

After a while, the fellow became so crafty that he began volunteering to
answer the teacher's questions, just to regale us with his arrant nonsense.
And if we had to write an essay, he'd stick together a string of communist
slogans: "Power in the hands of the people," "Communism will triumph
worldwide," "Long live the Party!" Finally, the teacher broke down, wrote
under one of these essays: "Hooray! Long live the Party!" and gave him
a D minus.

But compared to the years of internal exile to come, my time at high school was pretty much carefree. Once interned, I became leprous—I could infect anyone with my suffering. I was twenty, and every time I tried talking to a girl, she'd immediately cry: "Go away, you're an enemy of the people, I don't want anything to do with you!"

My background was repellent, like a slimy outer coating that pushed people away from me, preventing them from seeing what I was really like. Women treated me as if I didn't exist, because the hand I held out to them would have pulled them over the cliff. My mother was gone by now, but I wanted to love, just like everyone else. Loneliness was like a cocoon that I was trapped inside.

We, the bad boys, were constantly trodden into the ground. One time, when I was on my way to visit my father in Spaç, the bus stopped on the main road, and then I had to walk miles and miles along a remote, winding road. Finally I managed to get a lift on a timber truck. I was no fool, and to be on the safe side, I didn't talk too much, but the driver kept prying and asking questions. In the end, he managed to wring it out of me that I was going to the prison to see my father.

"Get out!" he roared. "Get out this minute, you enemy of the people!"

I walked for three hours, and when I finally reached the prison, visiting time was over. Night fell, and an icy wind bit into my cheeks. I fell asleep on the ground, curled in a ball, in front of the camp gates.

Yes, it really was like that. I can hardly believe it now.

I remember . . . Walking toward the prison that time, I saw them all in the distance: small figures in brown prison garb, circling the courtyard, identical in their suffering. I couldn't tell which man was my father, and suddenly it occurred to me that every one of them was him, and that I felt love for every single one. That love flooded me entirely, as I gazed at the tiny silhouettes of my fathers—each filled with more suffering than any human being can endure.

Brothers

One day, after my mother had died, the local policeman came up to me and unceremoniously declared: "I've heard your brothers are planning to flee the country."

Completely taken aback, all I could do was stammer: "No, that's not true."

"Come on, don't pretend," he hissed. "We both know it's true.

But you can still do something about it. If they get caught, the brats will go to prison for at least fifteen years, and what good will that do them?"

"Why are you telling me this?" I asked.

"Don't get the wrong idea. I'm retiring in four months' time, and I don't want any shit in my way."

I never saw him again. But my brothers took the inner tube out of a truck tire and tried sailing to Montenegro on it in the middle of the night. A fisherman saw them and raced off to the guards. They got seventeen years each. The perfect way to start a new life.

So now I was visiting not just my father but also my brothers in prison. I had company on the long trek to Qafë Bar, in the form of some friends who were going to visit their relatives, too. The road was endless—there were no buses, no chance of a lift, just a very long walk through the mountains. One time, we'd got all the way to the gate only to find that the guards were deliberately scheming not to let us in. They took as long as they could to inspect the food we'd brought, until finally they looked at my friend and said: "No, that man's sideburns are too long. He'll have to go back to town to get them cut."

We exchanged glances. If he had to go all that way and back again, he'd have no time left for the visit. And then my friend decided to settle the matter "the Albanian way." He picked up a piece of glass from the ground and started cutting his face with it; soon it was covered in blood, and the sideburns weren't visible anymore. When the guard saw that, he exclaimed: "All right, for fuck's sake, get inside! I can see that guy's off his head."

I'd had so much to do with people who worked for the regime that as soon as I saw one of them in the distance, I'd immediately cross to the other side of the street. And I'd stare at the ground, at the yellow, dusty sand, at children's faces, anything to avoid meeting his eye. Once I heard a policeman calling me by name, and I froze. I looked at that son of a bitch in uniform, and it took me a while to realize it was a friend of mine. My knees went weak, because that man knew more about me than anyone else.

"Come off it. . . ." He said, and sighed when he saw the look in my eyes. "I have to eat, too, don't I? I'm wearing a uniform, but otherwise nothing's changed."

Well, was I going to believe him? I backed away from him, because in that world you couldn't be sure of anything. But later on, when my brothers were arrested, that friend used to go and visit them in prison, too, with food and cigarettes, which in those days were worth their weight in gold. He wore that odious uniform, the sight of which made me feel faint, but under it he was still the same person.

Traitors and Friends

People used to say: If you're on your own, you're safe. If there are two of you, watch out. If a third person turns up—take to your heels and run. Because it was widely believed that one in four people was passing things on to the Sigurimi agents.

Four or five people were enough of a crowd for me to walk past them on tiptoe.

The extreme nature of the system brought out the worst in people, but it also forced them to make some extraordinary sacrifices. The dictatorship made us into monsters and saints. Some betrayed the person with whom they shared a bed, others risked their lives to help a stranger. Regardless of ideology, people always have both compassion and cruelty in them. You can never tell which side of a person will reveal itself to you.

I had two best friends, and three men could already be two too many. I gave one of them some poems to read—my first jottings on suffering and loneliness. I trusted him because I sensed that he hated the regime with all his heart: He was the son of a state official, his family had been interned just like mine, and we saved each other in our despair by talking endlessly about books.

"You're my first reader," I told him shyly when he came to give the poems back.

"Oh no, I'm not," he replied, with a glint in his eye. "I gave your poems to the head of our Sigurimi unit, because I've heard he's a great fan of poetry."

I was speechless with horror. I could feel the ground giving way beneath my feet.

"It's all right," said my friend with a smile. "I was joking."

And he took my notebook out of his pocket.

You could call it cruelty, but from then on we were united by a bond that no one can understand nowadays. Making friends with someone often meant risking your life. If someone plucked up the courage to complain about the regime, the repression, and the hopelessness, the person he was talking to often denounced him because he was convinced that degree of sincerity had to be a provocation by the Sigurimi. "The sly fox!" thought the poor wretch, on his way to grass on the other poor wretch. "He's testing my loyalty . . . They won't catch me out with that kind of trick!" Being frank and open was like a grenade that could explode between two people at any moment.

Imagine a society where it's extremely dangerous to be yourself, where you can never expose yourself to anyone. There were many cruel sides to the system, but now, when I look back, I think the worst thing was that everyday terror. We couldn't make any decisions—about where we were going to live or where we were going to work or, quite often, who we were going to love. There was no sphere of our lives where we were free. We couldn't even tell the people closest to us what a hard time we were having.

And as we couldn't trust anyone, we couldn't form any close bonds, either. The system knew that true friendship could kindle rebellion. Every revolt starts with people thinking alike and with a sense of solidarity forming among them. Nothing was as great a threat to Hoxha's regime as solidarity and friendship.

Forgiveness

Yes, let's say it loud and clear, Albanian communism was collective insanity. To carry on living after that kind of trauma, we needed to forget about it as quickly as possible. Except that the past is everywhere; we haul it around inside us. You can try to forget it, but you can't wipe it out.

The happiest day of my life was the day the system fell: February 20, 1991, when the golden Hoxha in the center of Tirana was toppled. All around me, people were crying with joy and despair; in particular, the ones who were involved with the regime were shaking in their shoes, because what they were most afraid of was retribution. And I regained my freedom twice over: First, because until then I'd been isolated in a tiny country called Albania, and second, because I'd been a social outcast, a lowlife, a louse.

And just as I'd always felt like everyone's enemy, suddenly I became a hero—the whole village came knocking at my door to hug me, even the ones who'd always refused to return my greeting. There was no mutual hatred between us—we all felt that there was only one enemy: the regime. The crowds in the streets cried: "Democracy! Fraternity! Solidarity!" We were drunk on freedom, intoxicated with joy. I thought that now anything was possible, and we'd create an Albania we'd never dared to imagine before. But in the first democratic elections, in March 1991, the communists won. We were still so insecure and afraid, especially in the countryside . . . It was only a year later, after a wave of strikes, that further elections brought victory to Sali Berisha's Democratic Party. We thought we were ready to be free people, but time has shown that we were wrong.

The enthusiasm completely dissipated in 1997, when the financial pyramid schemes crashed and a citizens' revolution broke out against the authorities—a minor civil war and a major national catastrophe. The masks fell away, pure violence reigned, and the random gunfire and gangland feuds killed two thousand people.

As the years went by, the victims and executioners became one and the same: the new Albanian society.

In the 1990s, I used to go to a chess club in Blloku, where I'd play against an elderly man who looked extremely respectable: His clothes were smart and subtle, and he wore a signet ring—a real old-fashioned gentleman, sleek and jovial, like a well-fed walrus. One time, he put the chess pieces away and said: "Let's have a chat. I'd like to know more about you."

I told him I'd been persecuted throughout my life, that I'd worked at a cooperative farm, and that my father had spent seven years in prison.

"And what did you do, sir?" I asked.

"I worked for the Sigurimi."

I almost leaped to my feet.

"I've been playing chess with a Sigurimi agent?"

"And where's the harm in that?" asked the man, his fingers forming a pyramid.

My hands clenched into fists.

"If I'd met you in 1991, I could have killed you! I was so full of rage about my ruined life!"

"You could have done," agreed the man. "But you didn't. Perhaps we deserved to die, but no one raised their hand against us, and we're not afraid of you anymore. At the end of the day, democracy has brought one good thing: It's made us brothers again, and now"—he swept a hand around the room—"we can play chess here together."

I never went there again.

In the early 1990s, when there was an ongoing debate about whether the victims should forgive their persecutors, the writer Arshi Pipa said: "Yes. We should forgive them. But how can we forgive someone who doesn't feel guilty?"

As there's no one to blame in the new democratic Albania, no one has been punished and no one is asking for forgiveness.

The Fortress Crumbles

ALBANIAN COMMUNISM WAS LIKE a crumbling fortress, losing a few stones every day. Or like a tumbledown wooden cottage with a rotten roof, mold on the walls, and flooded foundations, which by some miracle was still upright, despite the winds of history blowing hard at it.

First the chimney collapsed. Then the gale tore off the shutters and smashed the windowpanes; finally, the rusty hinges couldn't bear the weight of the door any longer. When the roof caved in with a crash, the people who lived in the cottage weren't sure if the building was still standing or if it had collapsed. Can we leave? Are we free?

Every Albanian has their own date marking the end of communism. And each one saw different harbingers of change.

"Things are getting better," people had been saying since 1987, when Ramiz Alia allowed them to keep two sheep for every cottage—but only of the same sex so they wouldn't multiply.

"They are!" agreed those who could finally listen to such excesses as the Beatles on the radio.

"Something's changing," said the citizens of Tirana with a sigh at the sight of the flamboyant youths walking down the street looking scruffy in their leathers and their jeans—the decadent West, to put it simply.

"It's as if someone's lifted the cover of a well and there's light shining in for the first time," said the people who were pleased in 1986, when the government launched the first international rail connection linking Tirana and Titograd, today's Podgorica in Montenegro.

But to make sure society didn't get too high-spirited, Ramiz Alia did his best to curb public enthusiasm, while the economy, in a state of total collapse, did a great deal to help him. If you did manage to get your hands on some cheese or butter, it tasted so disgusting that you lost the will to live.

Some say the first irrefutable signs of change appeared on August 17, 1989, when Anjezë Gonxhe Bojaxhiu, that is, Mother Teresa, arrived in Albania on a private visit. What an unusual guest for atheist Albania!

"For me, communism ended on November 4, 1990, when Father Simon Jubani conducted the first Mass at the Catholic cemetery in Shkodër," says Denis Gila, son of Kitty Harapi, the woman who sang Italian songs.

"On July 8, 1990, when I saw the workers in the streets of Kavajë shouting 'Freedom!,' I thought: 'It's the end! The end! The end at last!'" recalls Bibika Kokalari.

That same year, on a dark December night, two statues of Stalin disappeared from the streets of Tirana—it was the authorities, quietly paving the way for changes it could no longer hold back. The stately thirty-three-foot statue of Enver Hoxha was still standing in Skanderbeg Square, but the hand he held behind him was starting to shake.

The rage of the citizens of Shkodër, who, on January 14, 1990, tried to topple their statue of Stalin, was actually the rage of the entire country. Emboldened by their example, two weeks later the students of Tirana marched in the streets, demanding the removal of the name "Hoxha" from the title of their university and better conditions in their halls of residence.

Finally, on February 20, 1991, a swarm of people gathered in Skanderbeg Square chanting "Freedom! Freedom!" A dense crowd surrounded the plinth like boiling lava and got to work, pushing, bashing, yanking, and battering, until after some long minutes of fury and uproar the statue finally started to wobble, to sway and to rock, leaning ever closer to the ground, until suddenly—crash! Suddenly—bang! And it was down! The people flew at the corpse, trampling, kicking, and spitting at it—they couldn't believe it was really him, lying at their feet! Then triumphant hands seized the bronze cadaver and carried it across the square, across the heart of Albania, beating with euphoria, and loaded it onto a truck to take it to the university campus, to the students on hunger strike, who for the past two days had been demanding freedom for the entire country. Look, students, here lies the smashed husk of the dictator!

But there are others who claim the system bit the dust earlier, when a crazy guy drove a truck into the wall of the German embassy, and more than three thousand people dropped everything, ran into the embassy grounds, and demanded to be let out of Albania immediately.

That man was called Ylli Bodinaku, and he knew exactly what he was doing.

How I Demolished
Albania's Berlin Wall

SOMETIMES WE USED TO SEE HOUSES with swimming pools on Italian television, and we'd rack our brains: How do those sly Western foxes make fake swimming pools? Because the propaganda was constantly blaring that everything the foreigners showed was pure manipulation, designed to weaken our invincible country, and it barked and lied so stridently that even the wisest people gave it credence.

So when I went to the West for the first time, in July 1990, I wanted to cry out: "Hold on a minute, what's this? Is it all for real? You weren't joking about those swimming pools?" I traveled to Germany through Switzerland, and from a highway up in the mountains I gaped at the houses and the villages, and I couldn't get my head around all those bright blue spots below.

So that's why we're sitting here now, next to my own, pretty good swimming pool. It cost me thirty thousand euros, on credit, but so what? Why should I deprive myself? They don't make coffins with pools, do they? You're dead for all eternity, your suffering drags on relentlessly, while the good life goes flashing by as fast as an arrow.

They tortured me for eight months in cell number twelve; I was tortured by special services agents, which meant they had special techniques, too. And when I was sitting in that concrete cage, being kicked like a dog, I used a piece of metal to carve letter by letter into the wooden seat: "I'll make my dreams come true." That's what I decided. Whatever you do to me, you sons of bitches, know that you're not going to break me. You've got a whole fancy system designed to crush people, but I have my will. My body writhed in agony, but my mind was clear.

Because among those living shadows, I was the one who was always scheming and thinking. Do something—anything! Escape! Blow up the commie fortress! Destroy the wall! Protest! Even if it cost me my life. "If my life's going to be this miserable," I thought, "at least let me die with dignity!"

And that's why I decided to drive a truck through the wall of the German embassy. I knew I probably wouldn't survive such an act of madness, but I had to do something. There are those who live quietly and passively and then die, and all memory of them is lost. But there are also those whose actions speed up the course of history, who change the lives of others, and they leave their mark.

My mark is a hole in the wall and a breach in the system.

If you don't take risks, you'll never drink champagne. What shall we have, champagne or red wine? I've got a pretty decent vintage from 2010.

———

In the mid-1990s, a waiter from a nearby restaurant knocked on my door and, shifting from foot to foot, he said: "Ramiz Alia is asking for you. He found out you live here and he'd like to have a word . . ."

Oh hell, Ramiz Alia! The fireman who put out the fire! When he took power after Enver died, we were counting on something finally changing. And indeed—the system mellowed, by which I mean it killed less often and with greater forethought. Alia couldn't stop the transformation, but he didn't try to either. We crossed from one system to another without a river of blood, for the simple reason that Alia loosened the reins slowly and without shocks. Too slowly—for my taste.

So I nodded and trotted after the waiter. And I took my own raki with me, because it was better than the stuff they served at the restaurant.

"In that case, you drink first," said the old commie, pushing the glass toward me.

I downed it in one, just to make my point.

"I'm hardly going to stab you in the back," I said, "seeing I was brave enough to smash that wall with my own head."

Ramiz Alia tipped back his own glass, interlocked his fingers, and rested them on his chest.

"Yes, exactly . . . Why did you do it?"

Then I really let him have it. "Because I hated you!" I screamed. "Because I spent my whole life suffering! Because the biggest parasites had the best jobs, while everyone else had nothing to eat! Because you put me in prison for no reason! Because you shot my uncle in 1946!"

"Ah," sighed Alia. "So you did deserve to go to prison."

"And you deserve to have me kick you off that chair!"

Without another word, Ramiz Alia got on with his dinner. He devoured a whole chicken, which I paid for, and drank three double shots of raki. And he was quite long in the tooth by then. He evidently thought the devil looks after his own.

———

I was born in 1953, seven years after the death of my uncle, who was a policeman during the Italian occupation, and who was shot in 1946 for denouncing some partisans. As for my father, he had fought against the fascists, so a whole gang of partisans used to gather at our house, but the commies couldn't care less. When I was sent to prison a second time, to Spaç, they wrote in my papers that I'd inherited my dislike of the system from my uncle. The one I'd never laid eyes on . . .

The story of my wicked uncle cast a shadow over our entire family: my father, a newly qualified university professor, was forced to become a joiner, and all seven of us—six children and my mother—lived off his meager wages.

I loved my mother more than anything. I didn't get on with my father, because that demotion had utterly destroyed him, and he used to beat us to an impossible degree, and with my character, he could always find a reason. One time I jumped out of the window from the first floor, just to avoid being thrashed. I legged it—and came to a stop at a car repair shop, or rather a shabby garage, where a mechanic fixed state-owned vehicles. That guy changed my life.

I was quite a good pupil at high school, but as the nephew of an enemy of the people, I could forget about university, and in any case I'd always had itchy feet. If it weren't for that mechanic, a clever man with a heart of gold, I'd have ended up in prison much sooner—for assault or for attempting to escape the country. But he could see that my spirit was struggling inside me, and he directed all my energy into cars. From then on, I spent every waking hour poking around in engines at his garage.

One fine day he said: "You're going to take a driving test."

And later on he announced: "You're starting work as a van driver."

I was a driver for my whole life under communism, unless I happened to be in prison. The first time was for thumping a policeman who'd said something about my mother. Everyone has a moral compass and a red line no one should cross—keep your filthy hands off my mother! Besides, Albanian policemen think they've got your soul on a lead. I had to sock him one to remind him he wasn't God.

I was given three years for beating up a state official on duty, and I couldn't get over the fact that I'd ended up behind bars for such a human, perfectly natural reaction. Because, to be honest, I'd played the system lots of times before, and they'd never got onto me. For instance, I'd be driving a truckload of cement along snow-covered mountain roads in the middle of winter, and since Albanian snow chains were bloody useless, to make it lighter I'd pour away some of my cargo. Or, if I was transporting potatoes, I'd sell some along the way—which made people jump for joy. Or at night, I'd drive over to my neighbor with rocks from the riverbank and help him build his house.

All of that was illegal, and thus very risky, and I always felt like a sheep being hunted by a wolf. Whenever I wanted to nibble a bit of grass outside the pen, I had to look around in case the wolf was baring its fangs. But at the end of the day, that nibbling meant I could afford a television, a washing machine, and a fridge—in other words, you could say it paid off.

———

Two things changed my life: cars and an umbrella. In the late 1970s, I was working as a driver at a ministry, and one day the daughter of a famous Albanian left her umbrella there. I knew the authorities had her father in their sights. I stopped her in the street and gave back the umbrella, and she asked me if I wanted to go for coffee.

At the café table, she took out a packet of cigarettes. "Wow," I thought, "what a modern girl!" She was beautiful, she had enough personality for a hundred women. I fell in love as soon as I saw her smoking those ciggies. The only girl I knew who smoked! Later on, she told me she had relatives rotting in prison.

At the time, I'd started working at a mine in Krrabë, where I got to know two of my workmates. One of them was Aleksandër Meksi, who, after the fall of communism, became the first democratically elected prime minister. All three of us had good reasons to hate the system. I did because I'd had my ass kicked since I was a kid thanks to my uncle. Aleksandër did because he'd married a woman from a bad family, and although he had plenty of love in his life, the authorities succeeded in making it a misery. And Bashkim hated it because he'd been working his guts out in Krrabë since he was a boy to keep his family from starving. We were seething with hatred, and secretly we'd often fire each other up about how we ought to do something.

And so we reached a decision: We'd blow up the Central Committee building. Simple as that! Let's fill a truck with dynamite and drive it into the wall. Bashkim was in charge of the distribution and safe storage of explosives at the mine, so that was fine, he'd sort out the charge. Aleksandër Meksi was going to wire up the sticks of dynamite. I was going to be the driver, who'd get the truck up to speed and then leap out of the cab at the last minute, just before it hit the wall. And then there'd be a huge explosion that would send all those devils to hell. I wanted to die rather than go on living in their wretched system.

I told my girlfriend about it, because I loved her and I wanted her to stop worrying about her relatives. When we smash up the Committee, communism will fall in Albania. That's what I said to her, and she wept and nodded.

The next day she went straight to the Sigurimi to report me.

————

They used to tip potatoes into the bottom of a box, lay me down on top of them, cover my body with a board, and then go for nice little walks up and down on it. The pain was excruciating, inhuman. They used to chain my hands and feet together and leave me like that for ten days on end. Once a day, when the guard came to unshackle me so I could eat, I used to beg him not to, because when the circulation came back, the pain would rip my body apart. But he wouldn't listen, and then he'd put the handcuffs back on my swollen wrists. The suffering was endless.

They got nothing out of me. The Sigurimi had Bashkim in their sights, but I kept saying I barely knew him, and that I loathed him anyway. In the past, we used to have boxing matches for fun, but I told my interrogators I'd given that scum a real pasting, because he deserved it. By some miracle, the Sigurimi never got to Meksi . . . Perhaps it was a matter of luck, but perhaps not.

If one of us had confessed, they'd have shot all three of us the next day. Bashkim was no fool, so he kept repeating that if he'd ever had negative thoughts about the system, it was because of Freud, whom he'd read in secret. It was the despicable Freud who'd put ideas into his head! Assuming my girlfriend was cooperating with the authorities, I kept on saying she had made it all up to get her own back, because she was obsessed with the idea that I was cheating on her.

I saw her in the courtroom when she came to testify as a witness for the prosecution. She was shaking so badly the judge asked her if she was upset, or if she felt shy in front of the court.

"Seeing she has no qualms about telling lies in my presence, why would she feel shy in front of the court? She's shaking because she knows she's lying!" I shouted.

Apart from the woman's statement, they had nothing. So I only got eight years under Article 55, for agitation and propaganda—that article worked for anything.

The prison in Spaç was like something out of Dostoevsky's tales of hard labor and extreme cold. It was our own, Albanian version of the Gulag Archipelago, specially designed to drain and destroy us. Human life didn't count—the only thing that mattered was the output from the mine.

Luckily, I only spent two years rotting in there, because I qualified for the great amnesty of 1982, when anyone with a sentence of less than ten years was released.

I went straight to my girlfriend's house. The door was opened by her father. He called his daughter and disappeared. As soon as she was standing in the doorway, first I looked her straight in the eyes, and then I gave her a really good smack.

"All I could think about in prison was killing you, but Hoxha's let us out, so you're only getting a slap in the face for what you did to me."

I never saw her again.

Before I drove into the wall, I told my wife: "Darling, I'm extremely likely to die."

What did she say to that? It doesn't matter now. If I wasn't afraid of the state, I couldn't be scared of my own wife!

And I told my friends: "Whatever happens, the first thing you're going to do is carry my son into the grounds of the embassy!"

Because my youngest was only three months old at the time.

I was tipped off by a friend, who'd been tipped off by someone who worked at the German embassy, that there was one single spot where you could easily jump the wall and get inside. The embassy staff used to reflect light off mirrors to show us where it was, but that was exactly where the guards stood rooted to the spot. So I talked to a friend, who was also a driver, and we decided that instead of jumping over the wall, we'd try to smash it with a truck. We picked a date: July 2, 1990.

There were forty of us: thirty-eight in the back of the truck, my friend and I in the cab, and a bewildered sheep bleating with fear, which I took along in the hope there'd be something to celebrate. Demolishing the wall wasn't as big a challenge as rounding up that many people who wouldn't grass on us. They all knew about the plan in advance, but nobody breathed a word. Forty people and not a single spy! We were ready to die, if only to escape the country. By the late 1980s, we'd gone back to the Middle Ages—the factories stood idle for weeks, there was no petrol, and people were traveling around in horse-drawn carts. We dreamed of having a really good feed.

I thought it all through very carefully. I walked the length of the wall twice, feeling it and knocking on it in an attempt to estimate how thick it was, and I racked my brains: "How the hell are we going to do it?" The wall was ten feet high, and it was good and thick, too. I counted the steps from the turn in the road to calculate how fast the vehicle needed to be moving at the point of impact.

Yes, I was afraid of death, but that's a waste of breath.

On the ring road, not far from the 21 Dhjetori intersection, my team poured out of the truck and raced off toward the embassy, while my friend and I turned down Kavaja Street and then into Naim Frashëri Street. I took the corner at high speed, the truck almost keeled over, and then I stepped on the gas to take it up to seventy. My driver friend, who'd been navigating for me until then, was breathless with fear.

The guard on patrol outside the embassy roared: "Stop!" and fired a warning shot into the air, but I just shouted: "Fuck off! I'm going to Germany!"

At moments like that, your self-preservation instinct says: "What are you doing, you idiot? Save yourself!" but that was exactly why I smashed that truck into that thick wall—because I desperately wanted to live. And because I hated the regime with all my heart. It was my revenge for all the years of humiliation and suffering. "Freedom," I thought, "is even worth dying for."

A huge piece of concrete hit the front of the truck and then gashed my arm and shoulder. Look at that scar—it's my lifeline. The windshield shattered, and I was pouring with blood, but I couldn't feel a thing because adrenaline was flooding my brain. My only thought was that if that piece of concrete had hit me on the head, I'd be dead by now. We broke through the wall and I stepped out of the truck in a cloud of dust, my legs shaking. Soon after, my whole team ran in through the hole. The news got out immediately, and people in the vicinity dropped everything and ran to the embassy. Eventually there were more than three thousand people in the embassy courtyard. For several days they went on gathering there, because the German diplomats told the police chief to go hang. The place was packed to bursting . . . That's how desperate we were. We wanted the system to fall so badly.

———

Hans-Dietrich Genscher, the German foreign minister, sent us a congratulatory fax. "You have demolished the Berlin Wall of Albania!" it said. "You are harbingers of spring for the Albanian nation, the heroes of democracy."

He was spot on! They put me up in the ambassador's room, and for the first time in my life I saw a fireplace. I surfed the foreign channels on a huge TV set, and I couldn't believe that was what the world really looked like. I felt flooded with rage for all those lost years, for those decades of humiliation and poverty! I realized just what Albanian propaganda was. "How splendid it is to starve to death in Albania!"—that's what they'd been telling us all those years.

To tell you the truth, there were other people who'd already pulled a similar trick: On June 20, one guy jumped over the fence at the Greek embassy, then a few more broke down the Italians' gate with a truck, and, later on, twelve guys took refuge with the Turks. Some morons even got into the grounds of the Cuban embassy, but they were kicked out straightaway. But it was only when I smashed that truck into the Germans' wall that something snapped inside people and they rushed out to storm every possible embassy, from the Greek to the Italian to the Czechoslovak and the Polish! The foreigners actually helped them climb over the fences and immediately issued them passports. They understood that, after all those years in the bunker, we were quite simply entitled to our freedom.

———

More than three thousand people from our embassy immediately legged it to Germany, and I went with them. Soon after arriving, I saw a guy by the side of the road who needed to change a tire and was standing there like a fence post, waiting for someone to bring him some tools. I stopped and sorted it out with my bare hands, quick as a flash. The man was speechless, and he recommended me to a friend who worked at a Mazda factory. So, all well and good, I worked away there—everything was shipshape, on the level, but I was homesick for Albania. So when my mother fell ill, I decided to go back. Because just as passionately as I hated the regime, I loved my country, and I still do, more than those bastards in parliament do.

I had a capitalist head in communist Albania, so in the new system I was soon pulling in the money. First, I sold cars from Germany, then I opened my first car repair shop, then I bought an olive oil factory, then another repair shop, then I flogged some land, and so it went on. Nowadays I can't complain. Anyway, I'll show you everything in a moment, I've got a pretty good home cinema and a fantastic henhouse on the roof, a really big one, for guinea fowl, I check on them several times a day.

But when I returned to Albania in 1994, I realized life wouldn't be easy, because by way of welcome they ordered me to pay for destroying a state-owned truck. The one I'd crashed into the wall.

"Fine," I said. "I'll pay, but give me a statement saying exactly what I'm paying for, with a description of the incident."

I did that so I'd have it on paper that the system had changed but Albanians are still just as stupid.

The Sinking Ship

IN NOVEMBER 1989, EUROPE WATCHED as the Germans smashed the Berlin Wall to smithereens, and in December, Ramiz Alia announced to the Albanians: "To those who ask if similar changes are coming in this country, we say clearly and categorically: No, there will be no changes."

Meanwhile, Albania was crumbling to dust of its own accord. The factories were at a standstill, the land was being worked with plows, and people were sowing the fields by hand. Some were escaping across the hills to Greece, others were trying to cross the Yugoslav border, yet others were storming embassies. In March 1991, the first ship carrying twenty thousand refugees called at the port of Brindisi. People sailed for the promised land on anything that could float—they fired up the engines of clapped-out motorboats, built makeshift rafts, rowed across in rusty old boats, only to arrive in the Italian port of their dreams and collide head-on with reality: "No one wants you here, go home."

And then came August 7, 1991, the fateful day when a crowd that had gathered at the port in Durrës forced their way onto a ship named Vlora, which had just dropped anchor with a cargo of fraternal sugar from Cuba. People scrambled aboard in their thousands, until finally, the most desperate of them terrorized the captain and forced him to start the engine.

Some cried: "Let's sail to Switzerland, to Germany!," because they didn't know where those countries were.

"Let's sail to Italy!" cried others, because they had no idea what lay in store for them there.

"At the time I thought: 'Escape, escape, whatever happens, I've got to get out of this country, this sinking ship. Sail to that Italian paradise we've been watching for years on the sly, in fear.'

"My name is Ritmir Maloku, and after what happened to me, I've never left the country again.

"I'm from Durrës, and someone told me there was a ship taking people to Italy, so I ran straight off to the port and got on board the Vlora. I was just a kid, barely eighteen, the ship seemed so big and long to me. At home, I'd always done as my parents said, and suddenly here I was among strangers, each dreaming of a different part of the world, and each ready to do anything to reach their goal. At noon, I sat down on the deck and watched the crowd swelling below me—there were more and more of us, just like me, clinging to the masts and ropes, desperate to stay onboard. It felt as if the whole of Albania was trying to board the ship and get away. Everyone was pushing, shoving, and screaming. The ship expanded to titanic proportions—nobody would have thought ten thousand people could fit on it, but there may have been twenty thousand of us. 'The Vlora had better set sail,' I thought, 'or else we'll suffocate, trample each other, or sink . . .' But the hours went by and the ship stayed put. As people ran out of strength, the ropes slipped from their hands and they fell into the water, then at once other daredevils scrambled into their places. I didn't think the ship could ever move—or that we could possibly survive. Finally, at six o'clock, the sirens blared. Nobody tried to stop us.

"Now I know that people had threatened the captain with a screwdriver and that they'd simply hijacked the Vlora, but I had no idea about that at the time. I didn't think too hard about it. I just wanted us to sail away and never go back, and I was happy to feel the wind on my face.

"As the darkness and the waves rocked me steadily, the time came when I could no longer tell if I was dreaming, or if the ship had actually come to a halt. It was the middle of the night, and the people around me began shouting: 'What's going on, for God's sake?' Thousands of people on deck, but nobody knew a thing. Someone started waving a gun around, and someone called: 'Is there a mechanic onboard?' The rusty old Vlora was incapable of sailing across the Adriatic Sea of Albanian despair, just like that.

"I don't know who fixed the engine, but a few hours later we set off again. The ship sailed slowly, as if it were reluctant. People were playing with guns, and someone fired in the air. The words 'a better life' were being passed around. Before then, an ordinary trip from Durrës to Tirana had been a major undertaking and a source of anguish, and all of a sudden here we were on a ship sailing to another world . . .

"There was a helicopter flying above us the whole way. Finally, someone couldn't stand it any longer and threw a flip-flop at it. Then another. When the helicopter disappeared, we cheered as if we'd pulled off our first victory.

"The journey took hours and hours, because the Vlora was on its last legs—just like Albania. The whole time, no one had access to the toilets or showers, and all they had to eat and drink was whatever they'd brought with them. Imagine us after hours on end, anxious, hungry, tired, dirty . . . And the worst of it was yet to come.

"When it turned out the Italians weren't going to let us into the port at Brindisi, we sailed to Bari. Everyone was shouting: 'Italia!' And then, as we waited in the port for the Italians to make a decision, people simply started jumping off the deck, one by one, like stones into the water. They leaped from a height of eighty feet, because they thought that was the only thing separating them from the land of Italy, the promised land of their dreams . . . The coastguards fished them out of the water.

"Eventually, the Vlora was allowed to anchor. There was an awful crush—people were pushing and shouting, urging each other to get moving, faster, faster, hurry up about it! Some climbed down the mooring ropes, others fell into the water because someone else had pushed them.

Before us stood a double rank of soldiers, motionless, armed and ready to shoot. And behind them stood some buses. We relaxed for the first time.

"Except that the buses took us straight to the local stadium.

"What the hell? We've sailed all night, savoring the word 'freedom,' and the Italians pack us off to a stadium, to a locked cage?! Hey! We want to be free! People! We sailed here for a better life, didn't we?

"The gates of the stadium closed behind us. We were trapped again.

"The Italians threw food out of helicopters—either little plastic bags with small hamburgers in them or larger ones containing proper packed lunches. Except that we were so tightly crowded that we could hardly bend down to pick up the food. I was small and slight, so I kept darting between people's legs and scooping up whatever landed at their feet. The food was dropped at intervals, so whoever was lucky enough to get hold of something ate it, while the rest waited for the next airdrop.

"That's why there was so much fighting over those packets. Some people managed to grab big bags of food, while others got nothing to eat at all. There was never enough of it, so we became obsessed with getting our hands on some.

"And so the first day went by, and the second. Then the third, and the fourth . . .

"People slept on the bare ground, on the grass. During the day, they were painfully bored, so they concocted things to do. Eventually they found a storeroom full of clothes; they broke in and took shoes, T-shirts, and tracksuits . . . Everyone was trying to grab something for themselves, tearing those rags from each other's hands, ripping the seams, but we fought fiercely until we'd cleaned out the entire storeroom.

"The winners were very pleased they'd be bringing a T-shirt back from bloody Italy at the very least, while the rest had to settle for nothing.

"But what happened next? Yet another day dragged on mercilessly, while the sun blazed down on us.

"Out of boredom, we started exploring the stadium. Someone found some mopeds, someone else found some starting pistols, so we were off— on your marks, get set, go! The Albanian moped races at Bari stadium had begun. The competitors rode like mad, raising clouds of dust, to and fro, to and fro, until they ran out of gas. And once there was none left, they set fire to the mopeds. Just to make something happen. Just to get someone's attention.

"Our anger was growing, and so was our desperation . . . Day by day, we receded into a kind of bizarre brutality, into primitive violence. Someone snatched a sandwich out of my hand, right out of my hand! I looked in bewilderment at the face of the man who'd grabbed my bread. 'Has it really come to this, that people have started snatching food from one another?' I thought. 'How easily we've reached this point.'

"Someone stole my shoes while I was asleep. People stole each other's shoes because they didn't want to go back to Albania empty-handed. If only they could take something home with them, so this whole caper wouldn't be completely in vain . . .

"That's why after a while we split into groups: people from Tirana, people from Durrës, from Lushnjë, and from Elbasan. 'Our boys' stuck with 'our boys,' and protected each other. Because the mood was getting worse and worse, people had started robbing each other, and punches were being thrown.

"Isn't it weird? In a crisis situation, we instinctively recreated a tribal structure. It was only within our local groups that we felt safe. And yet we were all Albanians, brothers . . .

"People had lost hope of ever getting beyond the stadium. They knew the Italians would soon send us back to our country. So we began destroying everything—the benches, the barriers . . . That attack on the stadium was driven by fury and despair—it was a final act of revenge before we went back to our Albanian hopelessness. A trophy for the devastated victims after losing the battle.

"There were some fifteen thousand of us in the stadium—there we sat with no opportunity to wash or to change our clothes, completely cut off from the world, like in some kind of reserve for wild animals, like in Albania . . .

"A few guys managed to climb up the stadium flagpole and take a look at the city. They told us what they could see: some lovely colorful houses, some wonderful black street lamps, some shop windows, and girls in smart dresses . . . People were going crazy with despair, because they couldn't lay eyes on all those beautiful things. 'To hell with this!' they shouted. 'What was the point of taking a risk? They're treating us worse than in Albania!'

"But there were also some guys who found bedsheets in one of the storerooms, made ropes out of them, lowered themselves down the stadium fence, and escaped!

"By the seventh day, people were so furious and so hungry that they started pushing on the gate, but the policemen used their batons to strike the hands coming through the bars. 'Let us out or send us back to our country!' we shouted. 'We can't stand this any longer!'

"We couldn't believe there could be a place worse than Albania. In this country, which was supposed to be paradise . . . I don't know who said it, but they were right: Hell is standing at the gates of paradise and not being able to enter . . .

"Finally they selected several dozen people and packed them off in buses. Word went around that they were sending us back to Albania. Something snapped inside us. We had nothing else to lose. In a great surge, we rammed the stadium gates, which finally gave way. People started fighting with the soldiers, but they stood no chance. Anyone who came close to the Italians was instantly hit with a baton. At last, they packed us into the buses. One of them was so overloaded that it broke down immediately. Another was so full of people that the glass in the windows fell out.

"The picture of misery and despair. Like on the wretched *Vlora*.

"I was so very, very hungry. After a nine-day fight for survival, I had no strength left. The Italian authorities tried to tempt us with money, to get us to return to Albania voluntarily, but how much money would it take for someone to be willing to leave the promised land?

"We didn't know where they were taking us. Yet we were still hopeful.

"But they just took us to the airport. I knew there was a wonderful life going on all around the stadium, but so what? I could only see it for a moment, from the windows of the bus.

"The Italians kept us in the stadium for nine days, with no plan and to no purpose. They could have treated us like human beings, but they made us into animals. In the end, we had even turned on one another. I was going back to Albania barefoot—mistreated and barefoot . . .

"I've never left the country again. My dream of freedom and a better life was shattered. I'd tried it once, and I made up my mind: Never again would I put up with such awful humiliation. I'd rather suffer in Albania than let foreigners kick me around. It was only when I went abroad that I realized what hatred is. What it means to come face to face with people who hate you. They didn't see me as human, and for a while I stopped feeling human myself.

"Other boats from Albania weren't even allowed to enter the ports. They spent several days at anchor in the roadstead, but the Italians didn't send them any food, so the desperate people on board ripped open some bags of maggot-infested flour that they found below deck and used it to bake flatbread. They suffered even more than we did. Some were so distraught that they jumped into the sea, and many of them drowned.

"When I got home, my neighbors asked me: 'What did you see?' 'Nothing,' I replied truthfully. 'And what did you do?' 'I spent nine days fighting other people.' 'So what did you bring back?' 'Nothing. But they stole my shoes.' That was the end of my Italian dream.

"Yes, I used to think Albania was hell. But hell was standing at the gates of paradise and being unable to enter."

———

Six years later, when Albania was engulfed in mass riots, also known as the civil war, once again anyone who could tried to leave the country at all costs. On March 28, 1997, a small boat, the *Katër i Radës*, sailed out of the port in Vlorë with over one hundred people onboard, including forty children. Once the boat was close to Italian territorial waters, it was spotted by a patrol boat named the *Zefiro* and ordered to turn back. But the *Katër i Radës* kept going. So the Italian commanders summoned a naval vessel twenty times its size, the *Sibilla*, designed for antisubmarine warfare. Although what happened is unclear and has not been definitively established, it appears that first the *Sibilla*'s prow struck the starboard side of the *Katër i Radës*, then it sailed away, allegedly switched off its lights, and rammed the small boat in the darkness.

The *Katër i Radës* sank immediately.

At least eighty people died—almost all women and children, who were crowded below deck. The only survivors were those who had been on deck at the time of the first impact and were thrown into the sea—two women and thirty-two men. Fathers and husbands watched as the boat, which was meant to bring salvation, changed into a coffin for their wives and children.

After a trial lasting many years, the commander of the *Sibilla*, Captain Fabrizio Laudadio, was sentenced to three years in prison.

The Italian court found the captain of the *Katër i Radës*, an Albanian named Namik Xhaferi, more to blame. He was given four years.

The Red Can

IT'S NOT LIKE THAT ANYMORE, but once upon a time, every Albanian had his country carved into his face, into his sunken cheeks and his ruined hands. We wore shabby clothes, and we were small and thin after years of malnutrition. In 1992, when they hired me to work at the Kakavijë border crossing, I could always tell who was Albanian and who was Greek, because we had those years of communism stamped on our bodies—we were all skin and bones.

I used to dream of escaping the country, but now here I was, guarding the border. And the crowds kept on coming—whole crowds of people wanting to get out. Those who could went officially, but it wasn't easy, because who'd want Albanians in their country? And those who couldn't took a shortcut—that's to say they went by the longer route, over the mountains, an excruciating and arduous journey. Anyone with just a drop of courage went abroad, in order to change their destiny, because we hungered for the world and for life, and our longing turned into boldness that pushed us forward.

Everything amazed us . . . On the other side there was so much light, so many colors, girls who were so beautifully dressed you wanted to touch them just to make sure they were real. We were traveling between worlds divided by a border that used to be made of barbed wire but had now changed into a solid wall of documents and rubber stamps.

And while I guarded the crossing on one side, there were some well-fed Greeks on the other side, sitting on plastic chairs, full of the joys of spring. I didn't know a word of Greek back then, so I just watched as a few paces away my Greek colleagues roared with laughter and drank coffee; I couldn't have chatted with them even if I'd wanted to.

One day, one of them, my Greek mirror image, called out, beckoned to me and started walking in my direction. I noticed he was holding a red can.

The Greek was holding a red can!

"Oh my God!" I thought and froze in terror, because when I was a boy, my grandfather used to tell me how the Italians had dropped bombs on Albania in red cans.

"He wants to kill me!" That was my immediate thought. "But why?"

Though in fact I'm not sure I thought anything at all, I just stared at that red can in his hand. As the Greek came closer to me, I backed away. He'd take a step in my direction, and I'd take two steps back. I was trembling. Trembling from head to toe. Finally, the Greek realized I was afraid. He showed me a silver ring on the top of the can that you had to pull on to open it.

A firing pin! I legged it.

The bomb was hissing in the Greek's hands, but he calmly pressed it to his lips and started to drink. And then he put the can down on the pavement, pointed at it and took a few steps back.

Slowly I went up to it, keeping an eye on the Greek, while he watched me carefully. He raised a cupped hand to his mouth, as if he were drinking.

I picked up the can. I put the cold metal edge to my lips. I drank. I sighed.

When the Greek saw me smiling, he started to weep. He'd understood everything. And then I pointed to my stomach. To say it was good. God, how delicious I thought it was! As if I were drinking something from another world.

And then the Greek became my friend, I learned Greek, and a few years later, in his home village near Ioannina, when we told the story about how I'd been scared of a can of Coca-Cola, about how horribly isolated we were, the people listening to us had tears in their eyes. Just as you do now.

Come on, it's nothing to cry about. You only live once! Are you surprised I was scared? Imagine you've spent thirty years living in just one room. What do you know about life? You're afraid of everything; you find everything astonishing. You're afraid to go near a can of Coca-Cola, because how can you possibly know what it is? All you know is what someone told you. A bit of nonsense and a litany of lies.

I was dirt poor for years. I grappled with hunger throughout my childhood. I didn't know what wine or lemons or meat were. I used to cry from hunger. My mother would look at me and start crying, too. She'd give me half a slice of bread, because that was all she could get. We didn't have any shoes . . . We didn't have shoes, neither in summer nor in winter. We didn't have jackets. I was cold and hungry, and that's my memory of childhood. It wasn't a life.

It's only now that I'm truly alive, now that I can sit with you at table and drink wine. I don't give my children Coca-Cola, because it's filthy stuff. Sometimes, when they badger me or start whining, I tell them what life used to be like, to let them know how lucky they are. I tell them as much as it takes for them to start to cry. The stories have made them very sensitive to other people's pain. They understand everything in a flash. If they see a poor person, they come running to me to ask if we've got something for them to eat.

Don't forget, there's no need to cry. We should be happy that we can eat, laugh, and talk. Now at last we're alive, living this one short life.

AUTHOR'S ACKNOWLEDGMENTS

Writing this book took on new significance for me when I realized how important it was for victims of the regime to be heard. Some of the people I talked to had already published their own memoirs, while others had never spoken of their experiences before. It was easier to listen to the people who could talk about the past with dry eyes. But it's the interviews where the tears flowed that come back to my mind more often. Since 1991, many of my interviewees have made a life for themselves and started families, and the layer of pain has been covered by a new layer of peace and personal fulfillment. For others, the suffering of the past is so vivid that it feels as if it only ended yesterday. They're hurt by the failure to settle accounts or to provide compensation, and by the feeling that in today's Albania no one cares about the criminality of the old system.

When they heard what I was writing about, some of the young people said: "I've had it up to here with stories about communism." But when I asked them about the basic facts—the communist prisons, the role of Hoxha, or the ways in which people were persecuted—they couldn't tell me very much. For years there's been debate in Albania about the old regime. New books and memoirs are constantly being published and new facts are still coming to light; many people would like to talk about the past, but few are willing to listen. There's a widespread belief that everything has already been said. "We've been through our Golgotha, so now let's focus on how to get by in the new, democratic Albania, which hasn't turned out the way we imagined it would."

I wrote this book with the victims in mind, and also those who claim that the people who suffered are lying, exaggerating, and trying to extort money by stretching the truth. In Albania, no one who was responsible for issuing sentences and torturing prisoners has ever been convicted. The only exception was Nexhmije Hoxha, the dictator's wife, who spent four years in prison as the chief culprit and scapegoat of the system. Today, victims often pass their torturers in the street. And when the torturers are asked about their past crimes, they say they were only carrying out orders. They were tools in the hands of others. Conscious ones, yes, but just tools.

I'm afraid I can't list everyone who helped me write this book. It wouldn't have been possible without long conversations with all the kind people who at some point decided they'd do everything they could to help me.

In the first place, I'd like to thank Redi Muçi, my partner for almost four years of my life in Albania. In the early stages of work on this book, Redi was my interpreter, and later, once I was able to carry out the interviews myself, he read through them with me to make sure I didn't overlook any details. I'm immensely grateful to him for his dedication and patience.

Thank you to my other careful readers, too: Liri Kuçi, Steli Muçi, and Edlira Danaj. Edlira was also this book's good fairy, who often accompanied me to interviews to provide linguistic support.

For the great devotion and generosity they have shown me, thank you to the Kokalari-Ceka family from Gjirokastër, Arjeta Kokalari and Yzeir Ceka—cousins of the late writer Musine Kokalari. Without them, this book would not have been the same.

I'd also like to thank Frosi, Fredi, and Steli Muçi for the numerous conversations and anecdotes and for their warmth and support.

My thanks go to those with whom I've had so many conversations about Albania: Fatos Lubonja, Denis Gili, Vincent van Gerven Oei,

Enkelejd Zonja, Nick St. Oegger, Makis Hoxha, Kreshnik Merxhani, Wouter de Rooij, Severin Quick, Ervin Qafmolla, and Benet Nelku. I'd like to thank Wojciech Baranowski, the former Polish consul in Albania, his wife, Anna; Astrit Beqiri the interpreter at the Polish embassy in Tirana; and Agata Rogoś for helping me take my first steps in Tirana. I'm grateful to Jacek Multanowski, the Polish ambassador to Skopje, and his wife, Kinga Nettmann-Multanowska, for their endless enthusiasm and valuable conversations.

My sincere thanks go to Pjerin Mirdita for his patient support in collecting material in Shkodër, and to Father Andrzej Michoń for his help in discovering an Albania I'd never seen before.

Thank you also to my Polish friends in Tirana: Ola Kukuła, whom I was lucky enough to meet during my second year of Albanian life, Kasia Lasoń, and Maja Wawrzyk. Thank you also to the old guard: Ola Pavoni, Magda Malejczyk, and Magda Dorobińska. I am particularly grateful to Sylwia Jędrzejczyk and Magda Kicińska, who gave me lots of tips while I was working on the book. For his valuable advice—and not only—I am indebted to Łukasz Knap. In the final stages, my consulting editor Rigels Halili infused the book with a new spirit and encouraged me to reconsider some aspects, while at the same time showing himself to be an extremely kind person.

I'd also like to thank two wonderful women: my clever publisher Monika Sznajderman, who showed extraordinary patience while this book was being produced, and my incomparable editor, Magda Budzińska, who was always just an email away, alert, sensitive, and merciless.

Thank you also to Ania Nicolau, Ania and Piotrek Siemion, Maciek Grzybowski, Michał Szturomski, and Stefan Chitik for always being there for me.

And thank you to my Polish family—my mother Dorota; my father Robert; Piotruś; and Agata—for their care, understanding, and patience.

I'd also like to stress that this book would not have been possible without the Młoda Polska bursary that I received in 2014. I am especially grateful to Anna Rakowska and to everyone who wrote me a reference:

Andrzej Stasiuk, Dorota Horodyska, Mariusz Szczygieł, Kazimierz Jurczak, Andrzej Mencwel, Krzysztof Varga, and also the late Lidia Ostałowska, to whom I can no longer present this book.

The translators would like to thank Ani Gjika for her help with the translation of several of the Albanian poems quoted in this book.

BIBLIOGRAPHY

General texts

Albanian Identities: Myth and History, edited by Stephanie Schwandner-Sievers and Bernd-Jürgen Fischer. Bloomington and Indianapolis: Indiana University Press, 2002.

Albanistyka polska [Polish Albanian Studies (in Polish)], edited by Irena Sawicka. Toruń: Wydawnictwo UMK, 2007.

Aliçka, Ylljet. *Kompromisi* [The Compromise (short stories in Albanian)]. Tirana: Onufri, 2001.

Balkan Strongmen: Dictators and Authoritarian Rulers of South Eastern Europe, edited by Bernd-Jürgen Fischer. West Lafayette: Purdue University Press, 2007.

Czekalski, Tadeusz. *Alhania* (in Polish), Warsaw: Trio, 2003.

Elsie, Robert. *Albanian Literature: A Short History*. London and New York: I.B. Tauris, 2005.

———. *Classical Albanian Literature: A Reader*. Albanian Studies, vol. 18, London, 2015.

———. *An Elusive Eagle Soars—Anthology of Modern Albanian Poetry*. London and Boston: Forest Books, 1993.

Fevziu, Blendi. *Enver Hoxha: The Iron Fist of Albania*. Translated by Majlinda Nishku. London and New York: I.B. Tauris, 2016

Fischer, Bernd-Jürgen. *King Zog and the Struggle for Stability in Albania*. Boulder: East European Monographs, 1984.

Halili, Rigels. *Naród i jego pieśni. Rzecz o oralności, piśmienności i epice ludowej wśród Albańczyków i Serbów* [A Nation and Its Hymns: On orality, literacy and folk epics among Albanians and Serbs (in Polish)]. Warsaw: Warsaw University Press, 2012.

Lelaj, Olsi. *Nën shenjën e modernitetit. Antropologji e proceseve proletarizuese gjatë socializmit shtetëror* [Under the Sign of Modernity: Anthropology of proletarianization processes under state socialism (in Albanian)]. Tirana: Shtypur ne shtypshkronjen West Print, 2015

Lleshanaku, Luljeta. *Child of Nature.* Translated by Henry Israeli and Shpresa Qatipi. New York: New Directions Publishing, 2010.

Lubonja, Fatos. *Albania—wolność zagrożona. Wybór publicystyki z lat 1991–2002* [Albania—Endangered Freedom: Selected essays, 1991– 2002 (in Polish translation)]. Translated by Dorota Horodyska. Sejny: Fundacja Pogranicze, 2005.

Mëhilli, Elidor. *From Stalin to Mao: Albania and the socialist world.* Ithaca and London: Cornell University Press, 2017.

Pipa, Arshi. *Albanian Stalinism: ideo-political aspects.* Boulder: East European Monographs, 1990.

Studime aktuale dhe perspektiva të reja për historinë e Shqipërisë në shekullin XX [Current studies and new perspectives on the history of Albania in the 20th century (in Albanian)]. *Perpjekja* nos 32–33 (2014).

Vickers, Miranda. *The Albanians: A Modern History.* London and New York: Bloomsbury Academic, 2014.

Woodcock, Shannon. *Life is War: Surviving Dictatorship in Communist Albania.* Bristol: Hammeron Press, 2016.

Part One: Children of the Dictator

40 vjet Shqipëri socialiste. Të dhëna statistikore për zhvillimin e ekonomisë dhe të kulturës / 40 Years of Socialist Albania: statistical data on the development of the economy and culture (in Albanian and English)]. Tirana: 8 Nëntori Publishing House, 1984.

Amnesty International. *Albania: Political Imprisonment and the Law.* London: Amnesty International Publications, 1984.

Blumi, Isa. "Hoxha's Class War. The Cultural Revolution and State Reformation 1961–1971." *East European Quarterly* 33, no. 3 (1999): 303.

Elsie, Robert. *A Dictionary of Albanian Religion, Mythology and Folk Culture.* New York: New York University Press, 2000.

Manga, Nexhip. *Frymëzime të viteve të arta. Vjersha dhe poema* [Inspiration from the Golden Years: Poetry (in Albanian)]. Gjirokastër: Argjiro, 2012.

Organization for Security and Cooperation in Europe. "Citizens' understanding and perceptions of the Communist past in Albania and expectations for the future." (December 2016). osce.org/albania/286821.

Shehu, Bashkim. *Vjeshta e ankthit. Roman autobiografik* [The Autumn of Fear: autobiographical essays (in Albanian)]. Tirana: Albinform, 1994.

Part Two: Mud Sweeter than Honey

Dibra, Ridvan. *Gjumi mbi borë* [Sleeping on Snow (in Albanian)]. Tirana: Onufri, 2016.

Hajredin, Meçaj. "Toka është bujare" [The earth is generous (in Albanian)]. *Ylli* no. 3 (1968).

Saraçi-Mulleti, Fatbardha. *Kalvari i grave në burgjet e komunizmit* [The calvary of women in communist prisons (in Albanian)]. Tirana: ISKK, 2017.

Part Three: Circles

Blloshmi, Bedri. *Revolta e Spaçit* [The Spaç Revolt (in Albanian)]. Tirana: Mirgeeralb, 2015.

Czekalski, Tadeusz. *Zarys dziejów chrześcijaństwa albańskiego w latach 1912–1993* [An Overview of Albanian Christianity 1912–1993 (in Polish)]. Kraków: Zakład Wydawniczy Nomos, 1996.

Dervishi, Kastriot. *Internimi dhe burgimi komunist në Shqipëri. Të gjitha vendet në të cilat diktatura komuniste persekutoi dhe shfrytëzoi punën e të burgosurve dhe të internuarve* [Communist exile and imprisonment in Albania. All countries in which the communist dictatorship persecuted and exploited the labor of prisoners and internees (in Albanian)]. Tirana: Shtëpia Botuese 55, 2016.

Lubonja, Fatos. *Second Sentence: Inside the Albanian Gulag.* Translated by John Hodgson. London and New York: Bloomsbury Academic, 2009.

Pasha, Neim. *Bukë, mall dhe lot* [Bread, longing and tears (in Albanian)]. Gjirokastër: 2005.

———. *Trëndafilat e përgjakur* [Bloody Roses (in Albanian)], Gjirokastër: 2016.

Peters, Markus W. E. *Die Geschichte der Katholischen Kirche in Albanien seit der Pariser Friedenskonferenz 1919/20 bis zur Pastoralvisite Papst Johannes Paulus II. im Jahre 1993* [The History of the Catholic Church in Albania from the Paris Peace Conference 1919/20 to the pastoral visit of Pope John Paul II in 1991 (in German)]. PhD diss., Rheinische Friedrich-Wilhelms-Universität, Bonn, 2001.

Pllumi, Zef. *Live to Tell. A True Story of Religious Persecution in Communist Albania 1944–1951*, vol. 1. New York, Bloomington, Shanghai: iUniverse, 2008.

Vocaj, Gjet. *Takim fatal me diktatorin* [A Fatal Encounter with the Dictator (in Albanian)]. Lezhë: 2010.

Part Four: Stone on the Border

Barnes, Julian. *The Noise of Time.* London: Jonathan Cape, 2016.

Çapaliku, Stefan. *Secili çmendet simbas mënyrës së vet* [Everyone goes mad in his own way (in Albanian)]. Tirana: EBF, 2017.

Idrizi, Idrit. "'Magic Apparatus' and 'Window to the Foreign World'? The Impact of Television and Foreign Broadcasts on Society and State–Society Relations in Socialist Albania," in *Television Beyond and Across the Iron Curtain*, edited by Kirsten Bönker, Julia Obertreis, Sven Grampp. Newcastle upon Tyne: Cambridge Scholars Publishing, 2016.

Mai, Nicola. "'Looking for a More Modern Life. . .': The Role of Italian Television in the Albanian Migration to Italy," in *Westminster Papers in Communication and Culture* no. 1 (2004).

Vullnetari, Julie, and King, Russell. "'Women Here Are Like at the Time of Enver [Hoxha] . . .': Socialist and Post-Socialist Gendered Mobility in Albanian Society," in *Mobilities in Socialist and Post-Socialist States: Societies on the Move,* edited by Kathy Burrell and Kathrin Hörschelmann. Houndmills, Basingstoke, Hampshire: Palgrave-Macmillan, 2014.

Part Five: The Fortress Crumbles

Abrahams, Fred C. *Modern Albania: From Dictatorship to Democracy in Europe.* New York: NYU Press, 2015.

Carver, Robert. *The Accursed Mountains: Journeys in Albania.* London: Flamingo, 2009.

De Waal, Clarissa. *Albania Today: A Portrait of Post-Communist Turbulence.* London and New York: I.B. Tauris, 2005.

Kongoli, Fatos. *The Loser.* Translated by Robert Elsie and Janice Mathie-Heck. Bridgend: Seren, 2007.

"Mërgimi shqiptar pas vitit 1990" [Albanian Emigration after 1990 (in Albanian)], in *Perpjekja* nos 26–27 (2010).

Pettifer, James, and Miranda Vickers. *Albania: From Anarchy to a Balkan Identity.* London: C. Hurst and Co. Publishers Ltd., 1999.

———. *The Albanian Question: Reshaping the Balkans.* London and New York: I.B. Tauris, 2009.

Albanian newspapers and websites

arkivalajmeve.com

exit.algazetadita.al

iskk.gov.al

mapo.al

observatorikujteses.al

panorama.com.al

reporter.al

shekulli.com.al

tribunashqiptare.com

and others

PERMISSIONS

Illustrations

Front cover: Boy throwing crate in the air. Tirana, Albania, 1991. © Nikos Economopoulos/Magnum Photos

p. viii: Map © Bill Donohoe

p. xviii: The statue of Enver Hoxha erected in Gjirokastër in 1988 and destroyed by workers in February 1991. © Nikos Economopoulos/ Magnum

p. 48: A photographer's workshop in Durrës, 1984. © Ferdinando Scianna/Magnum Photos

p. 108: Men at a hunting club in Shkodër, 1984. © Ferdinando Scianna/ Magnum Photos

p. 176: The program to build a network of bunkers, shelters, and tunnels was launched in the early 1970s and lasted until 1984. According to various sources, from 173,000 to half a million bunkers were built. © Ferdinando Scianna/Magnum Photos

p. 226: In 1960, there were 1,900 passenger cars on Albanian roads. By the 1980s, this number had risen to 6,000 to 7,000. © Nikos Economopoulos/Magnum Photos

Excerpts

In *Mud Sweeter than Honey,* Margo Rejmer has quoted or incorporated words from a number of sources:

Lines from from Andon Zako Çajupi's *Baba Tomorri* (Tirana: Dituria, 1997), p. 23

Lines from Mitrush Kuteli's *The Muddy Albanian Soil* (*Balta shqipëtare, from the volume Sulm e lotë,* translated by Robert Elsie, 1944) pp. 55–57

Lines from Bakshim Shehu's *Vjeshta e ankthit* ["Autumn of Fear: Autobiographical Essays"] (Tirana: Albinform, 1994), in English in Blendi Fevziu's *Enver Hoxha: The Iron Fist of Albania* (London: I. B. Tauris, 2016), p. 164

Lines from *40 vjet Shqipëri socialiste. Të dhëna statistikore për zhvillimin e ekonomisë dhe të kulturës, Tiranë 1984* ["40 years of socialist Albania. Statistical data on the development of economy and culture, Tirana 1984"], p. 164

Lines from Nexhip Manga's *Frymëzime të viteve të arta. Vjersha dhe poema* ["Inspirations of the Golden Years: Verses and Poems"] (Gjirokastër: Argjiro, 2012), p. 169

Lines from "Auguries of Innocence" by William Blake

Lines from Martin Camaj's *Vendit tem,* from the volume *Lirika midis dy moteve,* Munich 1967, translated from the Albanian by Robert Elsie and first published in English in *An elusive eagle soars, Anthology of modern Albanian poetry* (London: Forest Books, 1993), p. 32

Lines from Stefan Çapaliku's *Secili çmendet simbas mënyrës së vet* (Tirana: Botimet Fishta, 2017), p. 75

ABOUT THE CONTRIBUTORS

MAŁGORZATA (MARGO) REJMER is an award-winning Polish novelist, reporter, and writer of short stories. She is the author of the novel *Toximia* and the nonfiction work *Bucharest: Dust and Blood*, which won the *Newsweek* Award for best book of 2013 and the Gryfia Literary Award. In 2018 she was awarded the Polityka Passport, the most prestigious prize in Poland for emerging artists, for *Mud Sweeter than Honey*. Her books have been translated into eight languages. She lives in Warsaw and Tirana.

ZOSIA KRASODOMSKA-JONES is a literary translator working from Polish. Since completing an Emerging Translators' Mentorship, she has translated several books for children and worked regularly with online journals. Her other collaboration with Antonia Lloyd-Jones, *Clementine Loves Red*, was shortlisted for the Warwick Prize for Women in Translation in 2017. *Mud Sweeter than Honey* is her first nonfiction translation for adults.

ANTONIA LLOYD-JONES has translated works by several of Poland's leading contemporary novelists and reportage authors, as well as crime fiction, poetry, and children's books. Her translation of *Drive Your Plow Over the Bones of the Dead* by 2018 Nobel Prize laureate Olga Tokarczuk was short-listed for the 2019 Man Booker International prize. She is a mentor for the Emerging Translators' Mentorship Programme, and former co-chair of the UK Translators Association.

TONY BARBER is European Affairs Columnist of the *Financial Times*. He is a former foreign correspondent in Austria, Belgium, Germany, Italy, Poland, the former Soviet Union, the US, and the former Yugoslavia.

RESTLESS BOOKS is an independent, nonprofit publisher devoted to championing essential voices from around the world whose stories speak to us across linguistic and cultural borders. We seek extraordinary international literature for adults and young readers that feeds our restlessness: our hunger for new perspectives, passion for other cultures and languages, and eagerness to explore beyond the confines of the familiar.

Through cultural programming, we aim to celebrate immigrant writing and bring literature to underserved communities. We believe that immigrant stories are a vital component of our cultural consciousness; they help to ensure awareness of our communities, build empathy for our neighbors, and strengthen our democracy.

Visit us at restlessbooks.org